Microsoft® Official Academic Course

Windows Operating System Fundamentals, Exam 98-349

WILEY

Credits

VP & PUBLISHER	Don Fowley
EDITOR	Bryan Gambrel
DIRECTOR OF SALES	Mitchell Beaton
EXECUTIVE MARKETING MANAGER	Chris Ruel
MICROSOFT PRODUCT MANAGER	Colin Klein of Microsoft Learning
EDITORIAL PROGRAM ASSISTANT	Jennifer Lartz
ASSISTANT MARKETING MANAGER	Debbie Martin
SENIOR PRODUCTION MANAGER	Janis Soo
ASSOCIATE PRODUCTION MANAGER	Joel Balbin
CREATIVE DIRECTOR	Harry Nolan
COVER DESIGNER	Jim O'Shea
TECHNOLOGY AND MEDIA	Tom Kulesa/Wendy Ashenberg

Cover photo: © I. Lizarraga/Getty Images, Inc.

This book was set in Garamond by Aptara, Inc. and printed and bound by Bind-Rite Robbinsville. The cover was printed by Bind-Rite Robbinsville.

ISBN 978-1-118-29527-4

Printed in the United States of America

10 9 8 7 6 5 4 3 2 1

www.wiley.com/college/microsoft *or*
call the MOAC Toll-Free Number: 1+(888) 764-7001 (U.S. & Canada only)

Foreword from the Publisher

Wiley's publishing vision for the Microsoft Official Academic Course series is to provide students and instructors with the skills and knowledge they need to use Microsoft technology effectively in all aspects of their personal and professional lives. Quality instruction is required to help both educators and students get the most from Microsoft's software tools and to become more productive. Thus our mission is to make our instructional programs trusted educational companions for life.

To accomplish this mission, Wiley and Microsoft have partnered to develop the highest quality educational programs for Information Workers, IT Professionals, and Developers. Materials created by this partnership carry the brand name "Microsoft Official Academic Course," assuring instructors and students alike that the content of these textbooks is fully endorsed by Microsoft, and that they provide the highest quality information and instruction on Microsoft products. The Microsoft Official Academic Course textbooks are "Official" in still one more way—they are the officially sanctioned courseware for Microsoft IT Academy members.

The Microsoft Official Academic Course series focuses on *workforce development*. These programs are aimed at those students seeking to enter the workforce, change jobs, or embark on new careers as information workers, IT professionals, and developers. Microsoft Official Academic Course programs address their needs by emphasizing authentic workplace scenarios with an abundance of projects, exercises, cases, and assessments.

The Microsoft Official Academic Courses are mapped to Microsoft's extensive research and job-task analysis, the same research and analysis used to create the Microsoft Technology Associate (MTA) and Microsoft Certified Information Technology Professional (MCITP) exams. The textbooks focus on real skills for real jobs. As students work through the projects and exercises in the textbooks they enhance their level of knowledge and their ability to apply the latest Microsoft technology to everyday tasks. These students also gain resume-building credentials that can assist them in finding a job, keeping their current job, or in furthering their education.

The concept of life-long learning is today an utmost necessity. Job roles, and even whole job categories, are changing so quickly that none of us can stay competitive and productive without continuously updating our skills and capabilities. The Microsoft Official Academic Course offerings, and their focus on Microsoft certification exam preparation, provide a means for people to acquire and effectively update their skills and knowledge. Wiley supports students in this endeavor through the development and distribution of these courses as Microsoft's official academic publisher.

Today educational publishing requires attention to providing quality print and robust electronic content. By integrating Microsoft Official Academic Course products, *WileyPLUS*, and Microsoft certifications, we are better able to deliver efficient learning solutions for students and teachers alike.

Joseph Heider

General Manager and Senior Vice President

Preface

Welcome to the Microsoft Official Academic Course (MOAC) program for Windows Operating System Fundamentals. MOAC represents the collaboration between Microsoft Learning and John Wiley & Sons, Inc. publishing company. Microsoft and Wiley teamed up to produce a series of textbooks that deliver compelling and innovative teaching solutions to instructors and superior learning experiences for students. Infused and informed by in-depth knowledge from the creators of Microsoft products, and crafted by a publisher known world-wide for the pedagogical quality of its products, these textbooks maximize skills transfer in minimum time. Students are challenged to reach their potential by using their new technical skills as highly productive members of the workforce.

Because this knowledge base comes directly from Microsoft, creator of the Microsoft Certified IT Professional, Microsoft Certified Technology Specialist (MCTS), and Microsoft Technology Associate (MTA) exams (www.microsoft.com/learning/certification), you are sure to receive the topical coverage that is most relevant to students' personal and professional success. Microsoft's direct participation not only assures you that MOAC textbook content is accurate and current; it also means that students will receive the best instruction possible to enable their success on certification exams and in the workplace.

■ The Microsoft Official Academic Course Program

The *Microsoft Official Academic Course* series is a complete program for instructors and institutions to prepare and deliver great courses on Microsoft software technologies. With MOAC, we recognize that, because of the rapid pace of change in the technology and curriculum developed by Microsoft, there is an ongoing set of needs beyond classroom instruction tools for an instructor to be ready to teach the course. The MOAC program endeavors to provide solutions for all these needs in a systematic manner in order to ensure a successful and rewarding course experience for both instructor and student—technical and curriculum training for instructor readiness with new software releases; the software itself for student use at home for building hands-on skills, assessment, and validation of skill development; and a great set of tools for delivering instruction in the classroom and lab. All are important to the smooth delivery of an interesting course on Microsoft software, and all are provided with the MOAC program. We think about the model below as a gauge for ensuring that we completely support you in your goal of teaching a great course. As you evaluate your instructional materials options, you may wish to use the model for comparison purposes with available products.

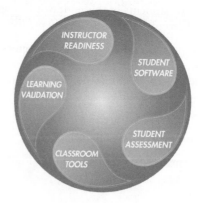

■ Pedagogical Features

The MOAC textbook for Windows Operating System Fundamentals is designed to cover all the learning objectives for that MTA exam 98-349, which is referred to as its "objective domain." The Microsoft Technology Associate (MTA) exam objectives are highlighted throughout the textbook. Many pedagogical features have been developed specifically for *Microsoft Official Academic Course* programs.

Presenting the extensive procedural information and technical concepts woven throughout the textbook raises challenges for the student and instructor alike. The Illustrated Book Tour that follows provides a guide to the rich features contributing to *Microsoft Official Academic Course* program's pedagogical plan. Following is a list of key features in each lesson designed to prepare students for success as they continue in their IT education, on the certification exams, and in the workplace:

- Each lesson begins with an **Exam Objective Matrix**. More than a standard list of learning objectives, the Exam Objective Matrix correlates each software skill covered in the lesson to the specific exam objective domain.

- Concise and frequent **Step-by-Step** instructions teach students new features and provide an opportunity for hands-on practice. Numbered steps give detailed, step-by-step instructions to help students learn software skills.

- **Illustrations:** Screen images provide visual feedback as students work through the exercises. The images reinforce key concepts, provide visual clues about the steps, and allow students to check their progress.

- **Key Terms:** Important technical vocabulary is listed with definitions at the beginning of the lesson. When these terms are used later in the lesson, they appear in bold italic type and are defined. The Glossary contains all of the key terms and their definitions.

- Engaging point-of-use **Reader Aids**, located throughout the lessons, tell students why this topic is relevant (*The Bottom Line*), provide students with helpful hints (*Take Note*). Reader Aids also provide additional relevant or background information that adds value to the lesson.

- **Certification Ready** features throughout the text signal students where a specific certification objective is covered. They provide students with a chance to check their understanding of that particular MTA objective and, if necessary, review the section of the lesson where it is covered. MOAC offers complete preparation for MTA certification.

- **End-of-Lesson Questions:** The Knowledge Assessment section provides a variety of multiple-choice, true-false, matching, and fill-in-the-blank questions.

- **End-of-Lesson Exercises:** Competency Assessment case scenarios and Proficiency Assessment case scenarios are projects that test students' ability to apply what they've learned in the lesson.

▪ Lesson Features

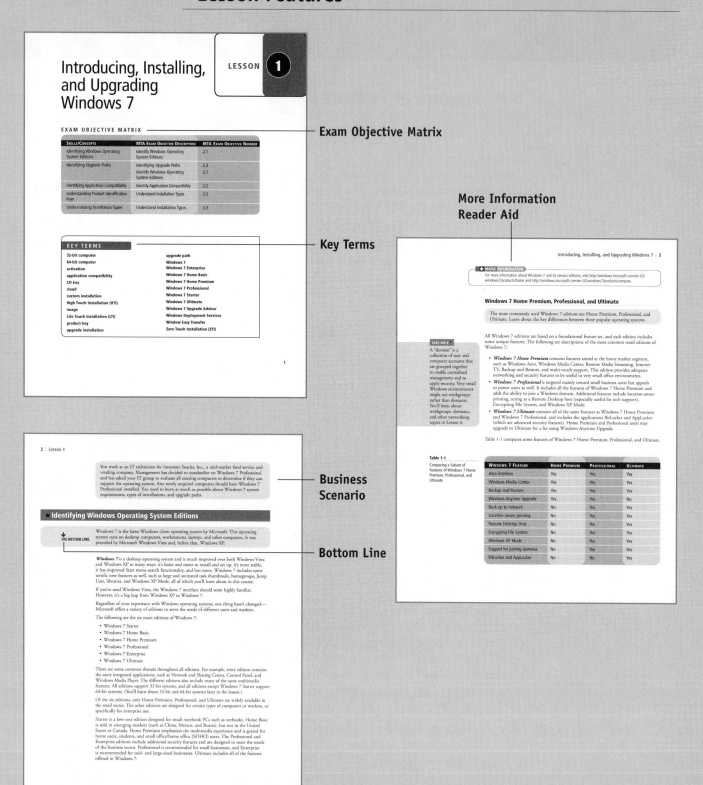

Exam Objective Matrix

More Information
Reader Aid

Key Terms

Business
Scenario

Bottom Line

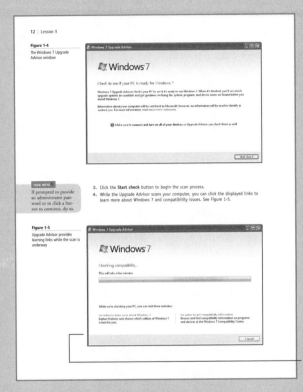

Screen Images

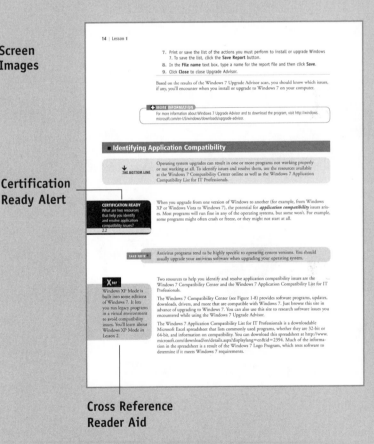

Certification Ready Alert

Cross Reference Reader Aid

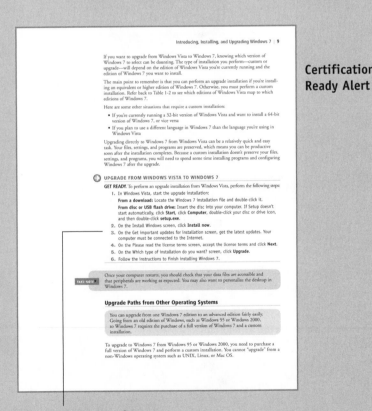

Step-by-Step Exercises

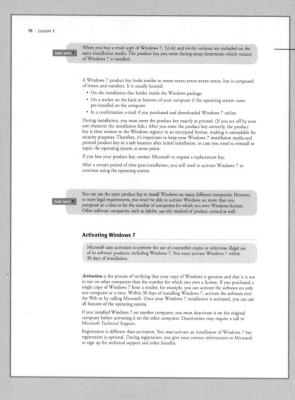

**Take Note
Reader Aid**

Easy-to-Read Tables

16 | Lesson 1

> When you buy a retail copy of Windows 7, 32-bit and 64-bit versions are included on the same installation media. The product key you enter during setup determines which version of Windows 7 is installed.

A Windows 7 product key looks similar to xxxxx-xxxxx-xxxxx-xxxxx-xxxxx, but is composed of letters and numbers. It is usually located:

• On the installation disc holder inside the Windows package
• On a sticker on the back or bottom of your computer if the operating system came pre-installed on the computer
• In a confirmation e-mail if you purchased and downloaded Windows 7 online

During installation, you must enter the product key exactly as printed. (If you are off by even one character the installation fails.) After you enter the product key correctly, the product key is then written to the Windows registry in an encrypted format, making it unreadable for security purposes. Therefore, it's important to keep your Windows 7 installation media and printed product key in a safe location after initial installation, in case you need to reinstall or repair the operating system at some point.

If you lose your product key, contact Microsoft to request a replacement key.

After a certain period of time post-installation, you will need to activate Windows 7 to continue using the operating system.

> You can use the same product key to install Windows on many different computers. However, to meet legal requirements, you won't be able to activate Windows on more than one computer at a time or for the number of computers for which you own Windows licenses. Other software companies, such as Adobe, use this method of product control as well.

Activating Windows 7

> Microsoft uses activation to prevent the use of counterfeit copies or otherwise illegal use of its software products, including Windows 7. You must activate Windows 7 within 30 days of installation.

Activation is the process of verifying that your copy of Windows is genuine and that it is not in use on other computers than the number for which you own a license. If you purchased a single copy of Windows 7 from a retailer, for example, you can activate the software on only one computer at a time. Within 30 days of installing Windows 7, activate the software over the Web or by calling Microsoft. Once your Windows 7 installation is activated, you can use all features of the operating system.

If you installed Windows 7 on another computer, you must deactivate it on the original computer before activating it on the other computer. Deactivation may require a call to Microsoft Technical Support.

Registration is different than activation. You *must* activate an installation of Windows 7 but registration is optional. During registration, you give your contact information to Microsoft to sign up for technical support and other benefits.

---

38 | Lesson 2

Table 2-1
Control Panel Categories

CATEGORY	DESCRIPTION
System and Security	Provides applets for maintaining the system and configuring security. This category includes Action Center, Windows Firewall, System, Windows Update, Power Options, Backup and Restore, Windows Anytime Upgrade, and Administrative Tools. Windows 7 Ultimate and Enterprise editions also offer BitLocker Drive Encryption (if installed).
Network and Internet	Provides applets for connecting to the Internet and other networks, setting up a local network (HomeGroup), and configuring wireless settings.
Hardware and Sound	Provides applets for configuring hardware (including printers), audio settings, power options, display settings, mobile options, and more.
Programs	Provides applets for installing/uninstalling software, setting default programs, and managing desktop gadgets.
User Accounts and Family Safety	Provides applets for creating and managing user accounts, configuring parental controls, and managing Windows credentials.
Appearance and Personalization	Provides applets for changing the Windows theme, desktop background, screen saver, display settings, desktop gadgets, and taskbar and Start menu. You can also open the Ease of Access Center, change folder options, and install fonts.
Clock, Language, and Region	Provides applets for changing your computer's date and time, time zone, language, and region/location.
Ease of Access	Provides access to the Ease of Access Center, where you can configure accessibility options; also provides access to the speech recognition feature.

Table 2-1 summaries the categories in Windows 7 Control Panel.

Let's look at a few Control Panel applets in more detail.

Configuring Administrative Tools

> Think of Administrative Tools as a well-rounded toolkit of utilities for power users and administrators. These utilities can help resolve most computer problems you may encounter and keep your system running optimally.

CERTIFICATION READY
What are Administrative Tools?
1.1

Administrative Tools is a set of utilities for managing advanced Windows features and diagnosing system problems. You can access the tools from the System and Security category of Control Panel. You can also click Start, type **admin tools** in the *Search programs and files* search box, and then select Administrative Tools from the resulting list. Figure 2-11 shows the Administrative Tools window on a Windows 7 Home Premium system. Windows 7 Professional, Ultimate, and Enterprise editions include the Local Security Policy and Print Management tools as well.

Within Administrative Tools, you can defragment your hard disk, monitor system performance, start and stop services, determine which programs run when Windows starts, and much more. Table 2-2 summarizes the tools.

Photos

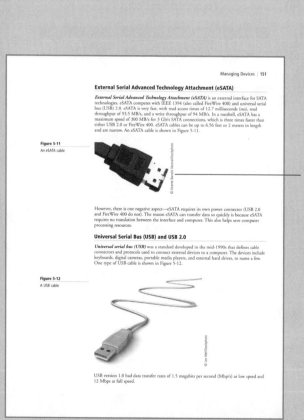

Managing Devices | 151

External Serial Advanced Technology Attachment (eSATA)

External Serial Advanced Technology Attachment (eSATA) is an external interface for SATA technologies. eSATA competes with IEEE 1394 (also called FireWire 400) and universal serial bus (USB) 2.0. eSATA is very fast, with read access times of 12.7 milliseconds (ms), read throughput of 93.5 MB/s, and a write throughput of 94 MB/s. In a nutshell, eSATA has a maximum speed of 300 MB/s for 3 Gb/s SATA connections, which is three times faster than either USB 2.0 or FireWire 400. eSATA cables can be up to 6.56 feet or 2 meters in length and are narrow. An eSATA cable is shown in Figure 5-11.

Figure 5-11
An eSATA cable

However, there is one negative aspect—eSATA requires its own power connector (USB 2.0 and FireWire 400 do not). The reason eSATA can transfer data so quickly is because eSATA requires no translation between the interface and computer. This also helps save computer processing resources.

Universal Serial Bus (USB) and USB 2.0

Universal serial bus (USB) was a standard developed in the mid-1990s that defines cable connectors and protocols used to connect external devices to a computer. The devices include keyboards, digital cameras, portable media players, and external hard drives, to name a few. One type of USB cable is shown in Figure 5-12.

Figure 5-12
A USB cable

USB version 1.0 had data transfer rates of 1.5 megabits per second (Mbp/s) at low speed and 12 Mbps at full speed.

Skill Summary Matrix

Maintaining, Updating, and Protecting Windows 7 | 257

2. Configure Forefront Endpoint Protection definition update methods based on the settings defined in the Forefront Endpoint Protection policies created in Step 1.
3. Deploy the Forefront Endpoint Protection installation package to client computers.

With Forefront Endpoint Protection deployed, you can perform a quick or full scan on one or more computers simultaneously from the Configuration Manager console.

MORE INFORMATION

For more information about Microsoft Forefront Endpoint Protection, visit http://www.microsoft.com/en-us/server-cloud/forefront/endpoint-protection.aspx.

SKILL SUMMARY

IN THIS LESSON YOU LEARNED:

- Windows 7 comes with many built-in maintenance tools that help to keep computers running at top performance. These tools include Disk Defragmenter, Disk Cleanup, Task Scheduler, and the Action Center Maintenance feature.
- Disk Defragmenter can speed up your computer's performance by defragmenting data on your hard disk. In Windows 7, the utility is set to automatically run once a week.
- Disk Cleanup helps you remove unnecessary files from your computer, such as downloaded program files, temporary Internet files and those that are left after running software, and much more.
- Task Scheduler enables you to automate tasks that don't have scheduling features built in. You can also use Task Scheduler to open programs on specific days and times, or at Windows startup.
- Windows 7 Action Center is an improvement upon Security Center in previous versions of Windows. Within Action Center, you can view the status of security features (firewall, antivirus software, etc.) and maintenance (backups, updates, etc.).
- System Information displays a wealth of information about your computer's hardware, drivers, and system software. If you're having any type of system-related issues, you should check System Information for possible clues as to the source of the problem.
- The Windows registry is a database of configuration settings for your computer. The registry is self-sufficient and rarely requires maintenance, but you can use a reputable registry cleaner occasionally to remove settings that are no longer used.
- Microsoft provides several ways to help you keep your Windows system patched and updated, using hotfixes, service packs, updated drivers, and more. Windows Update and Microsoft Update are the primary update tools.
- Windows Firewall is the native firewall in Windows 7 and many other versions of Windows. It monitors inbound and outbound traffic to allow safe traffic to flow and to prevent unsafe traffic from reaching your computer.
- Windows Defender is a free program from Microsoft that monitors your computer for spyware and quarantines or removes it upon detection.
- Microsoft Security Essentials is another free program from Microsoft that provides constant, real-time protection from viruses and other malware.
- If your anti-malware software cannot remove a virus or worm from a computer, try the Microsoft Windows Malicious Software Removal Tool.
- Microsoft Forefront Endpoint Protection works with System Center Configuration Manager 2007 to provide security for network-connected computers in the enterprise.

Knowledge Assessment Questions

258 | Lesson 7

Knowledge Assessment

Fill in the Blank

Complete the following sentences by writing the correct word or words in the blanks provided.

1. A disk that is _____ has file data spread across many different sectors.
2. _____ is a utility that removes many different kinds of unnecessary files from your computer.
3. In Task Scheduler, a _____ is an event that causes a task to run.
4. The _____ is a database in Windows that stores user preferences, file locations, program configuration settings, startup information, hardware settings, and more.
5. Microsoft provides regularly scheduled updates to the Windows operating system via the _____ feature.
6. _____ delivers updates for Microsoft software in addition to the Windows operating system.
7. _____ describes a wide variety of malicious software, such as viruses and worms, that attack computers.
8. A _____ is a collection of updates from Microsoft since the last version of Windows or another Microsoft product was released.
9. _____ is Microsoft's free antispyware program.
10. _____ enables you to centrally manage the security of client computers and devices in an enterprise.

Multiple Choice

Circle the letter that corresponds to the best answer.

1. Which Windows built-in utility helps you delete unnecessary files from your computer?
   a. Disk Defragmenter
   b. Disk Cleanup
   c. Task Scheduler
   d. Registry Editor
2. Which Windows built-in utility helps improve your computer's performance by moving sectors of data on the hard disk?
   a. Disk Defragmenter
   b. Disk Cleanup
   c. Task Scheduler
   d. Registry Editor
3. In Task Scheduler, which command creates a task using a wizard?
   a. Create Task
   b. Create Scheduled Task
   c. Create Task Automatically
   d. Create Basic Task
4. In Windows Defender and Microsoft Security Essentials, which of the following scans is not available?
   a. Quick
   b. Full

Competency Assessment

Understanding Operating System Configurations | 61

10. Which of the following correctly explains the abbreviation VHD?
   a. Variable Hex Determinant
   b. Virtual Home Directory
   c. Virtual Hard Disk
   d. Virtual Hard Drive

True / False

Circle T if the statement is true or F if the statement is false.

T | F | 1. A User Account Control dialog box displays when you open your data files.
T | F | 2. You cannot change the desktop resolution setting because it's a fixed value.
T | F | 3. Deleting a shortcut does not delete the resource it represents.
T | F | 4. A user account and a user profile are the same thing.
T | F | 5. Med-V delivers centrally managed virtual machines to authorized end users.

Competency Assessment

Scenario 2-1: Getting Administrative-Level Privileges

As an IT technician, you need to perform some maintenance tasks on an employee's computer that will require elevated privileges. When you go to the Manage Accounts window in Control Panel on that employee's computer, you see only the employee's standard user account. What do you do to be able to log on as a user with administrative-level privileges?

Scenario 2-2: Configuring Accessibility Features

Alexandra, an employee at your company, is visually impaired. Which features can you configure in Windows 7 to help her do her work more efficiently?

Proficiency Assessment

Proficiency Assessment

Scenario 2-3: Running a Legacy Application

Oscar is the warehouse manager for The OEM Connection, an auto parts business. Although the business standardized on Windows 7 Professional, Oscar needs to run a legacy parts lookup program that does not run in Windows 7. You provide technical support to The OEM Connection. What can you do to help Oscar?

Scenario 2-4: Creating a Better User Experience

Oscar at The OEM Connection asks you to help him speed up his computer, which now runs Windows 7 Professional. He doesn't care about all of the "nippy, new" features in the Windows 7 Aero interface—he just wants the computer to run a bit faster and be more responsive. He would also like to be able to quickly launch Microsoft Excel each time he logs on to his computer, and he does not want the Windows Media Player to be present on the taskbar. How do you meet Oscar's requests?

Conventions and Features Used in This Book

This book uses particular fonts, symbols, and heading conventions to highlight important information or to call your attention to special steps. For more information about the features in each lesson, refer to the Illustrated Book Tour section.

Convention	Meaning
↓ **THE BOTTOM LINE**	This feature provides a brief summary of the material to be covered in the section that follows.
CLOSE	Words in all capital letters indicate instructions for opening, saving, or closing files or programs. They also point out items you should check or actions you should take.
CERTIFICATION READY	This feature signals the point in the text where a specific certification objective is covered. It provides you with a chance to check your understanding of that particular MTA objective and, if necessary, review the section of the lesson where it is covered.
TAKE NOTE*	Reader aids appear in shaded boxes found in your text. *Take Note* provides helpful hints related to particular tasks or topics.
X REF	These notes provide pointers to information discussed elsewhere in the textbook or describe interesting features of Windows Server that are not directly addressed in the current topic or exercise.
Alt + Tab	A plus sign (+) between two key names means that you must press both keys at the same time. Keys that you are instructed to press in an exercise will appear in the font shown here.
Example	Key terms appear in bold italic.

www.wiley.com/college/microsoft *or*
call the MOAC Toll-Free Number: 1+(888) 764-7001 (U.S. & Canada only)

Instructor Support Program

The *Microsoft Official Academic Course* programs are accompanied by a rich array of resources that incorporate the extensive textbook visuals to form a pedagogically cohesive package. These resources provide all the materials instructors need to deploy and deliver their courses. Resources available online for download include:

- **DreamSpark Premium** is designed to provide the easiest and most inexpensive developer tools, products, and technologies available to faculty and students in labs, classrooms, and on student PCs. A free 3-year membership is available to qualified MOAC adopters.

  Note: Microsoft Windows 7 can be downloaded from DreamSpark Premium for use by students in this course.

- The **Instructor Guides** contains Solutions to all the textbook exercises and Syllabi for various term lengths. The Instructor Guides also includes chapter summaries and lecture notes. The Instructor's Guide is available from the Book Companion site (http://www.wiley.com/college/microsoft).

- The **Test Bank** contains hundreds of questions in multiple-choice, true-false, short answer, and essay formats, and is available to download from the Instructor's Book Companion site (www.wiley.com/college/microsoft). A complete answer key is provided.

- A complete set of **PowerPoint presentations and images** are available on the Instructor's Book Companion site (http://www.wiley.com/college/microsoft) to enhance classroom presentations. Approximately 50 PowerPoint slides are provided for each lesson. Tailored to the text's topical coverage and Skills Matrix, these presentations are designed to convey key concepts addressed in the text. All images from the text are on the Instructor's Book Companion site (http://www.wiley.com/college/microsoft). You can incorporate them into your PowerPoint presentations, or create your own overhead transparencies and handouts. By using these visuals in class discussions, you can help focus students' attention on key elements of technologies covered and help them understand how to use it effectively in the workplace.

- When it comes to improving the classroom experience, there is no better source of ideas and inspiration than your fellow colleagues. The **Wiley Faculty Network** connects teachers with technology, facilitates the exchange of best practices, and helps to enhance instructional efficiency and effectiveness. Faculty Network activities include technology training and tutorials, virtual seminars, peer-to-peer exchanges of experiences and ideas, personal consulting, and sharing of resources. For details visit www.WhereFacultyConnect.com.

DREAMSPARK PREMIUM—FREE 3-YEAR MEMBERSHIP AVAILABLE TO QUALIFIED ADOPTERS!

DreamSpark Premium is designed to provide the easiest and most inexpensive way for universities to make the latest Microsoft developer tools, products, and technologies available in labs, classrooms, and on student PCs. DreamSpark Premium is an annual membership program for departments teaching Science, Technology, Engineering, and Mathematics (STEM) courses. The membership provides a complete solution to keep academic labs, faculty, and students on the leading edge of technology.

Software available in the DreamSpark Premium program is provided at no charge to adopting departments through the Wiley and Microsoft publishing partnership.

And tools that professors can use to engage and inspire today's technology students.

Contact your Wiley rep for details.

For more information about the DreamSpark Premium program, go to:

https://www.dreamspark.com/

Note: Windows 7 can be downloaded from MSDN AA for use by students in this course.

■ Important Web Addresses and Phone Numbers

To locate the Wiley Higher Education Rep in your area, go to http://www.wiley.com/college and click on the "*Who's My Rep?*" link at the top of the page, or call the MOAC Toll Free Number: 1 + (888) 764-7001 (U.S. & Canada only).

To learn more about becoming a Microsoft Certified Technology Specialist and exam availability, visit www.microsoft.com/learning/mcp/mcp.

▪ Additional Resources

Book Companion Web Site (www.wiley.com/college/microsoft)

The students' book companion site for the MOAC series includes any resources, exercise files, and Web links that will be used in conjunction with this course.

Wiley Desktop Editions

Wiley MOAC Desktop Editions are innovative, electronic versions of printed textbooks. Students buy the desktop version for up to 40% off the U.S. price of the printed text, and get the added value of permanence and portability. Wiley Desktop Editions provide students with numerous additional benefits that are not available with other e-text solutions.

Wiley Desktop Editions are NOT subscriptions; students download the Wiley Desktop Edition to their computer desktops. Students own the content they buy to keep for as long as they want. Once a Wiley Desktop Edition is downloaded to the computer desktop, students have instant access to all of the content without being online. Students can also print out the sections they prefer to read in hard copy. Students also have access to fully integrated resources within their Wiley Desktop Edition. From highlighting their e-text to taking and sharing notes, students can easily personalize their Wiley Desktop Edition as they are reading or following along in class.

▪ About the Microsoft Technology Associate (MTA) Certification

Preparing Tomorrow's Technology Workforce

Technology plays a role in virtually every business around the world. Possessing the fundamental knowledge of how technology works and understanding its impact on today's academic and workplace environment is increasingly important—particularly for students interested in exploring professions involving technology. That's why Microsoft created the Microsoft Technology Associate (MTA) certification—a new entry-level credential that validates fundamental technology knowledge among students seeking to build a career in technology.

The Microsoft Technology Associate (MTA) certification is the ideal and preferred path to Microsoft's world-renowned technology certification programs, such as Microsoft Certified Technology Specialist (MCTS) and Microsoft Certified IT Professional (MCITP). MTA is positioned to become the premier credential for individuals seeking to explore and pursue a career in technology, or augment related pursuits such as business or any other field where technology is pervasive.

MTA Candidate Profile

The MTA certification program is designed specifically for secondary and post-secondary students interested in exploring academic and career options in a technology field. It offers students a certification in basic IT and development. As the new recommended entry point for Microsoft technology certifications, MTA is designed especially for students new to IT and software development. It is available exclusively in educational settings and easily integrates into the curricula of existing computer classes.

MTA Empowers Educators and Motivates Students

MTA provides a new standard for measuring and validating fundamental technology knowledge right in the classroom while keeping your budget and teaching resources intact. MTA helps institutions stand out as innovative providers of high-demand industry credentials and is easily deployed with a simple, convenient, and affordable suite of entry-level technology certification exams. MTA enables students to explore career paths in technology without requiring a big investment of time and resources, while providing a career foundation and the confidence to succeed in advanced studies and future vocational endeavors.

In addition to giving students an entry-level Microsoft certification, MTA is designed to be a stepping stone to other, more advanced Microsoft technology certifications, like the Microsoft Certified Technology Specialist (MCTS) certification.

Delivering MTA Exams: The MTA Campus License

Implementing a new certification program in your classroom has never been so easy with the MTA Campus License. Through the one-time purchase of the 12-month, 1,000-exam MTA Campus License, there's no more need for ad hoc budget requests and recurrent purchases of exam vouchers. Now you can budget for one low cost for the entire year, and then administer MTA exams to your students and other faculty across your entire campus where and when you want.

The MTA Campus License provides a convenient and affordable suite of entry-level technology certifications designed to empower educators and motivate students as they build a foundation for their careers.

The MTA Campus License is administered by Certiport, Microsoft's exclusive MTA exam provider.

To learn more about becoming a Microsoft Technology Associate and exam availability, visit www.microsoft.com/learning/mta.

▪ Activate Your FREE MTA Practice Test!

Your purchase of this book entitles you to a free MTA practice test from GMetrix (a $30 value). Please go to www.gmetrix.com/mtatests and use the following validation code to redeem your free test: **MTA98-349-39D88DDFE2F9.**

The **GMetrix Skills Management System** provides everything you need to practice for the Microsoft Technology Associate (MTA) Certification.

Overview of Test features:

- Practice tests map to the Microsoft Technology Associate (MTA) exam objectives
- GMetrix MTA practice tests simulate the actual MTA testing environment
- 50+ questions per test covering all objectives
- Progress at own pace, save test to resume later, return to skipped questions
- Detailed, printable score report highlighting areas requiring further review

To get the most from your MTA preparation, take advantage of your free GMetrix MTA Practice Test today!

For technical support issues on installation or code activation, please email support@gmetrix.com.

Acknowledgments

■ MOAC MTA Technology Fundamentals Reviewers

We'd like to thank the many reviewers who pored over the manuscript and provided invaluable feedback in the service of quality instructional materials:

Yuke Wang, University of Texas at Dallas

Palaniappan Vairavan, Bellevue College

Harold "Buz" Lamson, ITT Technical Institute

Colin Archibald, Valencia Community College

Catherine Bradfield, DeVry University Online

Robert Nelson, Blinn College

Kalpana Viswanathan, Bellevue College

Bob Becker, Vatterott College

Carol Torkko, Bellevue College

Bharat Kandel, Missouri Tech

Linda Cohen, Forsyth Technical Community College

Candice Lambert, Metro Technology Centers

Susan Mahon, Collin College

Mark Aruda, Hillsborough Community College

Claude Russo, Brevard Community College

Heith Hennel, Valencia College

Harold Lamson, Excelsior College

Zeshan Sattar, Zenos

Douglas Tabbutt, Blackhawk Technical College

David Koppy, Baker College

Sharon Moran, Hillsborough Community College

Keith Hoell, Briarcliffe College and Queens College—CUNY

Mark Hufnagel, Lee County School District

Rachelle Hall, Glendale Community College

Scott Elliott, Christie Digital Systems, Inc.

Gralan Gilliam, Kaplan

Steve Strom, Butler Community College

John Crowley, Bucks County Community College

Margaret Leary, Northern Virginia Community College

Sue Miner, Lehigh Carbon Community College

Gary Rollinson, Cabrillo College

Al Kelly, University of Advancing Technology

Katherine James, Seneca College

www.wiley.com/college/microsoft *or*
call the MOAC Toll-Free Number: 1+(888) 764-7001 (U.S. & Canada only)

Brief Contents

Contents

Introducing, Installing, and Upgrading Windows 7

EXAM OBJECTIVE MATRIX

SKILLS/CONCEPTS	MTA EXAM OBJECTIVE DESCRIPTION	MTA EXAM OBJECTIVE NUMBER
Identifying Windows Operating System Editions	Identify Windows operating system editions.	2.1
Identifying Upgrade Paths	Identify upgrade paths.	2.2
	Identify Windows operating system editions.	2.1
Identifying Application Compatibility	Identify upgrade paths.	2.2
Understanding Product Identification Keys	Understand installation types.	2.3
Understanding Installation Types	Understand installation types.	2.3

KEY TERMS

32-bit computer

64-bit computer

activation

application compatibility

CD key

cloud

custom installation

High Touch Installation (HTI)

image

Lite Touch Installation (LTI)

product key

upgrade installation

upgrade path

Windows 7

Windows 7 Enterprise

Windows 7 Home Basic

Windows 7 Home Premium

Windows 7 Professional

Windows 7 Starter

Windows 7 Ultimate

Windows 7 Upgrade Advisor

Windows Deployment Services

Window Easy Transfer

Zero Touch Installation (ZTI)

You work as an IT technician for Interstate Snacks, Inc., a mid-market food service and vending company. Management has decided to standardize on Windows 7 Professional and has asked your IT group to evaluate all existing computers to determine if they can support the operating system. Any newly acquired computers should have Windows 7 Professional installed. You need to learn as much as possible about Windows 7 system requirements, types of installations, and upgrade paths.

■ Identifying Windows Operating System Editions

 THE BOTTOM LINE Windows 7 is the latest Windows client operating system by Microsoft. This operating system runs on desktop computers, workstations, laptops, and other computers. It was preceded by Microsoft Windows Vista and, before that, Windows XP.

Windows 7 is a desktop operating system and is an improvement over both Windows Vista and Windows XP in many ways: it's faster and easier to install and set up, it's more stable, it has improved Start menu search functionality, and lots more. Windows 7 includes some terrific new features as well, such as large and animated task thumbnails, homegroups, Jump Lists, libraries, and Windows XP Mode, all of which you'll learn about in this course.

If you've used Windows Vista, the Windows 7 interface should seem highly familiar. However, it's a big leap from Windows XP to Windows 7.

Regardless of your experience with Windows operating systems, one thing hasn't changed—Microsoft offers a variety of editions to serve the needs of different users and markets.

The following are the six main editions of Windows 7:

- Windows 7 Starter
- Windows 7 Home Basic
- Windows 7 Home Premium
- Windows 7 Professional
- Windows 7 Enterprise
- Windows 7 Ultimate

There are some common threads throughout all editions. For example, every edition contains the same integrated applications, such as Network and Sharing Center, Control Panel, and Windows Media Player. The different editions also include many of the same multimedia features. All editions support 32-bit systems, and all editions except Windows 7 Starter support 64-bit systems. (You'll learn about 32-bit and 64-bit systems later in the lesson.)

Of the six editions, only Home Premium, Professional, and Ultimate are widely available in the retail sector. The other editions are designed for certain types of computers or markets, or specifically for enterprise use.

Starter is a low-cost edition designed for small notebook PCs such as netbooks. Home Basic is sold in emerging markets (such as China, Mexico, and Russia), but not in the United States or Canada. Home Premium emphasizes the multimedia experience and is geared toward home users, students, and small office/home office (SOHO) users. The Professional and Enterprise editions include additional security features and are designed to meet the needs of the business sector. Professional is recommended for small businesses, and Enterprise is recommended for mid- and large-sized businesses. Ultimate includes all of the features offered in Windows 7.

➕ **MORE INFORMATION**

For more information about Windows 7 and its various editions, visit http://windows.microsoft.com/en-US/windows7/products/home and http://windows.microsoft.com/en-US/windows7/products/compare

Windows 7 Home Premium, Professional, and Ultimate

The most commonly used Windows 7 editions are Home Premium, Professional, and Ultimate. In this section, you'll learn about the key differences between these popular operating systems.

All Windows 7 editions are based on a foundational feature set, and each edition includes some unique features. The following are descriptions of the most common retail editions of Windows 7:

TAKE NOTE ✱

A "domain" is a collection of user and computer accounts that are grouped together to enable centralized management and to apply security. Small Windows environments might use workgroups rather than domains. You'll learn about workgroups, domains, and other networking topics in Lesson 4.

- *Windows 7 Home Premium* contains features aimed at the home market segment, such as Windows Aero, Windows Media Center, Remote Media Streaming, Internet TV, Backup and Restore, and multi-touch support. This edition provides adequate networking and security features to be useful in small office environments.

- *Windows 7 Professional* is targeted mainly toward small business users but appeals to power users as well. It includes all the features of Windows 7 Home Premium and adds the ability to join a Windows domain. Additional features include location-aware printing, acting as a Remote Desktop host (especially useful for tech support), Encrypting File System, and Windows XP Mode.

- *Windows 7 Ultimate* contains all of the same features as Windows 7 Home Premium and Windows 7 Professional, but also includes the applications BitLocker and AppLocker (which are advanced security features). Home Premium and Professional users may upgrade to Ultimate for a fee using Windows Anytime Upgrade.

Table 1-1 compares some features of Windows 7 Home Premium, Professional, and Ultimate.

Table 1-1

Comparing a Subset of Features of Windows 7 Home Premium, Professional, and Ultimate

WINDOWS 7 FEATURE	HOME PREMIUM	PROFESSIONAL	ULTIMATE
Aero interface	Yes	Yes	Yes
Windows Media Center	Yes	Yes	Yes
Backup and Restore	Yes	Yes	Yes
Windows Anytime Upgrade	Yes	Yes	No
Back up to network	No	Yes	Yes
Location-aware printing	No	Yes	Yes
Remote Desktop Host	No	Yes	Yes
Encrypting File System	No	Yes	Yes
Windows XP Mode	No	Yes	Yes
Support for joining domains	No	Yes	Yes
BitLocker and AppLocker	No	No	Yes

Other Windows 7 Editions: Starter, Home Basic, and Enterprise

Some Windows 7 editions—Windows 7 Starter, Home Basic, and Enterprise—don't have a large retail presence for a variety of reasons. These include limited functionality, geographical restrictions, or a focus on larger business environments.

You won't find the following Windows editions on a retail shelf but they nonetheless fill a demand niche:

- **Windows 7 Starter** is available only as a pre-installed operating system on netbook-class PCs. This edition is designed to run well with relatively low memory and disk space. It does not include some Windows 7 features such as 64-bit system support, the Windows Aero theme, or Windows domain support for business users. Because it's essentially a stripped down version of Windows 7 Home Premium, Windows 7 Starter is built mainly for mobile users who only need to browse the Internet, check e-mail, and use a word processor or spreadsheet program.

- **Windows 7 Home Basic** supports the Windows Aero theme but does not include all Aero features. This edition is not available to North American users or those in other "developed technology markets" (such as Australia, Western and Central Europe, Hong Kong, or Saudi Arabia). Microsoft controls the geographical restrictions through the activation process (discussed later in this lesson). If you attempt to activate a computer running Home Basic in a country or region that's restricted from use, the activation process fails.

- **Windows 7 Enterprise** is geared toward enterprise environments. This edition contains all of the same features as Windows 7 Ultimate, but unlike the Ultimate edition, it is not available to home users on an individual license basis. Enterprise is available only through special corporate licensing agreements. Companies must have a Software Assurance Agreement with Microsoft to purchase software licenses. As a result, it includes benefits that are unique to the Software Assurance program, such as allowing operation of diskless PCs (nodes) and running multiple virtual machines.

32-Bit Computing versus 64-Bit Computing

The terms 32-bit and 64-bit refer to the way a computer's central processing unit (CPU) processes data. One of the significant differences is that a 64-bit computer can use much more random access memory (RAM) than a 32-bit computer. Operating systems also come in 32-bit and 64-bit versions, and it's important to match the correct operating system to its corresponding computer processor.

More memory and a faster processor helps an operating system run more efficiently, especially when running multiple programs or graphics-intensive applications. The end user has a much better computing experience using a computer that has ample memory.

A **32-bit computer**, also designated as x86, can use up to 4 gigabytes (GB) of RAM. A **64-bit computer**, often designated as x64, can handle much more RAM—the maximum is limited by the computer's motherboard. For example, Windows 7 Home Premium supports up to 8 GB of memory, which is typically the maximum the motherboard supports on new computers designed for the Windows 7 Home Premium market. If you install Windows 7 Professional, Ultimate, or Enterprise on the same computer, although they support up to 192 GB of memory, the motherboard will still use only 8 GB even if you try to install more memory.

TAKE NOTE*

Some computers have a 64-bit-capable processor, which is a 32-bit processor that can run 64-bit user-mode code.

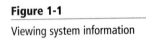

TAKE NOTE*

To check for the latest drivers, run Windows Update or go to Device Manager, double-click a specific hardware component, and click Update Driver on the Driver tab in the Properties dialog box. You can also visit the manufacturer's Web site and download the latest driver.

You can run a 32-bit operating system on a 64-bit computer, but you generally cannot run a 64-bit version of Windows on a 32-bit computer. (There are exceptions but they rarely apply nowadays.) In addition, a 64-bit computer requires 64-bit drivers for all of the hardware components. If you run a mix of 32-bit and 64-bit systems in an enterprise environment, you will need both types of drivers for networked printers, scanners, projectors, and other shared devices. You will also need to maintain multiple images—at least one image for the 32-bit computers and one for the 64-bit computers. An *image* is an exact replica of a computer system. You can use an image to quickly install an operating system with applications to a computer or to restore a crashed computer. You'll learn about images later in this lesson and in Lesson 8.

Finally, many computers today have multi-core processors. A 32-bit version of Windows 7 supports up to 32 processor cores; a 64-bit version of Windows 7 supports up to 256 processor cores.

DETERMINE IF YOUR PC IS RUNNING 32-BIT WINDOWS OR 64-BIT WINDOWS

GET READY. To find out if your computer is running a 32-bit or 64-bit version of Windows 7 or Windows Vista, perform the following steps:

1. Click the **Start** button, right-click **Computer**, and then click **Properties**. The System window displays.

2. Look in the System area to view the system type (see Figure 1-1).

Figure 1-1

Viewing system information

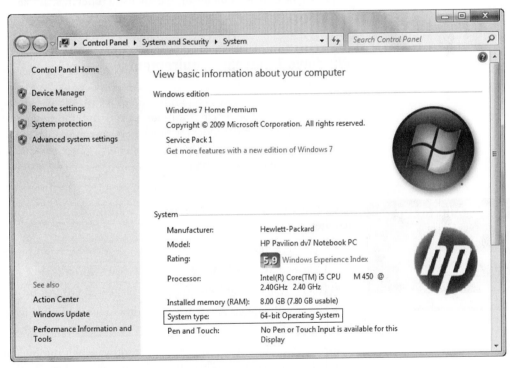

An alternative method is to check the System Information window. To do so, perform the following steps:

1. Click the **Start** button, type **system info** in the **Search programs and files** search box, and then click **System Information** in the resulting list.

2. Make sure **System Summary** is selected in the navigation pane on the left.

3. Look at the **System Type** value in the right pane (see Figure 1-2):
   - **x86-based PC** displays for a 32-bit operating system
   - **x64-based PC** displays for a 64-bit operating system

Figure 1-2

Viewing the System Type value on the System Information page

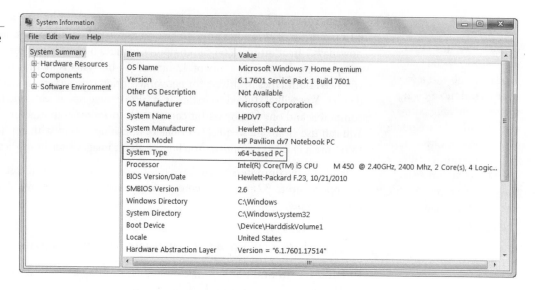

To check the operating system version in Windows XP:

1. Click **Start**.
2. Right-click **My Computer** and choose **Properties**. If "x64 Edition" is not listed, you're running the 32-bit version of Windows XP.

Windows 7 System Requirements

Software manufacturers, including Microsoft, list the system requirements needed to run their products. The specifications are usually minimum requirements; recommended requirements—which allow for much better performance of the OS and applications—are often much higher (in the case of memory, processor speed, or hard disk space) or involve more recent technology.

CERTIFICATION READY
What is the minimum amount of RAM a computer must have in order to run Windows 7 on a 32-bit processor?
2.1

According to Microsoft, a computer that will run Windows 7 must meet the following system requirements:

- 1 gigahertz (GHz) or faster 32-bit (x86) or 64-bit (x64) processor
- 1 gigabyte (GB) RAM (32-bit) or 2 GB RAM (64-bit)
- 16 GB available hard disk space (32-bit) or 20 GB (64-bit)
- DirectX 9 graphics device with Windows Display Driver Model (WDDM) 1.0 or higher driver

Hardware specifications usually mean the software will run but might not result in an optimal user experience. When preparing to run Windows 7, it's best to exceed the processor, RAM, and hard disk space requirements, if possible. For example, a user who wants to simultaneously run a Web browser, an e-mail client, and productivity software (such as a word processor and a spreadsheet application) will have a good user experience on a computer with a 2 GHz processor, 4 GB of RAM, and at least a 250 GB hard drive. A user who needs to run memory-intensive graphic programs along with other applications will find the computer highly responsive with at least 8 GB of RAM and 500 GB or more of hard disk space. Computers that don't have access to shared storage space on a network may also need secondary storage, such as an external flash hard drive. This is especially important if the user has a large number of image, video, or audio files, which tend to consume much more disk space than ordinary document files.

In addition, Microsoft lists the following items as required for using specific features or for optimal performance:

- Internet access (be aware that you may need to pay for the service)
- Additional memory and advanced graphics hardware for video playback, depending on the resolution required or desired
- A graphics card compatible with DirectX 10 or higher for certain games and programs; DirectX enhances the multimedia capabilities of a computer by enabling the graphics card to process some multimedia functions rather than the CPU.
- A TV tuner and additional hardware for some Windows Media Center functionality
- Specific hardware for Windows Touch and Tablet PCs
- A network and PCs running Windows 7 for HomeGroup utilization
- A compatible optical drive to burn DVDs/CDs
- Trusted Platform Module (TPM) 1.2 for BitLocker; TPM is a security chip on some motherboards that helps protect a computer from being used when the computer has been lost, stolen, or attacked by a hacker.
- A universal serial bus (USB) flash drive for BitLocker To Go
- An additional 1 GB of RAM and an additional 15 GB of available hard disk space for Windows XP Mode
- Audio output for music and sound

If you're not sure whether your computer will run Windows 7, see the "Using Windows 7 Upgrade Advisor" section in this lesson.

> **TAKE NOTE** *
>
> Remember, some features of Windows 7, such as BitLocker, do not ship with every version of Windows 7.

> **+ MORE INFORMATION**
>
> For more information about the Windows 7 system requirements, visit http://windows.microsoft.com/en-US/windows7/products/system-requirements

■ Identifying Upgrade Paths

THE BOTTOM LINE

Can you upgrade to Windows 7 from your current operating system? If so, what type of upgrade you can perform? Those answers depend on many factors. Learn about Windows 7 upgrade paths to fully understand your options.

> **CERTIFICATION READY**
> What type of upgrade path is necessary for upgrading from Windows Vista to Windows 7?
> 2.2

A retail version of Windows 7 is available as a full version or an upgrade version. You install the full version on a clean hard disk. You should purchase an upgrade version if your computer is currently running Windows XP or Windows Vista. The full and upgrade versions are essentially the same—they have the same features and integrated programs.

In the context of this lesson, an *upgrade path* is the set of options you have to upgrade from one Windows operating system to another. When upgrading to Windows 7 from Windows Vista, you have two primary choices: a standard upgrade or a custom installation. Windows XP users must perform a custom installation when "upgrading" to Windows 7.

An *upgrade installation* replaces your current version of Windows with Windows 7 while retaining your files, settings, and programs. This type of installation is sometimes called an "in-place" installation. A *custom installation* replaces your current version of Windows with Windows 7 but overwrites your files, settings, and programs. This is also referred to as a "clean" installation.

TAKE NOTE* You can use the upgrade or full version of Windows 7 to perform either a custom or upgrade installation. Regardless of the type of installation you plan to perform, you should first back up the files and settings on the computer to be upgraded as a safety precaution. Backups are covered in Lesson 8.

Table 1-2 shows the upgrade paths to Windows 7 Home Premium, Professional, and Ultimate.

Table 1-2

Windows 7 Upgrade Paths for Home Premium, Professional, and Ultimate

UPGRADING FROM	TO HOME PREMIUM	TO PROFESSIONAL	TO ULTIMATE
Windows XP	Custom	Custom	Custom
Windows Vista Home Basic	Upgrade	Custom	Upgrade
Windows Vista Home Premium	Upgrade	Custom	Upgrade
Windows Vista Business	Custom	Upgrade	Upgrade
Windows Vista Ultimate	Custom	Custom	Upgrade

+ MORE INFORMATION

For more information about upgrading to Windows 7, visit http://windows.microsoft.com/en-US/windows7/products/upgrade and http://windows.microsoft.com/en-US/windows7/upgrading-to-windows-7-frequently-asked-questions

Upgrade Paths from Windows XP

You don't have a lot of choices when upgrading from Windows XP. However, you can ease the process by following a few tips.

To upgrade from Windows XP to Windows 7, you must perform a custom installation. Because your files, programs, and settings will be overwritten, *back up all of your data files first.* A best practice is to create at least two backups and test both of them before proceeding with the upgrade.

You should also ensure you have the original installation media or downloaded installation files for all of the programs you plan to install after you upgrade to Windows 7.

 TAKE NOTE* You may be able to use Windows Easy Transfer to "move" files and settings from Windows XP to Windows 7. See the "Using Windows Easy Transfer" section in this lesson.

Upgrade Paths from Windows Vista

The upgrade path you must take from Windows Vista to Windows 7 depends on some key factors—mainly your current edition of Windows Vista and the edition of Windows 7 you want to run. There are a few other considerations too, such as 32-bit versus 64-bit environment and desired language.

If you want to upgrade from Windows Vista to Windows 7, knowing which version of Windows 7 to select can be daunting. The type of installation you perform—custom or upgrade—will depend on the edition of Windows Vista you're currently running and the edition of Windows 7 you want to install.

The main point to remember is that you can perform an upgrade installation if you're installing an equivalent or higher edition of Windows 7. Otherwise, you must perform a custom installation. Refer back to Table 1-2 to see which editions of Windows Vista map to which editions of Windows 7.

Here are some other situations that require a custom installation:

- If you're currently running a 32-bit version of Windows Vista and want to install a 64-bit version of Windows 7, or vice versa
- If you plan to use a different language in Windows 7 than the language you're using in Windows Vista

Upgrading directly to Windows 7 from Windows Vista can be a relatively quick and easy task. Your files, settings, and programs are preserved, which means you can be productive soon after the installation completes. Because a custom installation doesn't preserve your files, settings, and programs, you will need to spend some time installing programs and configuring Windows 7 after the upgrade.

UPGRADE FROM WINDOWS VISTA TO WINDOWS 7

GET READY. To perform an upgrade installation from Windows Vista, perform the following steps:

1. In Windows Vista, start the upgrade installation:

   From a download: Locate the Windows 7 installation file and double-click it.

   From disc or USB flash drive: Insert the disc into your computer. If Setup doesn't start automatically, click **Start**, click **Computer**, double-click your disc or drive icon, and then double-click **setup.exe**.

2. On the Install Windows screen, click **Install now**.

3. On the Get important updates for installation screen, get the latest updates. Your computer must be connected to the Internet.

4. On the Please read the license terms screen, accept the license terms and click **Next**.

5. On the Which type of installation do you want? screen, click **Upgrade**.

6. Follow the instructions to finish installing Windows 7.

TAKE NOTE* Once your computer restarts, you should check that your data files are accessible and that peripherals are working as expected. You may also want to personalize the desktop in Windows 7.

Upgrade Paths from Other Operating Systems

You can upgrade from one Windows 7 edition to an advanced edition fairly easily. Going from an old edition of Windows, such as Windows 95 or Windows 2000, to Windows 7 requires the purchase of a full version of Windows 7 and a custom installation.

To upgrade to Windows 7 from Windows 95 or Windows 2000, you need to purchase a full version of Windows 7 and perform a custom installation. You cannot "upgrade" from a non-Windows operating system such as UNIX, Linux, or Mac OS.

However, you can easily upgrade from one edition of Windows 7 to a more advanced edition using Windows Anytime Upgrade. Upgrading in this manner preserves your files, settings, and programs, so you can be up and running within minutes. Table 1-3 shows you the Windows 7 upgrade paths using Windows Anytime Upgrade.

Table 1-3

Windows Anytime Upgrade Options

UPGRADE FROM	TO HOME PREMIUM	TO PROFESSIONAL	TO ULTIMATE
Windows 7 Starter	Yes	Yes	Yes
Windows 7 Home Premium	No	Yes	Yes
Windows 7 Professional	No	No	Yes

To perform this type of in-place upgrade, you must buy an upgrade key from Microsoft or your preferred retailer.

Windows Anytime Upgrade (see Figure 1-3) will upgrade a 32-bit version of Windows 7 to a 32-bit version of Windows 7 and a 64-bit version to a 64-bit version. You cannot use Windows Anytime Upgrade when going from a 32-bit to a 64-bit version or vice versa.

Figure 1-3

The Windows Anytime Upgrade main window

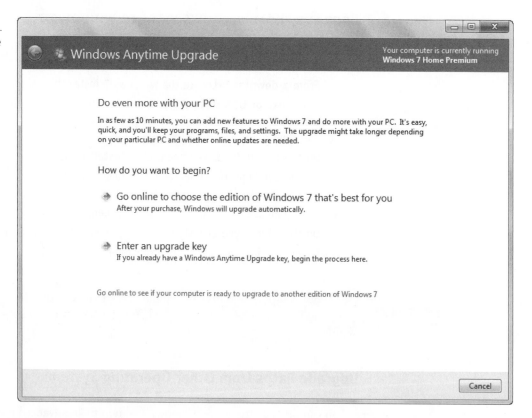

TAKE NOTE* Run Windows 7 Upgrade Advisor before purchasing an upgrade key to ensure your system is ready for the upgrade.

Once you install Windows 7 on a computer, all of the features for all editions of Windows 7 are stored on your computer. When you use Windows Anytime Upgrade to upgrade to an advanced edition of Windows 7, you are simply unlocking the features of that edition.

Using Windows 7 Upgrade Advisor

> Windows 7 Upgrade Advisor helps you determine if your computer can run Windows 7, which editions and features will work, and whether your computer has any compatibility issues. You may download the utility for free from the Microsoft Web site at http://windows.microsoft.com/en-US/windows/downloads/upgrade-advisor

If you've been running Windows Vista on your computer without any hardware problems, you'll probably be able to run Windows 7 too. The two operating systems run well on similar equipment. Upgrading from Windows XP to Windows 7 may result in more compatibility issues simply because the equipment may be older.

You should find out ahead of time if you need to upgrade hardware components or peripherals. *Windows 7 Upgrade Advisor* is a good preparation tool that checks your computer's hardware, attached devices, and installed programs for compatibility issues with Windows 7. The tool creates reports that list potential issues, such as an incompatible printer or a legacy application, and either recommends solutions or points to resources for further information. You also find out which version of Windows 7 is best for your computer.

⊙ INSTALL WINDOWS 7 UPGRADE ADVISOR

GET READY. To download and install Windows 7 Upgrade Advisor, perform the following steps:

1. Using a Web browser, go to the Windows 7 Upgrade Advisor Web page at http://windows.microsoft.com/en-us/windows/downloads/upgrade-advisor

2. Click the **Download** button to begin the download process. You may have to click two Download buttons on two different pages (just follow the on-screen instructions).

3. In the dialog box that displays, click **Save** and then save the setup file to a folder on your computer, such as the Downloads folder.

4. Open the folder and double-click **Windows7UpgradeAdvisorSetup.exe**.

5. If a Security Warning dialog box displays, click **Run** when prompted to start the installer.

> **TAKE NOTE***
> If prompted to provide an administrator password or to click a button to continue, do so.

> **TAKE NOTE*** You might be prompted to install .NET Framework or another program before continuing. Click Yes to install the program and follow the prompts. If using Windows XP, you may need to log on as an administrator to complete the installation.

6. The Windows 7 Upgrade Advisor Setup Wizard starts. Accept the license terms and then click **Install**.

7. When the installation is complete, click **Close**.

⊙ RUN WINDOWS 7 UPGRADE ADVISOR

GET READY. To run Windows 7 Upgrade Advisor and scan your computer for upgrade and compatibility issues, perform the following steps:

1. Plug in and power on external hard disks, printers, or any other peripheral devices that you use regularly with your computer.

2. Click **Start > All Programs > Windows 7 Upgrade Advisor**. The Windows 7 Upgrade Advisor window displays, as shown in Figure 1-4. (This example shows Windows 7 Upgrade Advisor running in Windows XP.)

Figure 1-4

The Windows 7 Upgrade Advisor window

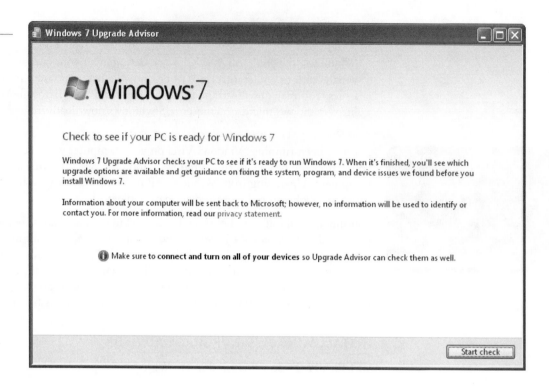

3. Click the **Start check** button to begin the scan process.

4. While the Upgrade Advisor scans your computer, you can click the displayed links to learn more about Windows 7 and compatibility issues. See Figure 1-5.

Figure 1-5

Upgrade Advisor provides learning links while the scan is underway

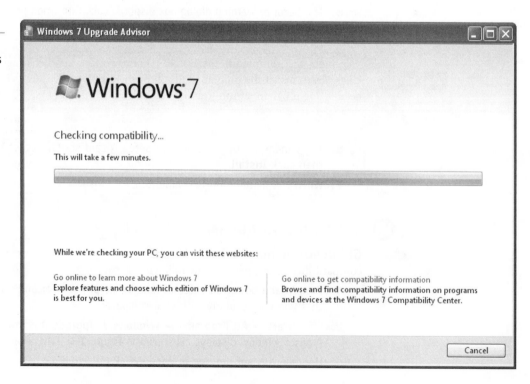

5. When the scan is complete, Upgrade Advisor displays the results of the scan. Parts of an example report are shown in Figure 1-6 and Figure 1-7.

Figure 1-6

The results of an Upgrade Advisor scan (displaying software issues)

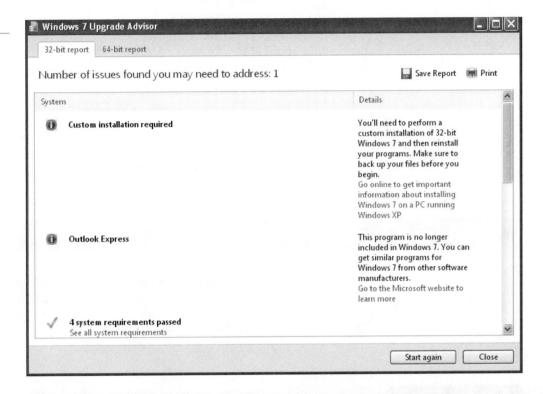

Figure 1-7

The results of an Upgrade Advisor scan (displaying device issues)

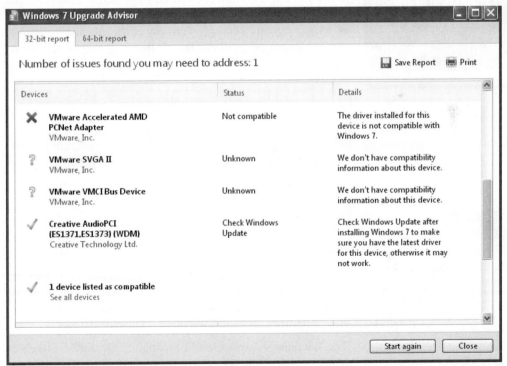

6. Click on any live links that appear in the window to see whether Upgrade Advisor has identified solutions to specific problems or to get more information about an action to be taken.

7. Print or save the list of the actions you must perform to install or upgrade Windows 7. To save the list, click the **Save Report** button.

8. In the **File name** text box, type a name for the report file and then click **Save**.

9. Click **Close** to close Upgrade Advisor.

Based on the results of the Windows 7 Upgrade Advisor scan, you should know which issues, if any, you'll encounter when you install or upgrade to Windows 7 on your computer.

> **➕ MORE INFORMATION**
>
> For more information about Windows 7 Upgrade Advisor and to download the program, visit http://windows.microsoft.com/en-US/windows/downloads/upgrade-advisor

■ Identifying Application Compatibility

↓ THE BOTTOM LINE

Operating system upgrades can result in one or more programs not working properly or not working at all. To identify and resolve issues, use the resources available at the Windows 7 Compatibility Center online as well as the Windows 7 Application Compatibility List for IT Professionals.

CERTIFICATION READY
What are two resources that help you identify and resolve application compatibility issues?
2.2

When you upgrade from one version of Windows to another (for example, from Windows XP or Windows Vista to Windows 7), the potential for *application compatibility* issues arises. Most programs will run fine in any of the operating systems, but some won't. For example, some programs might often crash or freeze, or they might not start at all.

TAKE NOTE*

Antivirus programs tend to be highly specific to operating system versions. You should usually upgrade your antivirus software when upgrading your operating system.

Windows XP Mode is built into some editions of Windows 7. It lets you run legacy programs in a virtual environment to avoid compatibility issues. You'll learn about Windows XP Mode in Lesson 2.

Two resources to help you identify and resolve application compatibility issues are the Windows 7 Compatibility Center and the Windows 7 Application Compatibility List for IT Professionals.

The Windows 7 Compatibility Center (see Figure 1-8) provides software programs, updates, downloads, drivers, and more that are compatible with Windows 7. Browse this site in advance of upgrading to Windows 7. You can also use this site to research software issues you encounter while using the Windows 7 Upgrade Advisor.

The Windows 7 Application Compatibility List for IT Professionals is a downloadable Microsoft Excel spreadsheet that lists commonly used programs, whether they are 32-bit or 64-bit, and information on compatibility. You can download this spreadsheet at http://www.microsoft.com/download/en/details.aspx?displaylang=en&id=2394. Much of the information in the spreadsheet is a result of the Windows 7 Logo Program, which tests software to determine if it meets Windows 7 requirements.

Figure 1-8

The Windows 7 Compatibility Center web site

➕ **MORE INFORMATION**

For more information about application compatibility with Windows 7, visit the Windows 7 Compatibility Center at http://www.microsoft.com/windows/compatibility/windows-7/en-us/default.aspx. The Windows 7 Application Compatibility List for IT Professionals may be downloaded from http://www.microsoft.com/download/en/details.aspx?displaylang=en&id=2394

■ Understanding Product Identification Keys

↓ **THE BOTTOM LINE**

A product key is essential to installing any Windows operating system. This digital key ensures you have a legal installation of the Windows software.

CERTIFICATION READY
What term is used to describe a unique, alphanumeric code required by many software programs during installation?

2.3

The product identification key, often called a ***product key*** or ***CD key***, is a unique, alphanumeric code required by many software programs during installation. The purpose of a product key is to help avoid illegal product installations. The product key you enter during Windows 7 installation is checked by Microsoft for legitimacy and whether it is already being used on a different computer.

TAKE NOTE ✱
When you buy a retail copy of Windows 7, 32-bit and 64-bit versions are included on the same installation media. The product key you enter during setup determines which version of Windows 7 is installed.

A Windows 7 product key looks similar to xxxxx-xxxxx-xxxxx-xxxxx-xxxxx, but is composed of letters and numbers. It is usually located:

- On the installation disc holder inside the Windows package
- On a sticker on the back or bottom of your computer if the operating system came pre-installed on the computer
- In a confirmation e-mail if you purchased and downloaded Windows 7 online

During installation, you must enter the product key exactly as printed. (If you are off by even one character the installation fails.) After you enter the product key correctly, the product key is then written to the Windows registry in an encrypted format, making it unreadable for security purposes. Therefore, it's important to keep your Windows 7 installation media and printed product key in a safe location after initial installation, in case you need to reinstall or repair the operating system at some point.

If you lose your product key, contact Microsoft to request a replacement key.

After a certain period of time post-installation, you will need to activate Windows 7 to continue using the operating system.

TAKE NOTE ✱
You can use the same product key to install Windows on many different computers. However, to meet legal requirements, you won't be able to activate Windows on more than one computer at a time or for the number of computers for which you own Windows licenses. Other software companies, such as Adobe, use this method of product control as well.

Activating Windows 7

Microsoft uses activation to prevent the use of counterfeit copies or otherwise illegal use of its software products, including Windows 7. You must activate Windows 7 within 30 days of installation.

Activation is the process of verifying that your copy of Windows is genuine and that it is not in use on other computers than the number for which you own a license. If you purchased a single copy of Windows 7 from a retailer, for example, you can activate the software on only one computer at a time. Within 30 days of installing Windows 7, activate the software over the Web or by calling Microsoft. Once your Windows 7 installation is activated, you can use all features of the operating system.

If you installed Windows 7 on another computer, you must deactivate it on the original computer before activating it on the other computer. Deactivation may require a call to Microsoft Technical Support.

Registration is different from activation. You *must* activate an installation of Windows 7 but registration is optional. During registration, you give your contact information to Microsoft to sign up for technical support and other benefits.

■ Understanding Installation Types

THE BOTTOM LINE

There are many different types of Windows 7 installations, from the manual DVD method to a fully automated setup effort over a network. Learn the various ways in which you can install Windows 7 and select the most efficient method for your needs.

CERTIFICATION READY
What is a cloud installation?
2.3

CERTIFICATION READY
What are the types of removable media installations?
2.3

TAKE NOTE*

An image file is an exact replica of the contents of a hard disk, saved to a file with an .iso extension, or a .wim extension if it's a Windows Imaging Format image.

TAKE NOTE*

For more information on building a WinPE image, visit http://technet.microsoft.com/en-us/library/dd799244(WS.10).aspx

Microsoft provides many different ways to install Windows 7, from manual methods like inserting a DVD to fully automated, "non-touch" installations performed over a network or even via the cloud. (The *cloud* generally refers to the Internet or to a server accessible over the Internet.) The method you choose depends mainly on the number of computers on which you need to install Windows and how much time you have to devote to the project.

Installing Windows 7 from removable media is common in smaller enterprise or home environments. When you think of removable media, you might think of DVDs, but many installations are performed from USB drives as well. Using a DVD or USB drive is considered a manual method of installation. If you're installing Windows on one, two, or even 10 computers, a manual method works well. If you must install Windows on many computers, you'll want to understand automated methods, in order to save time (and, thus, money).

The following are categories that correspond to the level of interaction required during an installation:

- High Touch Installation (HTI)
- Lite Touch Installation (LTI)
- Zero Touch Installation (ZTI)

High Touch Installation (HTI) may include retail media or a standard image (ISO file). Using this method, you use an installation DVD or USB drive and manually install the operating system on every computer. You must then also manually configure each system.

In a larger environment, where you have, say, 25 or more computers that require Windows 7 installations, you could use a tool called ImageX to create bootable media. The Windows Automated Installation Kit (AIK) includes ImageX. You would perform these general steps:

1. Install Windows 7 on a clean hard disk.
2. Configure it with settings that will apply to all computers.
3. Use the Sysprep utility to create an image of the installation.
4. Boot to the Windows Preinstallation Environment (WinPE) and use ImageX to save the image to a DVD, a USB drive, or whatever type of media you plan to use.
5. Install the image on the remaining computers.

Lite Touch Installation (LTI) requires some human intervention in the early phase of the installation, but is automated (or unattended) from that point on. This installation method works well in environments with more than 150 computers.

You need the Windows AIK, Windows Deployment Services, and the Microsoft Deployment Toolkit 2010 for LTIs. *Windows Deployment Services* is a server role for Windows Server 2008 or Windows Server 2008 R2. It allows a user to press the F12 key, log on, and select an image for installation. After that, the installation can be automated. For example, you can use an answer file to configure Windows settings during installation. The answer file contains all the settings that are required for an unattended installation. The Microsoft Deployment Toolkit 2010 is a free download used to automate high-volume operating system deployments.

Zero Touch Installation (ZTI) is a fully automated, "touchless" method of installing Windows. You need System Center Configuration Manager (SCCM) for ZTIs. You use SCCM to deploy and update servers, client computers, and all kinds of devices on a network.

The ZTI method is geared for environments with more than 500 computers, involves a fairly steep learning curve, and requires a considerable budget compared to HTIs.

Another form of automated installation is to use a cloud service such as Windows Intune. This particular service is geared toward business environments and enables you to manage and secure networked computers. In addition, you can upgrade client computers to Windows 7 Enterprise Edition. You need a Web browser and Internet connection along with appropriate licensing to deploy Windows 7 Enterprise Edition via Windows Intune.

⟶ INSTALL WINDOWS 7

GET READY. There are many ways to install Windows 7. This exercise shows you how to install Windows 7 from removable media. Perform the following steps:

1. Turn on your computer and start the installation:

   From a download: Locate the Windows 7 installation file and double-click it.

   From disc or USB flash drive: Insert the disc into your computer. If Setup doesn't start automatically, click the **Start** button, click **Computer**, double-click your disc or drive icon, and then double-click **setup.exe**.

2. On the Install Windows screen, click **Install now.** The installation program shows you its progress as it install files (see Figure 1-9).

Figure 1-9

The Install Windows screen

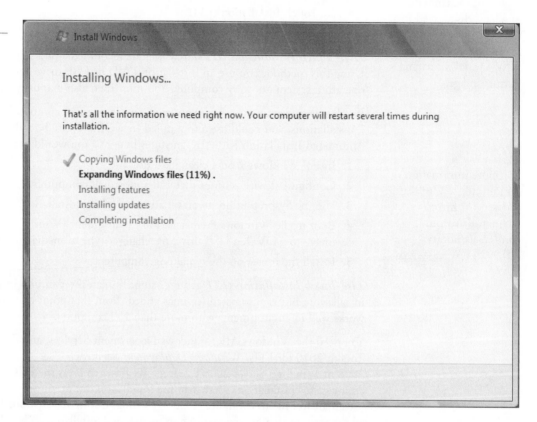

3. On the Get important updates for installation screen, if you have a live Internet connection, choose to get the latest updates to protect your PC.

4. On the Please read the license terms screen, accept the license terms and click **Next**.

5. On the Which type of installation do you want? screen, click **Custom**.

6. On the Where do you want to install Windows? screen, choose the partition that contains your previous version of Windows. Click **Next**.

7. In the Windows.old dialog box, click **OK**.

8. Follow any instructions and respond to prompts that appear, such as for naming your computer, creating a user account, and selecting a type of network (see Figure 1-10).

Figure 1-10

Selecting a type of network

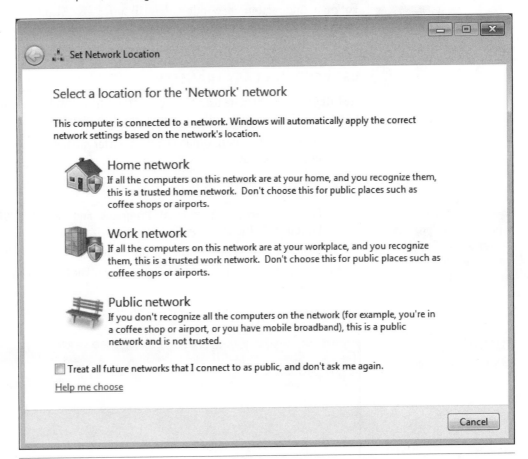

Be sure to run Windows Update immediately after installing Windows 7.

TAKE NOTE*

For more information on installing Windows 7, visit http://windows.microsoft.com/en-US/windows7/Installing-Windows-7-recommended-links and http://windows.microsoft.com/en-US/windows7/Installing-and-reinstalling-Windows-7

Using Windows Easy Transfer

Windows Easy Transfer helps you move files and settings from one computer running Windows to another. The "move" can occur on the same computer if you're upgrading to a different version of Windows that requires a custom installation. Either way, by transferring your files and settings, you get a jump start on your productivity.

If you've used your computer for a long time, you've probably accumulated hundreds or thousands of files, especially if you take photos or collect digital music. You've also, over time, tweaked user settings so they're most efficient for accomplishing work and running software. You shouldn't have to lose files or settings—and your efforts—to upgrade to Windows 7.

Use **Windows Easy Transfer** to save your files and settings on an external hard drive, and then "transfer" them to the new installation of Windows 7. You cannot transfer your programs, so make sure you have the original installation media so you can manually install them in Windows 7.

 TAKE NOTE ✱
For more information on Windows Easy Transfer, visit http://windows.microsoft.com/en-US/windows7/transfer-files-and-settings-from-another-computer

➔ **USE WINDOWS EASY TRANSFER**

GET READY. This exercise uses Windows XP as the example operating system. To perform the transfer with an external hard drive, perform the following steps:

1. Download the latest Windows Easy Transfer program from Microsoft.com and install it on your computer.
2. Reboot your computer and log on as an administrator. Make sure no programs are running.
3. Click the **Start** button, click **All Programs**, and then click **Windows Easy Transfer for Windows 7**. The Windows Easy Transfer Wizard starts.
4. Read the information on the opening screen, and then click **Next**.
5. Select a transfer method (see Figure 1-11). For this example, click **An external hard disk or USB flash drive**.

TAKE NOTE ✱
If prompted to provide an administrator password or to click a button to continue, do so.

Figure 1-11

Selecting a transfer method

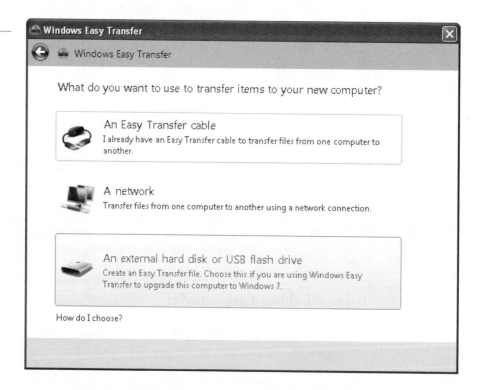

6. On the next screen, select **This is my old computer. I want to transfer files and settings from this computer.**
7. Windows Easy Transfer checks all user accounts, then displays a summary of what can be transferred (see Figure 1-12). Click **Next**.

Figure 1-12

Viewing content that can be transferred

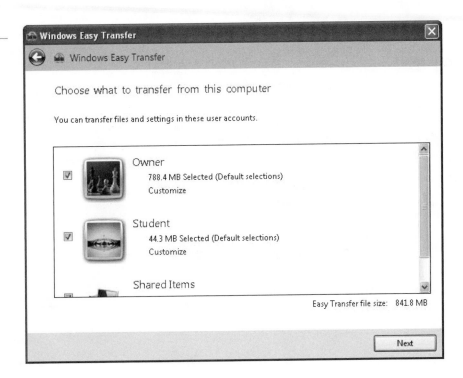

8. On the next screen, Windows Easy Transfer states it will save all files and settings to an Easy Transfer file. If you want to include a password, type it now. Otherwise, just click **Save**.

9. The Save your Easy Transfer file window displays. Select the external drive you are using for the transfer and click **Save**. A file with a .MIG extension is saved to the location you selected. The Save process may take several minutes or hours, depending on the amount of content you are transferring.

10. When the file is saved, click **Next**.

11. The Your transfer file is complete screen displays. Write down the location of the transfer file on your external drive. Click **Next**.

12. The Windows Easy Transfer is complete on this computer screen displays. Click **Close**.

After you install Windows 7 on the computer, perform the following steps:

1. Log on as an administrator and close any open programs.

2. Connect the external drive to your PC. You should be prompted to run Windows Easy Transfer. If not, open Windows Explorer, browse to your external drive, and then double-click the .MIG file. Windows Easy Transfer starts. If the program detects any open programs, it prompts you to close them. Click **Close all**.

3. The Choose what to transfer to this computer screen displays (see Figure 1-13). All items are checked by default. Uncheck any items you don't want transferred (if any) and click **Transfer**.

4. If you chose to password-protect your .MIG file, enter the password when prompted. The transfer process may take several minutes or several hours, depending on the amount of content you are transferring. A progress screen indicates at what stage the transfer is at. Do not close the window until the transfer is complete.

5. The Your Transfer is complete screen displays. To view the transferred files in Windows 7, click **See what was transferred** (see Figure 1-14).

Figure 1-13

Choosing what to transfer to the computer running Windows 7

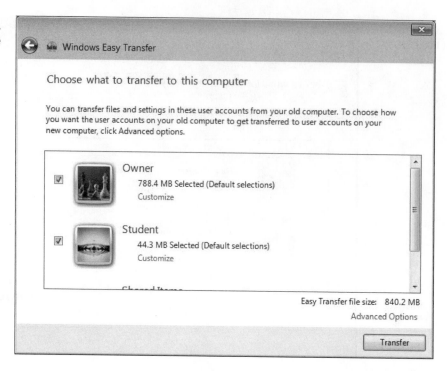

Figure 1-14

The Your Transfer is complete screen

6. The Windows Easy Transfer Reports window displays with the Transfer report tab displayed (see Figure 1-15). Browse the list and click **Details** in any of the categories for more information. Click the Close icon (X) in the upper-right corner when you're done.

7. Windows Easy Transfer remembers the programs you used previously and recommends those that should run in Windows 7. Click **See a list of programs you might want to install on your new computer**. The Windows Easy Transfer Reports window reappears, with the Program report tab displayed (see Figure 1-16). Browse the list of programs and note the recommendations. Click the **Close** icon in the upper-right corner.

Figure 1-15

The Transfer report tab

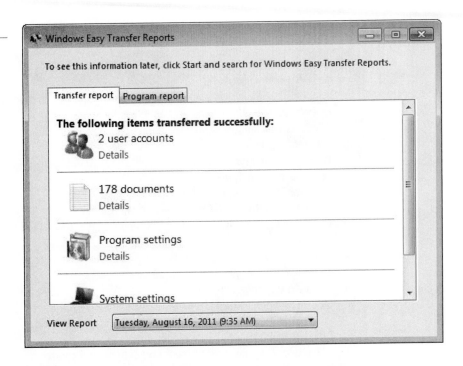

Figure 1-16

The Program report tab

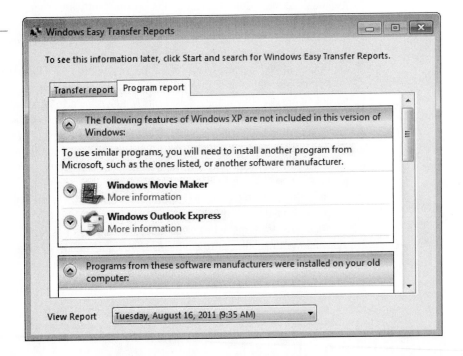

8. To end Windows Easy Transfer, click **Close**.

9. You're prompted to restart your computer. Click **Restart now** or **Restart later**.

The steps in this procedure will vary if you select different options; however, the basic process is the same.

SKILL SUMMARY

IN THIS LESSON YOU LEARNED:

- Windows 7 is a desktop operating system that improves on many aspects of its direct predecessors, Windows Vista and Windows XP.
- Windows 7 includes several new features, such as large and animated task thumbnails, homegroups, Jump Lists, libraries, and Windows XP Mode.
- The six main editions of Windows 7 are Starter, Home Basic, Home Premium, Professional, Ultimate, and Enterprise.
- Common computer architectures are 32-bit and 64-bit. A 32-bit computer can address up to 4 GB of RAM. A 64-bit computer can use much more RAM than a 32-bit computer. Operating systems also come in 32-bit and 64-bit versions, and it's important to match the correct operating system to the computer processor.
- You can run a 32-bit operating system on a 64-bit computer, but you generally cannot run a 64-bit version of Windows on a 32-bit computer.
- The main system requirements for running Windows 7 are: 1 GHz or faster 32-bit (x86) or 64-bit (x64) processor, 1 GB RAM (32-bit) or 2 GB RAM (64-bit), 16 GB available hard disk space (32-bit) or 20 GB (64-bit), and a DirectX 9 graphics device with Windows Display Driver Model (WDDM) 1.0 or higher driver.
- Windows 7 Upgrade Advisor helps you determine if your computer can run Windows 7, which editions and features will work, and whether your computer has any compatibility issues.
- The Windows 7 Compatibility Center provides software programs that are compatible with Windows 7, including updates, downloads, drivers, and more.
- An upgrade installation replaces your current version of Windows with Windows 7 while retaining your files, settings, and programs. A custom installation replaces your current version of Windows with Windows 7 but overwrites your files, settings, and programs. A custom installation is also referred to as a clean installation.
- The upgrade path you must take from Windows Vista to Windows 7 depends on some key factors, mainly your current edition of Windows Vista and the edition of Windows 7 you want to run. There are a few other considerations too, such as 32-bit versus 64-bit environment and desired language. You can easily upgrade from one edition of Windows 7 to a more advanced edition using Windows Anytime Upgrade.
- Installation methods fall into three main categories: High Touch Installation (HTI), Lite Touch Installation (LTI), and Zero Touch Installation (ZTI). HTI is mostly manual, and ZTI is almost completely automated.
- Windows Easy Transfer helps you move files and settings from one computer running Windows to another, or to a new installation of Windows 7 on the same computer.

■ Knowledge Assessment

Fill in the Blank

Complete the following sentences by writing the correct word or words in the blanks provided.

1. A(n) _____ is the set of options you have to upgrade from one Windows operating system to another.

2. _____ is the process of verifying that your copy of Windows is genuine and that it is not in use on more computers than the number for which you own licenses.

3. A _____-bit computer is also designated as x86.

4. A(n) _____ installation replaces your current version of Windows with Windows 7 while retaining your files, settings, and programs.

5. The _____ method involves manual installation of Windows 7 from media such as a DVD or USB drive.

6. Windows 7 _____ is targeted mainly toward small business users.

7. Windows 7 _____ is a retail version that includes BitLocker and AppLocker.

8. _____ is a fully automated, touchless method of installing Windows.

9. _____ is a server role for Windows Server 2008 or Windows Server 2008 R2 that allows for mostly automated installation of Windows 7 over a network.

10. To use Windows Anytime Upgrade to perform an in-place upgrade, you must buy an _____ from Microsoft or your preferred retailer.

Multiple Choice

Circle the letter that corresponds to the best answer.

1. Which edition of Windows 7 does *not* support x64 CPUs?
   a. Starter
   b. Home Basic
   c. Home Premium
   d. Professional

2. Which editions of Windows 7 are widely available in the retail sector? (Choose all that apply.)
   a. Home Premium
   b. Professional
   c. Ultimate
   d. Enterprise

3. Which edition of Windows 7 requires a Software Assurance Agreement with Microsoft?
   a. Home Premium
   b. Professional
   c. Ultimate
   d. Enterprise

4. Which of the following features is *not* included in Windows 7 Professional?
   a. Encrypting File System
   b. Windows XP Mode
   c. Support for joining domains
   d. BitLocker

5. Which tool scans your computer and produces a report of any Windows 7 compatibility issues with your computer?
   a. Windows 7 Compatibility Center
   b. Windows 7 Upgrade Advisor
   c. Windows Easy Transfer
   d. Windows Anytime Upgrade

6. Which Windows 7 installation method uses System Center Configuration Manager for deployment across a network?
   a. HTI
   b. LTI
   c. ZTI
   d. Windows Anytime Upgrade

7. Which Windows 7 installation method requires some human interaction but uses Windows Deployment Services to automate most of the installation?
   a. HTI
   b. LTI
   c. ZTI
   d. Windows Anytime Upgrade

8. You can use the upgrade installation method when upgrading from Windows Vista Business to which of the following? (Choose all that apply.)
   a. Windows 7 Home Basic
   b. Windows 7 Home Premium
   c. Windows 7 Professional
   d. Windows 7 Ultimate

9. What are two common methods for determining if your computer is running a 32-bit or 64-bit version of Windows 7 or Windows Vista? (Choose all that apply.)
   a. Run Windows 7 Upgrade Advisor.
   b. Open the Computer window.
   c. Open the System window.
   d. Run the System Information utility.

10. Where might a Windows 7 product key be located? (Choose all that apply.)
    a. On the installation disc holder inside the Windows package
    b. On a sticker on the back or bottom of your computer
    c. On the installation media itself
    d. In a confirmation e-mail if you purchased and downloaded Windows 7 online

True / False

Circle T if the statement is true or F if the statement is false.

T | F | 1. You must perform a custom installation to upgrade from Windows XP to Windows 7.

T | F | 2. A 1 GHz or faster 32-bit (x86) processor is required to run Windows 7.

T | F | 3. You must register Windows 7 to run it.

T | F | 4. The purpose of a Windows 7 product key is to help avoid illegal installations.

T | F | 5. The Windows 7 Logo Program tests software to determine if it meets Windows 7 requirements.

■ Competency Assessment

Scenario 1-1: Troubleshooting a Compatibility Problem

A remote employee reports that after he upgraded his computer to Windows 7, he is unable to use his USB printer. He says Windows 7 hangs whenever he plugs in his printer. How do you respond?

Scenario 1-2: Creating a Plan to Upgrade to Windows 7

The IT manager for your company informs you that senior management approved the budget for upgrading 20 networked client computers from Windows Vista Business to Windows 7. He asked you how to determine whether the computers can be upgraded to Windows 7 Professional, and which installation method will be most efficient and cost-effective. How do you answer?

■ Proficiency Assessment

Scenario 1-3: Converting a Small Office to Windows 7

Danielle provides IT support for Swish It Away, a small cleaning service in the Pacific Northwest. The company has eight computers. Four of the computers run Windows XP Professional Edition and the other four run Windows Vista Business Edition. The company president has asked her to make sure all eight computers are running Windows 7 Professional by the beginning of the next quarter. What type of installations must Danielle perform, and which additional steps (if any) must Danielle take to retain the users' files and settings?

Scenario 1-4: Selecting the Right Computer and Operating System

Swish It Away is beginning to grow. The president now wants Danielle to acquire computers for three new staff members. Randi has been hired as the president's personal assistant and will need to run a word processor, spreadsheet application, a Web browser, and an e-mail client. Pooja will provide marketing and graphics services, such as press releases, brochures, flyers, advertisements, and graphics for the new Web site. Stan is the new salesperson who will travel locally each day. When he's in the office, he will share a desktop computer with another salesperson, but Stan needs to be able to check e-mail and access the Internet while he's out of the office. What computer specifications should Danielle look for, and which editions of Windows 7 should run on each computer?

Understanding Operating System Configurations

EXAM OBJECTIVE MATRIX

SKILLS/CONCEPTS	MTA EXAM OBJECTIVE DESCRIPTION	MTA EXAM OBJECTIVE NUMBER
Understanding User Accounts and User Account Control (UAC)	Understand user account control (UAC).	3.2
Configuring Control Panel Options	Configure Control Panel options.	1.1
Configuring Desktop Settings	Configure desktop settings.	1.2
Understanding Virtualized Clients	Understand virtualized clients.	2.4
Understanding Application Virtualization	Understand application virtualization.	3.5

KEY TERMS

accessibility options

Administrative Tools

Administrator account

Aero

Aero Peek

Aero Shake

Aero Snap

application virtualization

authentication

cached credentials

color depth

Control Panel

desktop settings

display settings

Ease of Access Center

elevated permissions

font size

gadget

Guest account

guest operating system (guest OS)

Jump List

live preview

Microsoft Enterprise Desktop Virtualization (Med-V or MED-V)

Microsoft Management Console (MMC) snap-ins

permissions

pin	user profile
Quick Start definitions	virtualization
resolution	virtual computer
shortcuts	virtual desktop infrastructure (VDI)
Standard user account	virtual machine (VM)
user account	virtualized client
User Account Control (UAC)	Windows XP Mode

As an IT technician at Interstate Snacks, you're responsible for setting up new computers and helping users adjust their existing computer settings. Your duties include creating user accounts, optimizing display settings, creating shortcuts, and so on. In addition, because your company uses a legacy program that doesn't run in Windows 7, some of your employees need an alternative way to access the program. So, you plan to show those employees how to use Windows XP Mode.

■ Understanding User Accounts and User Account Control (UAC)

THE BOTTOM LINE

Microsoft introduced the security feature User Account Control (UAC) in Windows Vista and improved the feature in Windows 7. UAC constantly monitors activity on your computer and notifies you when changes are about to be made that affect your computer's security or that affect other user accounts on the computer.

A *user account* is a collection of information that defines the actions that can be taken on a computer and which files and folders can be accessed (rights, policies, and *permissions*). An account also keeps track of user preferences, such as the desktop background, window color, and screen saver. Several users can share a computer and each user should have her own account. With separate accounts, each user can personalize her desktop, keep her files and settings protected from other users, and so on.

There are three types of user accounts in Windows 7:

- Administrator
- Standard user
- Guest

Each account has a different level of control over the computer.

Understanding Standard User Accounts and Administrative User Accounts

The two most commonly used account types in Windows 7 are Standard user and Administrator. A standard account is generally used for everyday tasks, and an administrative-level account is used for troubleshooting, installation, and similar tasks that require more rights and permissions.

The *Guest account* type is simply an account with few permissions and no password that allows a user to use a computer without requiring a unique user account. The Guest account is intended mainly for a user who needs temporary use of a computer, and is disabled by default.

The *Standard user account* type has fewer permissions than an administrative-level account but enough permissions to be productive. You should use a standard account for day-to-day work. When you're logged on as a standard user, you can surf the Web, read e-mail, create documents, and listen to music, as well as perform other rather basic tasks.

The *Administrator account* type provides the broadest permissions and therefore the most control over the computer. This includes changing all settings, installing programs, and modifying the Windows registry. Use an administrative-level account only when you need to make changes or perform maintenance that requires elevated permissions. (*Elevated permissions* generally refer to administrative-level permissions.) Using an administrative account for ordinary (Standard-level) computing tasks leaves the computer at a much greater risk of attack. For example, if you visit a malicious Web site by accident, the site can easily install and execute a Trojan horse program on the computer because of the broad permissions of the administrative account.

A computer administrator can use a Standard user account for most tasks and use the Run as administrator command to start certain tasks or programs with full administrator-level permissions. For example, let's say you want to run a program but get an Access denied error message. Depending on the program, you might be able to right-click the program's menu item or icon and then select Run as administrator from the shortcut menu. The program will run with full administrator rights. Before running any tasks or programs with elevated privileges, make sure the computer is protected by a firewall and up-to-date antivirus program or that it's disconnected from the Internet.

There's another, special account to be aware of: the default Administrator account. It is the name of the default administrative-level account that's created when you install Windows. Think of it as the ultimate master local (i.e., non-domain) account in Windows. You shouldn't use this account for anything other than troubleshooting or for specific activities that you can't perform with any other account.

The default Administrator account is automatically hidden (disabled) in Windows 7, but you can enable it if necessary. You must first open a command prompt window in administrator mode by clicking the Start button, typing **cmd** in the *Search programs and files* search box, right-clicking cmd.exe in the resulting list, and then selecting *Run as administrator*. In the command prompt window that displays, type **net user administrator /active:yes** and press Enter. When you're finished using the account and want to disable it, open a command prompt window as described and type **net user administrator /active:no**.

When you create a new user account or modify an existing account, you can choose Standard or you can choose Administrator. The Guest account type does not show up as an option in the Create a New Account window.

 CREATE A USER ACCOUNT

GET READY. To create a new user account, perform the following steps:

1. Click **Start** and then click **Control Panel**. In the main Control Panel window, in the User Accounts and Family Safety section, click **Add or remove user accounts** (see Figure 2-1).

2. If you're logged on as a standard user, a User Account Control dialog displays. Enter an administrator password and click **Yes**.

3. The Manage Accounts window displays (see Figure 2-2). Click **Create a new account**.

Figure 2-1

Selecting Add or remove user accounts in Control Panel

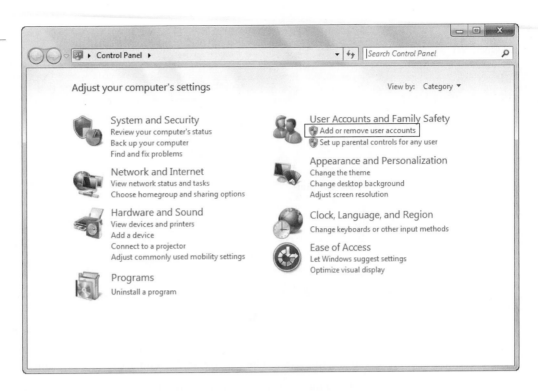

Figure 2-2

The Manage Accounts window

4. In the Create New Account window (Figure 2-3), in the **New account name** text box, type a name. Use just letters, numbers, and optionally spaces or hyphens.

5. If you want to create an administrative-level account, select **Administrator**; otherwise, leave **Standard user** selected.

Figure 2-3

The Create New Account window

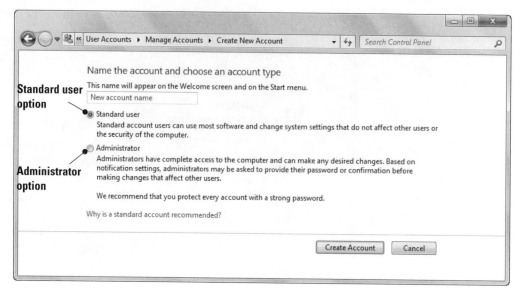

6. Click **Create Account**.

The new user displays in the Manage Accounts window. To change an account's settings, click an account name. The Change an Account screen displays and lists the following tasks:

- **Change the account name:** Edits the account's username. (This changes the name of the user's profile folder in the \Users folder. You will learn about user profiles later in the lesson.)
- **Create the password:** Creates or changes the account's password. For security purposes, it's recommended that you set a password on every user account.
- **Remove the password:** Deletes the password from this user's account.
- **Change the picture:** Selects a different picture to appear on the Start menu and the Welcome screen.
- **Set up Parental Controls:** Controls which applications and games the user can use and which days and times this user can use the computer.
- **Change the account type:** Changes the account type from Standard user to Administrator or vice versa.
- **Delete the account:** Removes the user account. You can choose to keep or delete a user account's files (such as pictures, music, documents, and so on).
- **Manage another account:** Returns to the Manage Accounts window and click another account.

Understanding User Account Control (UAC)

User Account Control (UAC) is a security feature in Windows Vista and Windows 7 that helps protect a computer from unauthorized changes. When a user, application, or even an attacker or malicious software attempts to modify certain system settings, a dialog box displays that requires confirmation or an administrative-level password to continue.

User Account Control (UAC) is a feature in Windows Vista and Windows 7 that requires administrative-level permission to make changes to your computer that affect security or affect settings for other user accounts. If you're logged on as a standard user and you attempt to make a change that requires administrative-level permissions, UAC displays a dialog box. A user with an administrator account on the computer must enter his password for you to continue (see Figure 2-4). You are then temporarily given the rights of an administrator to

Figure 2-4

A User Account Control dialog box requesting an administrative-level password

complete the task. Once you're finished, your permissions as a standard user once again apply. If you are logged on as an administrator and the UAC dialog box appears, click Continue or Yes to continue (see Figure 2-5).

Figure 2-5

A User Account Control dialog box requesting permission to continue

Some of the actions that can trigger a User Account Control dialog box include the following:

- Installing and uninstalling programs
- Changing system-wide settings
- Changing UAC settings
- Adding or removing user accounts
- Changing a user's account type
- Viewing or changing another user's folders and files
- Configuring Windows Update
- Running a program as Administrator (right-clicking a program name and selecting Run as administrator)
- Installing device drivers
- Changing settings for Windows Firewall

The point of UAC is to prevent potentially damaging, unauthorized changes to a computer, whether the changes are made accidentally, by malicious software, or by hackers accessing your system.

Understanding Types of UAC Prompts and Levels

> There are four levels of UAC control. Each produces different sets of alerts or notifications to users. Any user can choose the level that works best for her, although the default settings are highly recommended.

CERTIFICATION READY
What are the four notification levels in Windows 7?
3.2

In Windows 7, UAC has four notification levels, each of which has a different prompt (which means it displays a different dialog box). Each notification level varies slightly depending on whether you're logged on as a standard user or whether you're logged on as an administrator. The following levels pertain to an administrator account, unless noted otherwise:

- **Always notify me:** This is the most secure setting, which results in the most notifications. You are notified when programs try to install software or make changes to the computer, or when you make changes to Windows settings. (This is the default for a standard user account in Windows 7.)

- **Notify me only when programs try to make changes to my computer:** A UAC dialog box displays when installing software or making changes to system-wide computer settings, but no notification occurs when changing Windows settings. (This setting is the default for administrator Windows 7 accounts.)

- **Notify me only when programs try to make changes to my computer (do not dim my desktop):** Dimming the desktop is a visual indicator that an important change is pending. This setting does not open a UAC dialog box if you're making changes to your Windows settings. You must be logged on as an administrator to select this setting. This option is less secure but might be used by an administrator if the computer is highly secure.

- **Never notify me of installations or changes:** This is the least secure setting. You must be logged on as an administrator to select this setting. After restarting your computer, UAC is turned off. If you log on as a standard user, changes that require administrative-level permissions are denied (you are not prompted for an administrator password). This option should be used only in highly controlled and secure environments, such as test environments.

Microsoft highly recommends leaving UAC turned on for the safety and security of your computer.

 CHANGE UAC SETTINGS

GET READY. To modify UAC settings, perform the following steps:

1. Click **Start > Control Panel > System and Security > Change User Account Control settings** (see Figure 2-6). (Or, click the **Action Center** icon (the flag) on the right side of the Windows taskbar along the bottom of the screen, click **Open Action Center**, and then, in the left pane, click **Change User Account Control settings**.)

2. The User Account Control Settings window displays (see Figure 2-7). Move the slider up or down to raise or lower the number of UAC notifications you receive.

3. Click **OK** to save your changes.

Although Microsoft highly recommends that you leave UAC enabled, some users choose to turn it off to avoid the UAC notifications, especially if they're performing tasks (safely) that trigger UAC prompts. To turn off UAC, move the slider to the *Never notify* position and click OK. If you're prompted for an administrator password or confirmation, type the password or provide confirmation, and then restart your computer.

Figure 2-6

The System and Security window in Control Panel

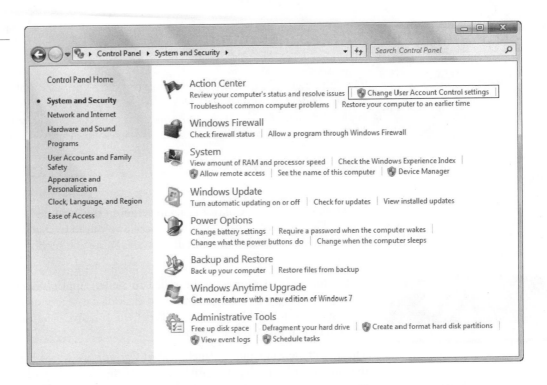

Figure 2-7

The User Account Control Settings window

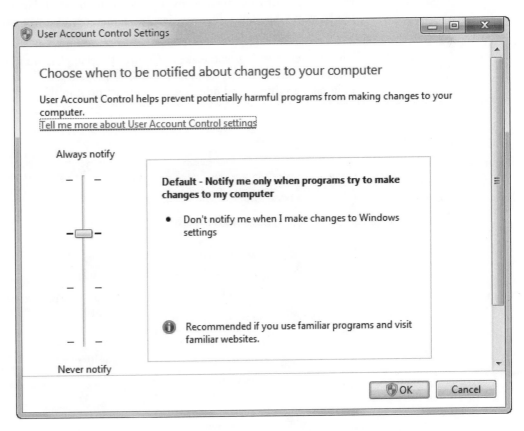

➕ **MORE INFORMATION**

For more information about User Account Control, visit http://windows.microsoft.com/en-US/windows7/products/features/user-account-control or http://technet.microsoft.com/en-us/library/cc709691(WS.10).aspx

■ Configuring Control Panel Options

THE BOTTOM LINE

The Windows 7 Control Panel provides access to the primary tools and utilities used to manage devices, settings, and system behaviors on Windows PCs. You'll find control applets (small applications) for everything from system administration to Windows Update; you will also find specific controls for system devices, displays, and more.

You've already seen the Control Panel in action in this lesson, but you will learn more about it now. The *Control Panel* is a utility that allows you to configure operating system features, set up hardware, install and uninstall software, create and modify users, and perform system maintenance.

CERTIFICATION READY
What is the purpose of Control Panel?
1.1

Each "program" in Control Panel is called an applet. Applets are organized by categories. Categories and applets are hyperlinked, so clicking a category or applet link in Control Panel opens a new window. One of Control Panel's most convenient aspects is that you can access many applets from multiple categories.

The default view in Control Panel is called Category view (see Figure 2-8). You can open the pull-down list in the upper-right corner of the Control Panel window to select two other views: Large icons and Small icons. The views are shown in Figure 2-9 and Figure 2-10, respectively. Choosing a different view can sometimes help you navigate through Control Panel applets more easily.

The preference settings you make in Control Panel applets are stored in the Windows registry. Therefore, you must have administrative-level access to modify many of the settings (such as uninstalling software and other system-wide settings) in the Control Panel.

Figure 2-8

The Category view in the Control Panel window

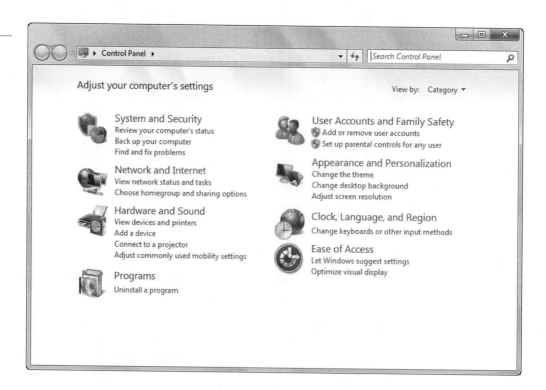

Figure 2-9

The Large icons view in the Control Panel window

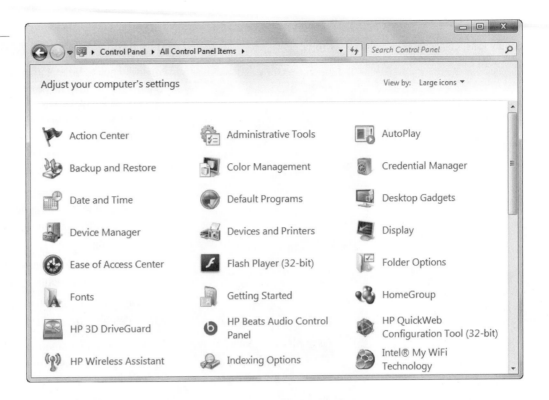

Figure 2-10

The Small icons view in the Control Panel window

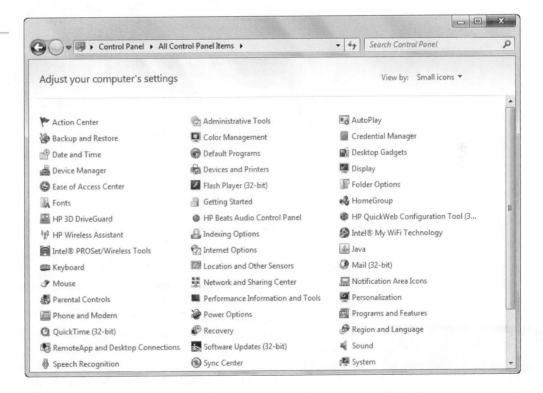

Table 2-1

Control Panel Categories

CATEGORY	DESCRIPTION
System and Security	Provides applets for maintaining the system and configuring security. This category includes Action Center, Windows Firewall, System, Windows Update, Power Options, Backup and Restore, Windows Anytime Upgrade, and Administrative Tools. Windows 7 Ultimate and Enterprise editions also offer BitLocker Drive Encryption (if installed).
Network and Internet	Provides applets for connecting to the Internet and other networks, setting up a local network (HomeGroup), and configuring wireless settings.
Hardware and Sound	Provides applets for configuring hardware (including printers), audio settings, power options, display settings, mobile options, and more.
Programs	Provides applets for installing/uninstalling software, setting default programs, and managing desktop gadgets.
User Accounts and Family Safety	Provides applets for creating and managing user accounts, configuring parental controls, and managing Windows credentials.
Appearance and Personalization	Provides applets for changing the Windows theme, desktop background, screen saver, display settings, desktop gadgets, and taskbar and Start menu. You can also open the Ease of Access Center, change folder options, and install fonts.
Clock, Language, and Region	Provides applets for changing your computer's date and time, time zone, language, and region/location.
Ease of Access	Provides access to the Ease of Access Center, where you can configure accessibility options; also provides access to the speech recognition feature.

Table 2-1 summarizes the categories in Windows 7 Control Panel.

Let's look at a few Control Panel applets in more detail.

Configuring Administrative Tools

Think of Administrative Tools as a well-rounded toolkit of utilities for power users and administrators. These utilities can help resolve most computer problems you may encounter and keep your system running optimally.

CERTIFICATION READY
What are Administrative Tools?
1.1

Administrative Tools is a set of utilities for managing advanced Windows features and diagnosing system problems. You can access the tools from the System and Security category of Control Panel. You can also click Start, type **admin tools** in the *Search programs and files* search box, and then select Administrative Tools from the resulting list. Figure 2-11 shows the Administrative Tools window on a Windows 7 Home Premium system. Windows 7 Professional, Ultimate, and Enterprise editions include the Local Security Policy and Print Management tools as well.

Within Administrative Tools, you can defragment your hard disk, monitor system performance, start and stop services, determine which programs run when Windows starts, and much more. Table 2-2 summarizes the tools.

Figure 2-11

The Administrative Tools window in Windows 7 Home Premium

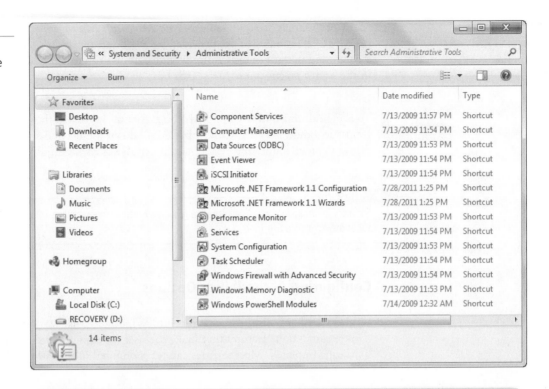

Table 2-2

Administrative Tools Utilities

CATEGORY	DESCRIPTION
Component Services	Used mainly by software developers; allows you to manage COM+/DCOM objects.
Computer Management	Allows you to manage local or remote computers by configuring hard disks and their partitions, monitoring system events, and managing system performance.
Data Sources (ODBC)	Used mainly by program developers and network database integrators, allows you to use ODBC to move data from one type of database to another.
Event Viewer	Allows you to view computer event information, such as program starting and stopping (including program crashes), security problems, and more.
iSCSI Initiator	Allows your computer to connect to network-attached storage.
Microsoft .NET Framework 1.1 Configuration/Wizards	Allows you to configure assemblies, services, and code access security policies related to .NET Framework. The Wizards tool gives you one-click access to configuration wizards.
Performance Monitor	Allows you to view and track system performance.
Services	Allows you to manage software and hardware services that work in the background.
System Configuration	Allows you to manage programs that run when Windows starts or when you log on.
Task Scheduler	Allows you to schedule programs and other tasks to run at certain times, automatically.
Windows Firewall with Advanced Security	Allows you to configure the built-in Windows Firewall.
Windows PowerShell Modules	Allows you to open a Windows PowerShell window and runs diagnostics.

Many of the tools listed in Table 2-2 are **Microsoft Management Console (MMC) snap-ins**. An MMC snap-in is a utility provided by Microsoft or a third party that's accessible through a common interface such as Administrative Tools. You can also access MMC by typing **MMC** in the *Search programs and files* search box.

> **TAKE NOTE** *
>
> To show Administrative Tools in the Start menu, right-click the Start button, click Properties, and then click Customize. Scroll down the list and select *Display on the All Programs menu* (under the System administrative tools heading).

> ➕ **MORE INFORMATION**
>
> For more information about Administrative Tools, visit http://windows.microsoft.com/en-US/windows-vista/What-are-Administrative-Tools

Configuring Accessibility Options

Microsoft has built many features into Windows 7 that work with assistive technologies or as stand-alone features that make the user experience better for the visually and hearing impaired. Most features can be configured in the Ease of Access Center.

The **Ease of Access Center** (see Figure 2-12) provides many **accessibility options**, which help visually and hearing impaired users use Windows more easily and efficiently. The primary tools include Magnifier, Narrator, On-Screen Keyboard, and High Contrast.

Magnifier helps visually impaired users see a selected portion of the screen or the entire screen more clearly by increasing the size of text and graphics. The Magnifier application window

Figure 2-12

The Ease of Access Center tools

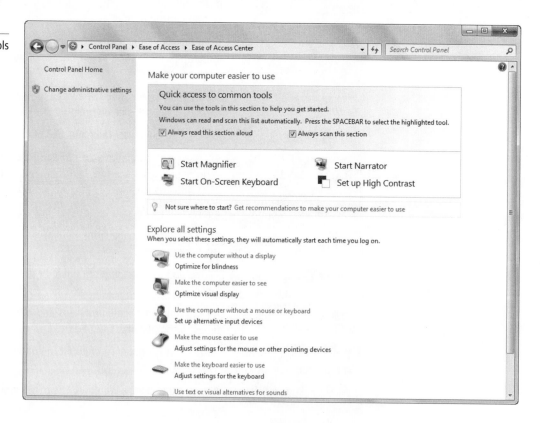

is quite small and provides you with access to Magnifier settings. Here you can set a certain magnification level and choose how the magnification "lens" follows the mouse pointer and text cursor. The lens looks like a magnifying glass icon on the screen.

Narrator is a text-to-speech program that reads aloud the actions you take, such as clicking and typing. This feature can also narrate certain events, such as error messages.

On-Screen Keyboard (see Figure 2-13) presents a keyboard on your screen from which you can type and enter data (rather than using a keyboard). You can use a mouse, stylus, or another pointing device to "press" keys.

Figure 2-13

The On-Screen Keyboard presents a fully functional keyboard

Another accessibility feature is the High Contrast theme (see Figure 2-14), a color scheme that makes some text easier to read and some images easier to identify on-screen.

Figure 2-14

The High Contrast settings

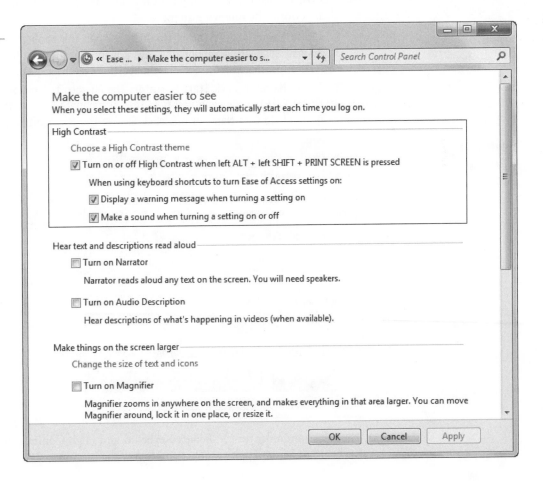

The bottom portion of the Ease of Access Center window includes other accessibility options you can configure for visually or hearing impaired users, including:

- Using the computer without a display
- Making the computer easier to see
- Using the computer without a mouse or keyboard
- Making the mouse easier to use
- Making the keyboard easier to use
- Using text or visual alternatives for sounds
- Making it easier to focus on tasks

Speech Recognition is an accessibility feature that you access in the Ease of Access category in Control Panel. This tool allows a user to speak commands into a microphone, which Windows then processes. All speech recognition programs require a sometimes lengthy training period in which the user "teaches" the computer to recognize the user's voice. You can learn more about the Windows Speech Recognition feature in Help and Support (click the Start button, click Help and Support, type **speech recognition** in the search box, and then press Enter).

+ MORE INFORMATION

For more information about accessibility options and the Ease of Access Center, visit http://windows.microsoft.com/en-US/windows7/introducing-accessibility-in-windows or http://www.microsoft.com/enable/training/windowsvista/eoa.aspx

USE ACCESSIBILITY FEATURES

GET READY. To enable accessibility features, open the Ease of Access Center in Control Panel and then perform the following steps:

1. To use Magnifier, click **Start Magnifier.** When the application name displays, click it. A small application window displays a magnifier glass icon. Select the level of magnification in the window and then move the magnifier glass icon around the screen.

2. To use Narrator, click **Start Narrator.** The Microsoft Narrator dialog box displays (see Figure 2-15). Now when you type text or navigate text on the screen, Narrator reads it aloud. To turn Narrator off, click **Exit** in the Microsoft Narrator and then click **OK.**

Figure 2-15

The Microsoft Narrator dialog box

The steps are similar for On-Screen Keyboard and High Contrast. Just click Start On-Screen Keyboard or Set up High Contrast and follow the prompts.

■ Configuring Desktop Settings

Windows *desktop settings* is a broad term that refers to many different settings you can configure to personalize Windows, such as the Windows theme, the desktop background, mouse clicks and pointer speeds, gadgets, shortcuts, and more. All settings are customizable—choosing the right mix will make your Windows experience more enjoyable and more productive.

The Windows desktop is a flexible, configurable part of the Windows environment. You can grab the taskbar and move it to either side of the screen, to the top, or back to its default location at the bottom (the taskbar must be unlocked to move it—right-click the taskbar and, if Lock the taskbar is checked, select the box to deselect it). You can also choose which items appear in the notification area on the right side of the taskbar by configuring the taskbar Properties dialog box. To access this dialog box, right-click the taskbar and select Properties.

CERTIFICATION READY
How are desktop settings configured?
1.2

New in Windows 7 is the ability to *pin* program shortcuts directly to the taskbar; when you pin a program, the icon for that program displays on the taskbar even when the program isn't running. This provides you with quick access to your frequently used programs. Shortcuts for Internet Explorer, Windows Explorer, and Windows Media Player appear there by default. You can unpin programs from the taskbar as well. You'll learn about shortcuts later in the lesson.

When you open a program in Windows 7, an icon for that program displays on the taskbar. To activate a program, just click its icon on the taskbar. When you right-click a program's icon on the taskbar, a menu appears above the icon that contains a list of recently used files (if the application has an associated file type). The menu is called a *Jump List*. If you have several programs open at once, you can press and hold the Alt key and then press the Tab key repeatedly to switch between windows and see *live previews* of the window for each open program (see Figure 2-16).

Figure 2-16

Viewing live previews of open programs with Alt+Tab

Figure 2-17

The Windows 7 Personalization window

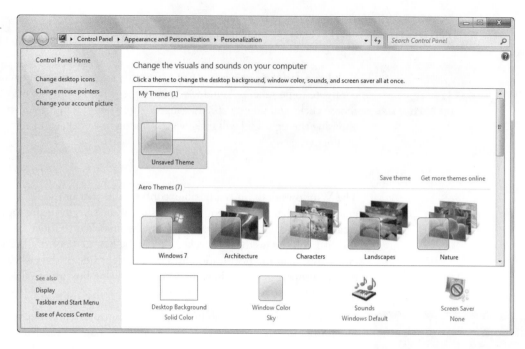

Many Windows 7 desktop settings are available when you right-click a blank area of the desktop and choose Personalize. The Personalization window is shown in Figure 2-17.

The main part of the window displays various themes you can use. Although there are many themes to choose from, a few of the most commonly used themes include the following:

- **Windows 7:** This is the default theme in Windows 7, which is an Aero theme. The Aero interface includes translucent borders and animations. You'll learn about the Aero interface in detail in the next section.
- **Windows Classic:** This theme is the same user interface used in Windows 2000 and earlier versions. The Windows Classic theme disables some of the high-end graphic features to provide better performance.
- **Windows 7 Basic:** This theme looks like Aero but doesn't include the semitransparent effect that can tax some older video cards. Selecting Windows 7 Basic can make the operating system seem more responsive.

Just click the theme of your choice and see the changes take effect immediately.

You can also change the background of any theme. Just click Desktop Background. In the Desktop Background window, open the **Picture location** drop-down list, and then select a different background image, a solid color, or a picture from your digital picture collection.

Clicking the Sounds link opens the Sound dialog box (see Figure 2-18). From here you can choose different sounds to accompany Windows events, such as when you connect a device or when you close Windows. The computer's sound volume must be set at an appropriate level to actually hear the sound.

Click the Screen Saver link to open the Screen Saver Settings dialog box. Then open the Screen saver drop-down list, select a screen saver, and click OK.

You'll learn about the Window Color link in the next section.

Figure 2-18

The Sound dialog box

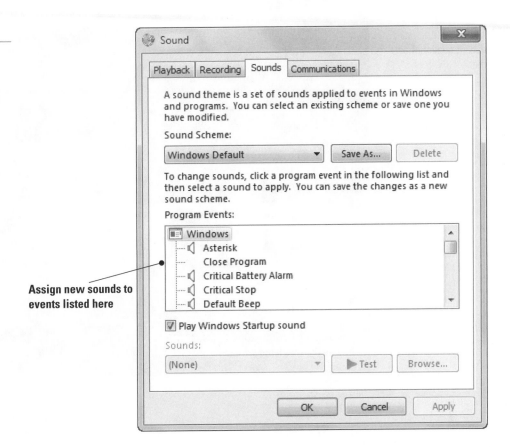

Assign new sounds to events listed here

Exploring and Configuring the Aero Interface

The Aero interface was introduced in Windows Vista and has been improved in Windows 7 with new features such as Aero Shake, Aero Peek, and Aero Snap. You can tweak some Aero settings to improve computer performance and customize it for personal appeal.

CERTIFICATION READY
What is the default theme in Windows 7?
1.2

The default theme in Windows is Windows 7, which is an *Aero* theme. Aero themes have a translucent "glass" design and provide your display with a three-dimensional look.

When you apply an Aero theme, window borders are partially transparent, allowing you to see what lies beneath them (see Figure 2-19). Aero themes also provide some animation within the interface. If you run the mouse over a button, the button glows. When you minimize a window, it fades and shrinks downward. The Aero theme is also customizable, as you'll learn in the exercise that follows. First, let's looks at some of the Aero features.

Aero Shake allows you to quickly minimize all open windows except the active one. Point the mouse at the title bar of the active window, click the hold and left mouse button, and then quickly move the mouse back and forth to shake it. (If you're new to Aero Shake, it can take a little practice to use it properly.)

To minimize all open windows at once, click the Show Desktop button. This button is the small shaded rectangle at the far right end of the taskbar. Pointing at it with your mouse

Figure 2-19

The translucent quality of an Aero theme

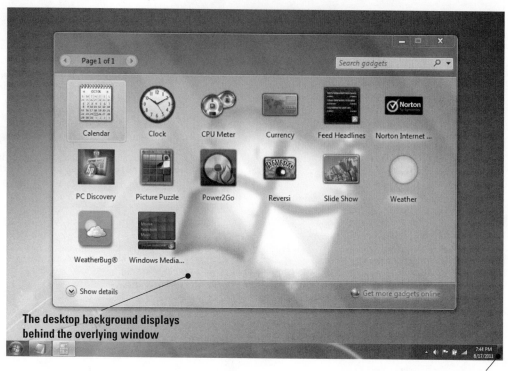

The desktop background displays behind the overlying window

Show Desktop button

pointer displays a preview of the desktop. This is called peeking at the desktop and is part of the *Aero Peek* feature. If you click the Show Desktop button, all open windows are minimized.

Windows 7 Aero also includes *Aero Snap*, which allows you to quickly resize and arrange windows on the desktop. To use Aero Snap, drag the title bar of an open window to either side of the desktop to align it there, or drag it to the top of the desktop to maximize the window.

 CHANGE AERO SETTINGS

GET READY. You can modify many settings to affect Aero behavior. For example, to change the color of the Aero interface, perform the following steps:

1. Right-click an empty part of the desktop, select **Personalize**, then click **Window Color**. The Window Color and Appearance window displays (see Figure 2-20).
2. Click a color box to change the color of Windows borders.
3. Uncheck the **Enable transparency** check box if you want to retain most of the Aero look and feel but you want to disable the semi-transparent effect.
4. Move the **Color intensity** slider to make the Windows border color more or less intense.
5. To create your own border color, click the **Show color mixer** arrow and then adjust the Hue, Saturation, and Brightness sliders (see Figure 2-21).
6. Click **Save changes**.

Figure 2-20

The Window Color and Appearance window

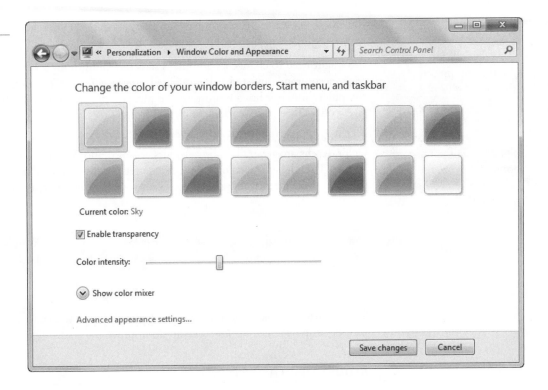

Figure 2-21

Adjusting the color mixer settings

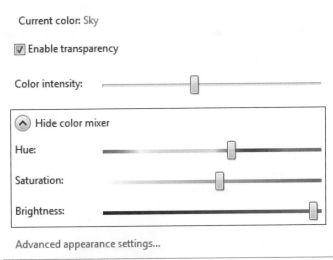

Configuring Display Settings

Windows 7 has several *display settings*, but you're likely to modify the resolution, color depth, and font size most often. You can modify each setting to suit a particular application.

CERTIFICATION READY
What are some of the display-related settings you can adjust using the Screen Resolution window?
1.2

The Windows 7 Screen Resolution window allows you to configure many display-related settings. This is where you choose which monitor to use (if your computer is connected to two or more monitors) and whether to display content in a landscape or portrait orientation. You can also configure settings to connect a projector to your computer. Three other important display settings you might want to adjust for specific purposes are resolution, color depth, and font size.

Resolution refers to the number of pixels that create the "image," that is, everything you see on the screen. **Resolution** has a horizontal value and a vertical value, such as 1200 x 768 or 1600 x 900. The Windows desktop expands itself to fit whichever resolution you select, so

X REF

If Windows 7 does not have the appropriate driver for the display, you might need to download and install a new driver to make the best use of your monitor. Lesson 5 covers drivers and how to install them.

you always have a full background. Similarly, the taskbar stretches across the bottom of the screen, regardless of the resolution you choose.

You might need to change a computer's screen resolution for a variety of reasons, such as when you're accommodating a visually impaired user or when you're using an external projector. Your computer's monitor has a minimum and a maximum resolution it can display, so Windows 7 gives you a range of resolutions to choose from.

Color depth refers to the number of bits that represents the color for each pixel on the screen. Color depths are generally 8 bits, 16 bits, 24 bits, and 32 bits; newer systems offer only 24 or 32 bits. The higher the color depth, the better photos and similar objects will look. You set color depth in the Advanced settings window of the Display control.

TAKE NOTE* You seldom need to change resolution or color depth settings. Windows chooses the best settings for your monitor. The two primary monitor types are LCD and CRT.

Screen fonts are usually measured in dots per inch (dpi). You can enhance the appearance of your desktop by adjusting **font size** dpi to improve the readability of pixelated or illegible fonts.

ADJUST DISPLAY SETTINGS

GET READY. To adjust display settings, perform the following steps:

1. To set screen resolution, right-click the desktop and select **Screen resolution**. Click the **Resolution** drop-down arrow and then drag the slider to change the resolution (see Figure 2-22).

Figure 2-22

Selecting a screen resolution

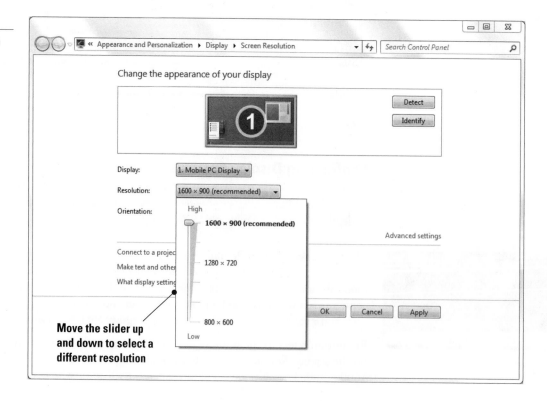

2. To adjust color depth, right-click the desktop, choose **Screen resolution,** and then click **Advanced settings**. Click the **Monitor** tab in the resulting properties window, click the **Colors** drop-down arrow, and then select the color depth of your choice (see Figure 2-23).

Figure 2-23

Selecting a color depth

Colors list

3. To adjust screen font size, right-click the desktop, select **Personalize**, and then click **Display** in the left pane. The options are **Smaller**, **Medium**, and **Larger**.

Windows might prompt you to confirm your selections. The changes should take effect without requiring you to restart Windows.

Creating and Managing Shortcuts

Shortcuts are icons you can click to start a program or go to a location without requiring any extra steps. Shortcuts save time because you don't have to use several keystrokes or click several menus or commands.

An icon is a small, visual symbol of a computer resource, such as a program, folder, file, or drive. To access an actual computer resource, click or double-click its icon. Some icons are located on the desktop, others are in the Start menu, and still others might appear in the list of files and folders in Windows Explorer.

A *shortcut* (see Figure 2-24) is an icon or link that gives you quick access to an original resource. The links you see in Control Panel are also considered shortcuts. Because a shortcut only points to a resource, deleting a shortcut does not delete the actual item. You can usually distinguish a shortcut icon from the original item it refers to because the shortcut has a small arrow in the shortcut icon's lower-left corner.

Figure 2-24

An example of a shortcut icon

If you regularly access a particular folder, you can create a shortcut to that folder on the desktop. Whenever you want to open that folder, double-click the icon instead of launching Windows Explorer and navigating to the folder to open it.

 CREATE AND DELETE A SHORTCUT

GET READY. To create a folder shortcut on the desktop, perform the following steps:

1. In Windows Explorer, point to the folder for which you want to create a shortcut.
2. Right-click the folder and choose **Send To > Desktop (create shortcut)** (see Figure 2-25). The shortcut now displays on your desktop.

To delete a shortcut icon:

1. Right-click it, choose **Delete**, and then click **OK**. The shortcut is removed and sent to the Recycle Bin.

Figure 2-25

Creating a shortcut on the desktop

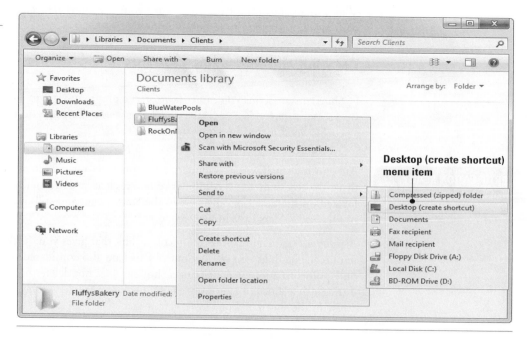

Configuring Gadgets

Gadgets are small, versatile applications that are run from the Windows 7 desktop. Gadgets are similar to mobile apps on a smartphone. A *gadget* is a small, single-purpose application that can be installed on the Windows 7 desktop. There are all kinds of gadgets available, such as calendars, clocks, games, newsfeeds, and weather reports and forecasts.

In Windows Vista, gadgets were displayed in the Windows Sidebar, which by default was located on the right side of the desktop. Windows 7 doesn't use the Windows Sidebar, so you can spread gadgets around your desktop wherever they're convenient to use. If open windows cover your gadgets, you can use Aero Peek to quickly reveal the desktop.

To open the Windows 7 gadget gallery, right-click an empty portion of the desktop and select Gadgets. The Windows 7 gadget gallery displays, as shown in Figure 2-26. The number of gadgets that install with Windows 7 is limited, but you can add gadgets to your gallery. Just click the *Get more gadgets online* link in the lower-right corner of the window. Your default Web browser opens to the Microsoft desktop gadgets Web site; the gadgets are free to download and install. Many gadgets are geared toward consumers, such as consumer shopping and auction sites and horoscope gadgets. However, some gadgets are useful in a business setting, such as the CPU meter, drive meter, and battery meter gadgets. As your gadget gallery grows, you can use the right and left arrows in the upper-left corner to scroll through available gadgets.

Figure 2-26

The Windows 7 gadget gallery

Click these arrows to scroll through available gadgets

➕ MORE INFORMATION

For more information about Windows gadgets, visit http://windows.microsoft.com/en-US/windows7/products/features/gadgets

➡ ADD A GADGET TO YOUR DESKTOP

GET READY. To add a gadget to your desktop, perform the following steps.

1. Right-click a blank area of the desktop and select **Gadgets**.

2. Browse the gadget gallery. To get information about a particular gadget, click the gadget and then click the **Show details** link in the lower-left corner of the gallery.

3. Right-click a gadget of your choosing and click **Add** (see Figure 2-27). That gadget displays on your desktop. You can also drag-and-drop a gadget onto your desktop.

Figure 2-27

Adding a gadget to your desktop

4. To move a gadget or change its size, hover your mouse pointer over the gadget and then use the menu that displays next to the gadget (see Figure 2-28).

Figure 2-28

A menu displays alongside a gadget when you hover your mouse pointer over the gadget

To remove a gadget from the desktop (but leave it in the gallery for later use), click the X at the top of the menu next to the gadget.

Configuring Profiles

All of a user's personal preferences—from theme choice to screen saver to shortcuts—are saved in a user profile. Windows relates a user's preferences to the user account. Each time a user logs on to Windows, the user's profile is loaded.

Now that you've learned how to change all kinds of desktop settings, create shortcuts, and add gadgets, you might wonder how Windows remembers all of those settings. Windows uses user profiles to do so. Your *user profile* contains your desktop settings (your theme, desktop background, screen saver, and so on) and other personal preferences. The purpose of a user profile is to maintain your preferences so they appear each time you log on to Windows.

User profiles can be local or roaming. A local profile is available only on the computer on which it was created. A roaming profile enables a user to use any computer to connect to a Windows domain and access her profile. (Remember, a domain is a collection of user and computer accounts that enable an administrator to manage and apply security to them as a group.) User preferences load upon domain log-on, giving the user a consistent desktop experience. A user with a lot of data and many personalized settings can experience a delay while the roaming profile loads.

In a domain, a server called a domain controller authenticates users at log on. *Authentication* means the domain controller checks the user's credentials, which are generally a user name and password. The user name entered must match the password on file. The domain controller also checks the permissions a user has to resources on the network. The credentials are saved to the computer's hard disk—referred to as *cached credentials*—which allow the user to access resources when a domain controller is unavailable. A domain controller might be unavailable because the server is down or because a user is attempting to access the network from a remote location.

Don't confuse a user profile with a user account. A user account is used to log on to Windows. Every user account has a subfolder in the C:\Users folder and each account has at least one user profile associated with it.

■ Understanding Virtualized Clients

THE BOTTOM LINE

Virtualization is a technology that creates an abstract version of a complete operating environment (including a processor, memory, storage, network links, a display, and so forth) entirely in software. Because the resulting runtime environment is completely software-based, the software produces what's called a *virtual computer* or a *virtual machine* (*VM*). Virtualization is a term used to describe the work involved in setting up all the data structures necessary to represent and run a VM on a physical computer of some kind.

In Windows, a *virtualized client* is a VM that's set up specifically to run some kind of application that typically runs in an older version of Windows (such as Windows 2000 or Windows XP). On a Windows 7 PC, a virtualized client runs as a VM inside what's called a *guest operating system* or *guest OS* within a virtual runtime environment (such as Windows Virtual PC or VMware Workstation).

Virtualization becomes necessary when users need to run applications that won't work on modern Windows operating systems. By running an older version of Windows (such as Windows XP) in a VM on Windows 7, users can continue to work with software that's incompatible with the host OS inside a compatible guest OS.

Understanding Windows XP Mode

As presented in the lesson case for Interstate Snacks at the outset of this chapter, users need access to a legacy program that doesn't work in Windows 7. Fortunately, it does work in Windows XP and that builds an ironclad case to make Windows XP Mode available to the Interstate Snacks user community. Although Windows Virtual PC runs on all Windows 7 versions, Windows XP Mode works only on Windows 7 Professional, Enterprise, or Ultimate. Be sure to factor that into your OS selection and deployment plans!

Windows XP Mode is an add-on that Microsoft makes available as an extension to Windows Virtual PC. When you install this virtual machine environment on a Windows 7 computer, users can run applications inside the VM that won't work on Windows 7.

Visit http://www.microsoft.com/windows/virtual-pc/download.aspx to grab a copy for your users' PCs. Figure 2-29 shows the download page with a download for 64-bit Windows 7 Professional selected. The download confers a free Windows XP Mode license to those who put it to work, which helps companies avoid license infringement trouble with Microsoft.

Figure 2-29

Selecting the Windows XP Mode download to match a Windows 7 version

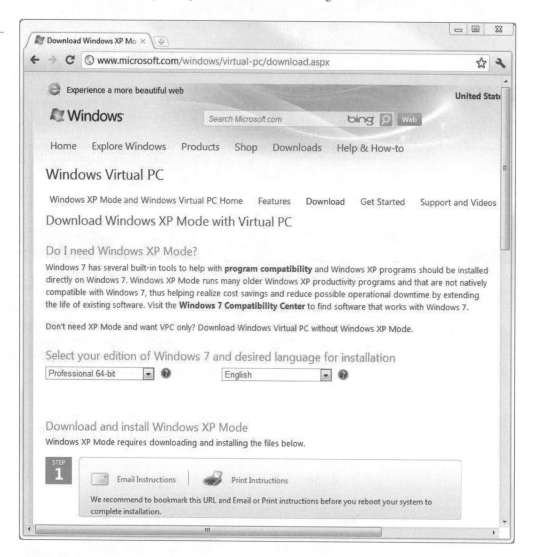

Once Windows XP Mode is installed, you must then install the applications that are not compatible with Windows 7 into the Windows XP VM that's created. Users can launch this VM directly from their desktops or menus to access the applications they need.

INSTALL WINDOWS XP MODE

GET READY. Visit the Microsoft Web page where you'll download the files you need to install Windows XP mode on your user machines. To install Windows XP Mode, perform the following steps:

1. Check the system requirements prior to downloading Windows XP Mode.
2. Select the appropriate Windows version and language for your target PC or PCs. As shown in Figure 2-29, our example is 64-bit Windows 7 Professional and English.

3. On the Web page shown in Figure 2-30, for **Step 2**, click **Download**. Once Windows validation completes successfully, Internet Explorer requests permission to download a file named **WindowsXPMode_en-us.exe**. Grant permission and run the file. This sets the stage for WindowsVirtual PC to be installed in a subsequent step.

Figure 2-30

Once you download the XP Mode file, you'll step through its installation process

4. In stepping through the Windows XP Mode install, you'll work through a Setup program. You'll start by clicking **Next** to start the installation, designating a target directory (the Program Files default target is usually suitable, as shown in Figure 2-31), waiting through a virtual hard disk install, and then clicking **Finish** to complete the XP Mode setup.

5. With XP Mode installed, you must return to the Web page and move on to Step 3. This is where you download and install Windows Virtual PC. When you click the **Download** button for Step 3, you grant permission to download and run the file named Windows6.1-KB9598559-x64-RefreshPkg.msu. (Refer to Figure 2-30 if necessary).

6. When you execute the Windows Virtual PC file, you run a standalone Windows Update file. Once it gets going, it looks like any other ordinary Windows Update file. And, like many other such updates, it forces a restart of your system when it completes; it also goes through an update configuration before and after the reboot.

7. When the PC reboots, click **Start** and in the **Search programs and files** search box, type **XP**. In the results list displayed, click the Windows XP Mode entry. This completes the Windows XP Mode installation and initialization process and usually takes

Figure 2-31

Designating a target directory while installing Windows XP Mode software

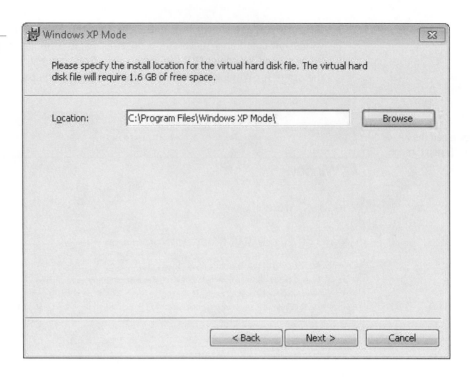

at least several minutes to complete. During this process, you'll need to agree to license terms and define a login password for the default xpmuser account that the program creates to finalize installation.

Now XP Mode is up and running and available as an entry named Windows XP Mode through the Virtual PC element in the Start Menu program listings. Before users can take advantage of this environment, you must complete your normal installation processes—which usually means installing anti-malware applications, standard programs, and of course the legacy applications that don't work under Windows 7.

Windows XP Mode makes it easy for users to run legacy applications, even on newer computers and inside otherwise incompatible operating systems. Programs installed inside the Windows XP Mode environment also show up in the standard Windows 7 Program menus, so users can access them without first launching the XP Mode Virtual Machine. Shortcuts to these programs can even be dropped on the desktop, if that's how users like to run things.

➕ MORE INFORMATION

For more information about Windows XP Mode, visit http://windows.microsoft.com/en-us/windows7/products/features/windows-xp-mode

■ Understanding Application Virtualization

THE BOTTOM LINE

Application virtualization adds the ability to install and manage legacy applications and virtual machines centrally. This capability sometimes relies on additional Microsoft technologies, including a *virtual desktop infrastructure* (*VDI*) that runs a desktop OS within a virtual machine (VM) running on a server.

Microsoft and several third parties support remote access tools whereby users load and display carefully constructed VMs on their desktops, and these VMs provide them with remote access to tools that are located on servers that might be located off site. This approach simplifies the management and deployment of legacy applications for IT professionals, but still makes them readily accessible to end users, on and off corporate networks.

Microsoft's Remote Desktop Services (RDS) permit users to access and run VMs in a variety of situations. This includes obtaining access to remote servers designed to create and deliver VMs to users on corporate networks, as needed. These same technologies can also provide remote access to mobile workers in the field or telecommuters in their homes. You will learn more about RDS in Lesson 3.

Understanding Med-V

Microsoft Enterprise Desktop Virtualization (aka *Med-V* or *MED-V*) is the part of the Microsoft Desktop Optimization Pack (MDOP), which delivers legacy applications to Windows 7 users in the form of Windows-XP based virtual machines. It provides a mechanism for providing uninterrupted access to legacy applications while Windows 7 upgrades and transitions are underway.

Med-V consists of several client components that must be installed on Windows 7 client computers. These include the Med-V Management Server that communicates with a central server to obtain information about and access to pre-defined VMs for use with Med-V. Clients also have installed a specific Med-V Client program and a Med-V Management Console to handle and run Med-V VMs.

CERTIFICATION READY
What is Med-V?
3.5

Med-V also works with Windows Virtual PC, and is often used to deploy that software in large organizations. An important advantage of Med-V is that it provides centralized management and uses policies to provide and deliver virtual images to client machines. Med-V also supports Windows XP Mode. In fact, Windows XP Mode lets administrators set up icons for applications inside Windows XP Mode that launch from the Windows 7 desktop just like native application, although they run inside the Windows XP VM.

Users access special pre-defined virtual hard disks (VHDs) to run Med-V VMs. These are made accessible through Med-V Workspaces and specific downloads. The Med-V Management Console is what enables *Quick Start definitions* for Med-V VMs (and the programs they contain), through a special Quick Start Group Policy file.

From an end-user perspective, these elements of Med-V infrastructure are unobtrusive and almost entirely invisible. Though system and desktop administrators have to set up and configure this infrastructure, Med-V creates an end-user experience that is best described as "click and go," even though it uses the basic elements of Windows XP Mode in a centrally controlled and managed fashion.

Understanding VDI and App-V

Microsoft's Virtual Desktop Infrastructure (VDI) depends on a special, licensed access right that permits users to access a virtual machine running a Windows client. This technology permits users to access secure, centrally-managed desktops running in a datacenter.

Microsoft VDI provides unified management of centralized desktops and corporate data using Microsoft System Center server technology. This approach permits IT to extend existing management tools and processes to virtual desktop environments. The goals are to reduce management overhead and enable rapid deployment and quick patching.

This is possible because VDI relies on desktop images that are created, managed, and maintained centrally. System Center Configuration Manager can orchestrate rapid delivery of operating systems and applications as well as driver and software updates for physical and virtual desktop platforms. It even works with self-service applications packaged using Microsoft App-V technologies.

CERTIFICATION READY
What is the purpose of Microsoft VDI and App-V?
3.5

App-V extends virtualized applications from central servers to authorized users on any authorized PCs without requiring application installs. Users simply request access to an application; virtualization technology running in the background brokers a connection to a suitable server and delivers direct access to the application with minimal delay. The environment preserves virtual applications and user settings whether users are active online or inactive and offline. With App-V, users need only to click to launch applications; they don't need to wait for installations or reboots. Updates are automatically applied and immediately available the next time a program is launched.

App-V also helps to minimize conflicts between applications because they run in separate runtime containers that do not interfere with one another. This reduces application compatibility testing requirements and can further speed deployment times. App-V is designed to make applications available anywhere, anytime to users as long as they have Internet access available.

⊕ MORE INFORMATION

For more information about desktop virtualization and VDI, visit http://www.microsoft.com/virtualization/en/us/products-desktop.aspx and http://technet.microsoft.com/en-us/edge/microsoft-virtual-desktop-infrastructure-vdi-explained.aspx

SKILL SUMMARY

IN THIS LESSON YOU LEARNED:

- The two primary types of user accounts in Windows 7 are Standard user and Administrator. You generally use a standard account for everyday tasks and an administrative-level account for troubleshooting, installation, and similar tasks that require more rights and permissions.

- User Account Control (UAC) is a security feature in Windows Vista and Windows 7 that helps protect a computer from unauthorized changes. When a user, malicious software, or even an attacker attempts to modify certain system settings, a dialog box displays that requires confirmation or an administrative-level password to continue.

- There are four levels of UAC control, which result in different types of alerts or notifications to the user. Each user can choose the level that works best for them, although the default settings are highly recommended.

- The Control Panel is a utility that allows you to configure operating system features, set up hardware, install and uninstall software, create and modify users, and perform system maintenance.

- The Ease of Access Center provides many accessibility features to help visually and hearing impaired people use Windows more easily and efficiently. The primary tools include Magnifier, Narrator, On-Screen Keyboard, and High Contrast.

- Windows desktop settings is a broad term that refers to many different settings you can configure to personalize Windows, such as the Windows theme, desktop background, mouse click and pointer speed, gadgets, shortcuts, and more. All settings are customizable, and choosing the right mix will make your Windows experience more enjoyable and more productive.

- Windows XP Mode is a free download available to users of Windows 7 Professional, Enterprise, and Ultimate versions. It permits administrators to create and package Windows XP-based VMs, to support legacy applications that don't work on Windows 7. Windows XP Mode programs are available directly through the Windows 7 Start menu, and are easy and convenient for users to launch and run.

- Application Virtualization (App-V) permits users to launch and run applications on their desktops without installing or rebooting their machines. Microsoft's App-V technology makes instant use available through System Center and special centralized configuration and management utilities. A virtual desktop infrastructure (VDI) makes delivery of VMs and virtual applications possible.

- Microsoft Enterprise Desktop-Virtualization (Med-V) provides another way to deliver legacy applications to end users, on centrally configured and managed VMs. This allows for administrators who need only manage master copies in the data center, while users put copies of the master to work on their desktops.

■ Knowledge Assessment

Fill in the Blank

Complete the following sentences by writing the correct word or words in the blanks provided.

1. A _____ is a collection of information that defines the actions you can take on a computer and which files and folders you can access.

2. The _____ account type is best for everyday use.

3. The _____ interface, which is the basis for the default theme in Windows 7, includes translucent borders and animations.

4. To configure accessibility options, open the _____.

5. To minimize all open windows at once, click the _____ button.

6. _____ includes several applets, including System and Security, Programs, and User Accounts and Family Safety.

7. Use _____ to troubleshoot and resolve computer problems, and to keep your system running optimally.

8. The Windows 7 _____ window allows you to configure several display-related settings, such as choice of monitors or content orientation (landscape or portrait).

9. _____ is a free download for Windows 7 Professional, Enterprise, and Ultimate versions that supports legacy applications inside a virtual Windows XP machine running on Windows 7.

10. _____ allows applications to run without being installed on desktop systems.

Multiple Choice

Circle the letter that corresponds to the best answer.

1. Which of the following is *not* an account type in Windows 7?
   a. Guest
   b. Limited user
   c. Standard user
   d. Administrator

2. Which of the following can you perform in the Manage Accounts window? (Choose all that apply.)
   a. Change the account type
   b. Create a password
   c. Delete the account
   d. Set up Parental Controls

3. Which of the following actions is most likely to trigger a User Account Control dialog box?
   a. Uninstalling a program
   b. Creating a shortcut
   c. Changing resolution
   d. Adding a gadget

4. Where can you directly access Event Viewer?
   a. Gadgets window
   b. Programs applet in Control Panel
   c. Administrative Tools
   d. User Account Control dialog box

5. Which of the following is *not* a UAC notification level?
   a. Always notify me
   b. Notify me only when users try to access my files
   c. Notify me only when programs try to make changes to my computer
   d. Never notify me of installations or changes

6. Which Aero feature allows you to quickly minimize all open windows except the active one?
   a. Shake
   b. Snap
   c. Peek
   d. Show Desktop

7. Which of the following settings is *not* configurable from the Screen Resolution window?
   a. Orientation
   b. Font size
   c. Display
   d. Windows theme

8. Which of the following allows you to manage programs that run when Windows starts or when you log on?
   a. Task Scheduler
   b. Performance Monitor
   c. Programs applet in Control Panel
   d. System Configuration

9. Which versions of Windows 7 support Windows XP Mode? (Choose all that apply.)
   a. Starter
   b. Home Premium
   c. Professional
   d. Ultimate
   e. Enterprise

10. Which of the following correctly explains the abbreviation VHD?
   a. Variable Hex Determinant
   b. Virtual Home Directory
   c. Virtual Hard Disk
   d. Virtual Hard Drive

True / False

Circle T if the statement is true or F if the statement is false.

T | F **1.** A User Account Control dialog box displays when you open your data files.

T | F **2.** You cannot change the desktop resolution setting because it's a fixed value.

T | F **3.** Deleting a shortcut does not delete the resource it represents.

T | F **4.** A user account and a user profile are the same thing.

T | F **5.** Med-V delivers centrally managed virtual machines to authorized end users.

■ Competency Assessment

Scenario 2-1: Getting Administrative-Level Privileges

As an IT technician, you need to perform some maintenance tasks on an employee's computer that will require elevated privileges. When you go to the Manage Accounts window in Control Panel on that employee's computer, you see only the employee's standard user account. What do you do to be able to log on as a user with administrative-level privileges?

Scenario 2-2: Configuring Accessibility Features

Alexandra, an employee at your company, is visually impaired. Which features can you configure in Windows 7 to help her do her work more efficiently?

■ Proficiency Assessment

Scenario 2-3: Running a Legacy Application

Oscar is the warehouse manager for The OEM Connection, an auto parts business. Although the business standardized on Windows 7 Professional, Oscar needs to run a legacy parts lookup program that does not run in Windows 7. You provide technical support to The OEM Connection. What can you do to help Oscar?

Scenario 2-4: Creating a Better User Experience

Oscar at The OEM Connection asks you to help him speed up his computer, which now runs Windows 7 Professional. He doesn't care about all of the "zippy, new" features in the Windows 7 Aero interface—he just wants the computer to run a bit faster and be more responsive. He would also like to be able to quickly launch Microsoft Excel each time he logs on to his computer, and he does not want the Windows Media Player to be present on the taskbar. How do you meet Oscar's requests?

3 LESSON

Understanding Native Applications, Tools, Mobility, and Remote Management and Assistance

EXAM OBJECTIVE MATRIX

SKILLS/CONCEPTS	EXAM OBJECTIVE DESCRIPTION	EXAM OBJECTIVE NUMBER
Understanding Windows Internet Explorer	Understand native applications and tools.	1.3
Introducing Accessory Programs	Supplemental	
Using the Snipping Tool	Understand native applications and tools.	1.3
Playing Back and Recording to Media	Understand native applications and tools.	1.3
Understanding Sync Center	Understand mobility.	1.4
	Understand libraries.	4.4
Using Windows Mobility Center	Understand mobility.	1.4
Understanding Remote Desktop Services	Understand virtualized clients.	2.4
	Understand mobility.	1.4
Understanding Remote Management and Assistance	Understand remote management and assistance.	1.5

KEY TERMS

ActiveX Filtering

cookies

Computer Management

cross-site scripting attack

cross-site scripting (XSS) filter

domain highlighting

InPrivate Browsing

Internet Explorer 9

Microsoft Management Console (MMC)   SmartScreen filter

New Tab page   snap-in

Notification bar   Snipping Tool

offline files   Sync Center

One Box   Tracking Protection

pinned site   Windows Media Center

playlist   Windows Media Player 12

Pop-up Blocker   Windows Mobility Center

Remote Desktop Connection   Windows PowerShell

Remote Desktop Services   Windows Remote Assistance

screen shot

Your IT manager has asked you to find ways to help computer users be more productive and provide support services to them without requiring you to purchase third-party tools and software. You decide to brush up on the native applications in Windows 7, such as Internet Explorer 9, Snipping Tool, Windows Media Player, and Windows Media Center. To help remote users who run into problems with their software or who just need quick tutorials, you'll begin using Windows Remote Assistance. Finally, you plan to show frequent travelers how to use Remote Desktop Connection to access files from their home or work computers.

■ Understanding Windows Internet Explorer

THE BOTTOM LINE

Although Windows 7 usually ships with Internet Explorer 8, the most current Microsoft Web browser as of this writing is Internet Explorer 9, which is also the version that the 98-349 exam focuses on. Microsoft made many improvements to Internet Explorer 9—the Web surfing experience is now much easier, safer, and private than ever before.

Internet Explorer 9 is the latest Web browser from Microsoft. The browser is faster and less cluttered than previous versions, and it includes several privacy, security, and interface features that enhance the user browsing experience with a focus on usability and safety.

CERTIFICATION READY
What are some of the improved features of Internet Explorer 9?
1.3

Microsoft introduced tabbed browsing in Internet Explorer 7 and has improved the feature in Internet Explorer 9. This feature allows you to keep all your favorite Web sites open within one Internet Explorer window. The Internet Explorer 9 interface also includes a large Back button, a consolidated menu, and a combined Address bar and search box (see Figure 3-1).

The *New Tab page* (see Figure 3-2) in Internet Explorer 9 appears when you click the **New Tab** button or press **Ctrl+T**. This page initially provides some thumbnails of Web sites you might

Figure 3-1

The Windows Internet Explorer 9 interface

be interested in visiting. As you use Internet Explorer 9, the sites you visit most often appear on this page, giving you one-click access to frequently visited sites. You can remove sites from the New Tab page by right-clicking a site's thumbnail and selecting **Remove this page** from the shortcut menu.

Figure 3-2

The New Tab page

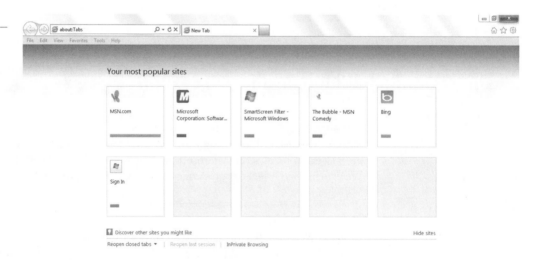

The New Tab page also provides commands for reopening closed tabs and starting InPrivate Browsing, which is explained later in this section.

Internet Explorer 9 introduces **One Box**, a feature that combines search functionality into the Address bar. One Box saves you time by using AutoComplete to help you complete Uniform Resource Locators (URLs), and allows you to enter search terms directly in the text box like you would in a search engine. Relevant suggestions for your search appear in a drop-down list (see Figure 3-3) that you can select or you can continue typing and then press Enter to see results in the default search engine.

Figure 3-3

Searching within One Box

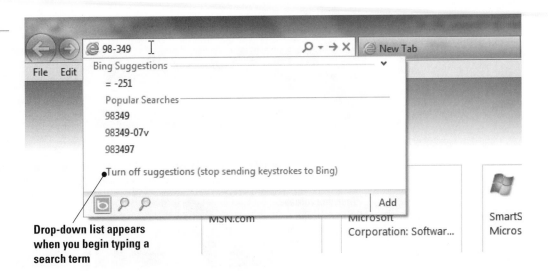

Drop-down list appears
when you begin typing a
search term

TAKE NOTE ★ For privacy reasons, search suggestions are turned off by default. To enable search suggestions, select *Turn on suggestions* in the drop-down list.

Another new feature of Internet Explorer 9 is the ***Notification bar***, which displays at the bottom of the browser window. All notifications, such as blocked pop-up windows and error messages, display in the Notification bar rather than in pop-up windows. You can click the options in the Notification bar or ignore them, depending on your preference.

➕ MORE INFORMATION

For more information about Windows Internet Explorer 9, visit http://windows.microsoft.com/en-US/internet-explorer/products/ie/home

Using Pinned Sites

Pinned sites makes it easy for users to get to frequently visited Web sites.

A ***pinned site*** is an Internet Explorer 9 Web site you "attach" to the Windows 7 taskbar. A pinned site is simply a quick way to open a Web site, much like you open a program that's pinned to the taskbar. Pinned sites let you access Web sites without having to open and navigate your Favorites list, or even open Internet Explorer first.

➲ PIN A WEB SITE TO THE WINDOWS 7 TASKBAR

GET READY. To pin a Web site to the Windows 7 taskbar, perform the following steps:

1. Launch Internet Explorer 9 and browse to any Web site.
2. Click the tab for the Web site and drag it to the taskbar (see Figure 3-4). You can also click and drag the Web site's thumbnail that appears on the New Tab page.
   An icon for the pinned site also appears to the left of the Back button in Internet Explorer 9. The site also shows up as a thumbnail on the taskbar (see Figure 3-5). When you hover your mouse pointer over a pinned site, a preview appears if an Aero theme is enabled. If the pinned site is for e-mail, such as Microsoft Hotmail, you may see brief status messages such as the number of new e-mails that have arrived since you last checked your account.

Figure 3-4

Pinning a Web site to the taskbar

Figure 3-5

A pinned site appears in Internet Explorer 9 and on the taskbar

To pin additional Web pages to a pinned site so all pages open by clicking a single thumbnail, perform the following steps:

1. Open the pinned Web site.
2. Open the site you want to add, and then click its tab.
3. Right-click the pinned Web site's icon to the left of the Back button, and then click **Add as a home page** (see Figure 3-6).

To unpin a site from the taskbar, right-click the pinned site's icon and select *Unpin this program from taskbar.*

Figure 3-6

Adding a site as a home page

© Danita Delimont/Gallo Images/Getty Images

➕ **MORE INFORMATION**

To learn more about pinned sites, visit http://windows.microsoft.com/en-US/internet-explorer/products/ie-9/
features/pinned-sites

Managing Security Features

The Internet is a great place to find useful information and entertainment, but it's also a
vehicle for viruses, worms, and more dangerous attacks on users. Microsoft has included
a lot of security and privacy features in Internet Explorer 9 to make Internet browsing a
safer experience.

Internet Explorer 9 includes many features that help you protect your computer and privacy
while surfing the Web. Some features have been around for a while, such as Pop-up Blocker,
while others have been introduced in Internet Explorer 9. With the millions of viruses,
worms, and other threats lurking on the Internet, it's highly recommended that you, at minimum, use the default Internet Explorer 9 security settings. You should even choose *more*
secure settings for your safety.

You can change a variety of options for safety and security and general default behaviors
in Internet Explorer 9 by clicking the Tools icon and then clicking Internet options. The
Internet Options dialog box displays; this dialog box features tabs that allow you to customize
your Web browsing experience. Let's look at the Security tab and the Privacy tab.

The Security tab (see Figure 3-7) is where you select a security zone, which is a group of
security settings for a type of site: Internet, Local intranet, Trusted sites, or Restricted sites.
For each zone, you can move the slider up or down to select higher or lower security settings.
You can also click the Custom level button to customize individual security settings, such as
scripts, ActiveX controls, .NET Framework, and more.

The Privacy tab (see Figure 3-8) also uses a slider to select levels of privacy controls, mainly
for blocking or allowing cookies.

The ***Pop-up Blocker*** check box (selected by default) automatically prevents pop-up windows
from appearing. Most pop-up windows are created by advertisers and appear when you first
open a Web site. However, their content can be malicious, so the Pop-up Blocker feature
prevents them from opening.

Figure 3-7

The Security tab

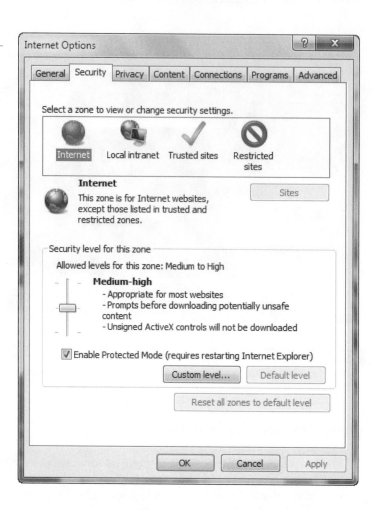

In Internet terms, "malicious" refers to viruses, worms, spyware, and other content that can harm your computer. Many of the security features in Internet Explorer 9 prevent malicious content from invading your computer.

Many other Internet Explorer 9 security controls are accessible from the Tools menu on the menu bar or the Safety menu on the command bar (if enabled). The first menu item is Delete browsing history, which allows you to erase Temporary Internet files, cookies, history, and many other "trails" of information all from a single dialog box (see Figure 3-9).

When you visit Web sites, your browser might store *cookies* (small text files that Web sites save to a computer's hard disk that contain information about the user and his or her browsing preferences), temporary Internet files, user names, passwords, and other data for your convenience. When you visit the sites again in the future, this information is already available to your browser so you don't have to reenter data. It's also meant to personalize the visit by remembering your information. However, the information can pose a security risk, especially if you share your computer with others, whether at home or work, or if you use a shared computer at the library, for example. *InPrivate Browsing* helps prevent personal information and browsing history from being stored by Internet Explorer 9. When you use InPrivate Browsing, a new tab appears in which you browse the Internet (see Figure 3-10). When you're finished and close the browser window, the session ends and any cookies or temporary files that were used during the session are cleared from your browsing history. A network administrator, however, can view Internet traffic that's generated with InPrivate Browsing.

Figure 3-8

The Privacy tab

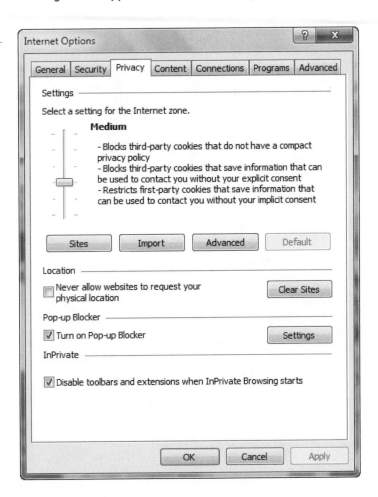

TAKE NOTE*

Some Web sites store a lot of information about your browsing sessions in cookies. For example, if you visit a shopping site, one or more cookies on your PC might include information about specific items you viewed or purchased. Advertising networks use cookies to "follow" you on the Web and display targeted advertising. After visiting a social networking site like Facebook, for example, a cookie might contain information related to what you typed on a friend's wall. If, for example, you mentioned you bought a great pair of Nike running shoes, the right side of your Facebook page might display an ad from a sporting goods retailer that sells Nike running shoes or you might even see an ad from Nike.com.

Tracking Protection helps you control which Web sites can track your online browsing activity and receive that information. This is accomplished with a Tracking Protection list. You can create your own Tracking Protection lists or download lists from the Internet Explorer Gallery Tracking Protection Lists Web site at http://iegallery.com/en/trackingprotectionlists/.

ActiveX Filtering blocks ActiveX controls, which are created for interactivity on the Web and commonly used on sites that display animations or offer multimedia such as videos. ActiveX is meant to enhance the user experience on the Web, but it can slow your computer. In addition, some attackers use ActiveX to push harmful content to unsuspecting users. ActiveX Filtering allows you to block ActiveX completely, or to trust certain sites and block all others.

Figure 3-9

The Delete Browsing History dialog box

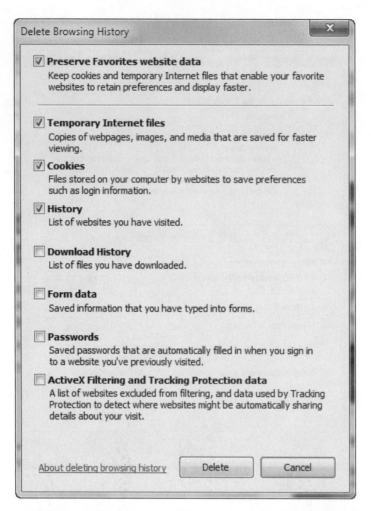

Figure 3-10

InPrivate Browsing runs in a new browser session

Other important security features include:

- **SmartScreen Filter:** The *SmartScreen Filter* detects threats on Web sites, such as phishing attacks and malware downloads, and prevents them from running. When Internet Explorer 9 detects a malicious Web site, it blocks the entire site from being accessed. It can also block malicious portions of legitimate Web sites, allowing the rest of the site to display as normal. SmartScreen Filter is enabled by default.

- **Cross-site scripting (XSS) filter:** A *cross-site scripting attack* occurs when you visit a compromised Web site that runs a script that installs a keylogger program on your computer. The installation occurs without your knowledge. After that, the keylogger records your keystrokes, including when you enter user names and passwords into other sites. The information is usually sent to a third party, who may access your accounts. The *cross-site scripting (XSS) filter* prevents the keylogger script from running.
  - **Domain highlighting:** Some Web sites use deceptive Web addresses, making you think you're visiting a legitimate site when you're actually on a phishing site or another danger-ous site. *Domain highlighting* shows you the true Web address of any Web site you visit by highlighting the domain in the Address bar.

Many Internet Explorer 9 security features are available in various forms in third-party Internet security suites.

➕ MORE INFORMATION

To learn more about ActiveX filtering, visit http://windows.microsoft.com/en-US/internet-explorer/products/ie-9/features/activex-filtering. Information on the cross-site scripting filter is available at http://windows.microsoft.com/en-US/internet-explorer/products/ie-9/features/cross-site-scripting-filter. Need extra help understanding InPrivate Browsing? Go to http://windows.microsoft.com/en-US/internet-explorer/products/ie-9/features/in-private. Finally, you can learn more about SmartScreen Filter at http://windows.microsoft.com/en-US/internet-explorer/products/ie-9/features/smartscreen-filter

---

 USE AND CONFIGURE INTERNET EXPLORER 9 SECURITY FEATURES

GET READY. To configure security features in Internet Explorer 9, perform the following steps:

1. Launch Internet Explorer 9.
2. To access Pop-up Blocker settings, click the **Tools** icon in the upper-right corner of the Internet Explorer 9 window, and then click **Internet options**.
3. In the Internet Options dialog box, click the **Privacy** tab, and then click the Pop-up Blocker **Settings** button. To allow pop-ups from a particular trusted Web site, such as your bank, type the URL in the **Address of website to allow** text box and then click **Add**.
4. Click **Close** to close the dialog box.
5. To enable ActiveX Filtering, click the **Tools** icon in Internet Explorer 9, point to **Safety**, and then click **ActiveX Filtering**. A check mark appears next to ActiveX Filtering to indicate the feature is enabled (see Figure 3-11).
6. To use Tracking Protection, click the **Tools** icon, point to **Safety**, and then click **Tracking protection**. In the Manage Add-ons dialog box (see Figure 3-12), click a Tracking Protection list (if available), and then click **Enable**.
7. To download a Tracking Protection list, click the **Get a Tracking Protection List online** link and then follow the prompts.
8. To use InPrivate Browsing, click the **Tools** menu, point to **Safety**, and then click **InPrivate Browsing**. A new browser session opens, which keeps your browsing actions private.
9. When you're finished, just close Internet Explorer to end the InPrivate Browsing session.

Figure 3-11

ActiveX Filtering is enabled

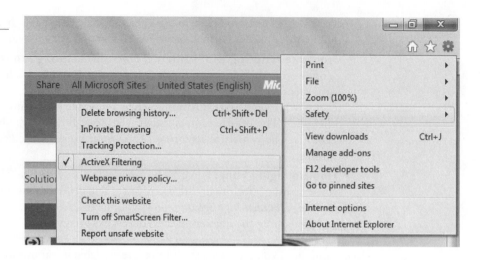

Figure 3-12

The Manage Add-ons dialog box

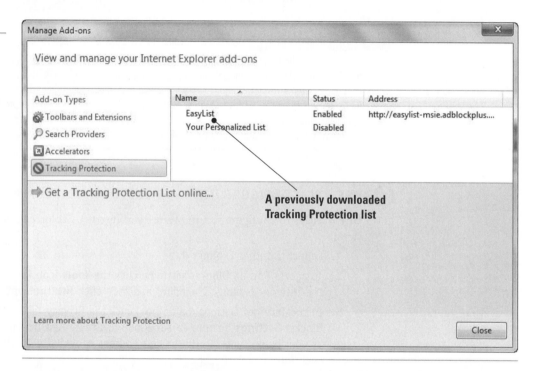

Some security features, such as Tracking Protection, might require you to close Internet Explorer 9 and then reopen it to see the features in action.

■ Introducing Accessory Programs

THE BOTTOM LINE

Microsoft provides a wealth of free programs and utilities in Windows to help you be more productive, creative, and efficient. The Accessories folder in the All Programs list is your starting point for lots of handy tools.

Windows 7 comes bundled with many useful accessory programs, such as Calculator, Notepad, Paint, Snipping Tool, Windows Media Player, WordPad, and many more. The programs allow you to be productive in Windows without purchasing third-party programs.

To access these programs, click Start > All Programs > Accessories. Table 3-1 lists the programs in the Windows 7 Accessories folder. Not all programs are available in every edition of Windows 7.

Table 3-1

Window 7 Accessory Programs

Program	Description
Calculator	Performs basic mathematical functions such as addition, subtraction, multiplication, division. Also includes scientific, programmer, and statistics functions, along with unit conversions, date calculations, and worksheets to determine mortgage payments, vehicle lease payments, and fuel economy.
Command Prompt	Opens a window in which you run MS-DOS and other computer commands.
Connect to a Projector Connect to a Network Projector	Allows you to expand your screen to use another monitor or external projector.
Math Input Panel	Allows you to write and correct free-hand math equations using your mouse or other pointing device.
Notepad	Serves as a simple text editor.
Paint	Allows you to perform basic image editing.
Remote Desktop Connection	Connects two computers over a network or the Internet, allowing one computer to see and use the other computer's desktop. Remote Desktop Connection is covered later in this lesson.
Run	Allows you to run commands from the Start menu. Some commands require elevated or administrative privileges; to run these commands, use the *Run as administrator* command.
Snipping Tool	Allows you to capture, annotate, and save screen shots. Snipping Tool is covered later in this lesson.
Sound Recorder	Allows you to record sound from different audio devices, such as a microphone that's plugged into the sound card on your computer.
Sticky Notes	Allows you to keep notes on the desktop to help you remember important items. Available in different colors.
Sync Center	Allows you to sync any folder in your computer with a folder on an external drive connected to your computers or a network drive. Sync Center is covered later in this lesson.
Windows Explorer	Allows you to access files and folders on your computer, copy and move items, search for items, and more. This graphical file management system is built into many versions of Windows.
Windows Mobility Center	Allows you to control many different computer settings, such as screen brightness, volume, power/battery, WiFi, Bluetooth, sound, and so on. Windows Mobility Center is covered later in this lesson.
WordPad	Serves as a word processor, with many more features than Notepad.
Ease of Access	Allows you to open the Ease of Access Center to configure accessibility options, and gives you access to the speech recognition feature. See Lesson 2.

(continued)

Table 3-1

Continued

Program	Description
System Tools	Gives you access to Control Panel, Disk Cleanup, Disk Defragmenter, Resource Monitor, System Restore, and much more.
Tablet PC	Gives you access to tools to use a tablet PC's input device.
Windows PowerShell	Opens a command window useful for IT professionals. Windows PowerShell is covered later in this lesson.

TAKE NOTE * This lesson covers Snipping Tool, Sync Center, Windows Mobility Center, and Windows PowerShell in detail because they're listed as measureable skills for the 98-349 exam.

■ Using the Snipping Tool

THE BOTTOM LINE Home and business users alike need to capture screen shots occasionally for many different reasons. Windows 7 includes the Snipping Tool, an easy-to-use screen capture program with a few editing features.

A *screen shot*, also referred to as a snip or screen grab, is a snapshot of whatever is displayed on the computer screen. You might take a screen shot of an error message to help troubleshoot a computer problem, you might capture screen shots of a process in a program to create a how-to guide, or you might capture a screen shot to save as an image to use in a report or other document.

CERTIFICATION READY
What is the Snipping Tool used for?
1.3

The *Snipping Tool* (see Figure 3-13) is an accessory program that comes with Windows 7 that allows you to take screen shots, annotate them, and save them. When using Snipping Tool, you can capture the entire screen, a window, a rectangular portion of the screen, or a free-form image. The free-form capture allows you to use your mouse pointer or other pointing device to draw around a non-rectangular object on the screen.

Figure 3-13

The Snipping Tool window

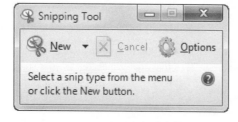

You can save images in GIF, JPG, PNG, or HTML format, then use Snipping Tool to add freehand annotations, highlight or erase part of the image, or send it to a recipient via e-mail. If you select the HTML format, Snipping Tool saves the screen shot as a Web archive file in MHT format, which you can open in a Web browser such as Internet Explorer.

TAKE NOTE * The Snipping Tool is available in Windows 7 Home Premium, Professional, Ultimate, and Enterprise editions.

USE THE SNIPPING TOOL TO CAPTURE A SCREEN SHOT

GET READY. To capture a screen shot with the Snipping Tool and save it as a graphics file, perform the following steps:

1. Open or display a file, program, window, Web page, or anything that contains an object or picture you want to capture in a screen shot.
2. Click **Start** > **All Programs** > **Accessories** > **Snipping Tool.**
3. Click the **New** drop-down menu and choose **Free-form Snip**, **Rectangular Snip**, **Window Snip**, or **Full-screen Snip** (see Figure 3-14). The default is Rectangular Snip, which is used in this example.

Figure 3-14

Selecting the type of screen shot to capture

4. A white overlay appears on your screen. Click and drag the mouse pointer over the area you want to capture (see Figure 3-15). An editing window appears, displaying the captured image.

TAKE NOTE ✻ You can turn off the Snipping Tool overlay. Just click **Options**, uncheck the **Show screen overlay when Snipping Tool is active** check box, and click **OK.**

Figure 3-15

The captured image

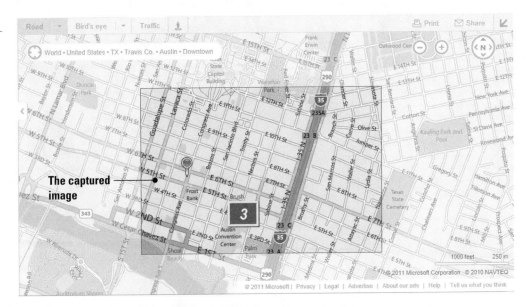

5. To save the image, click the **Save Snip** icon on the toolbar, which looks like a floppy diskette.
6. In the Save As dialog box, navigate to the location where you want to save the screen shot. In the **File name** text box, type a descriptive name for the file.
7. Click the Save as type drop-down menu and select **GIF**, **JPG**, or **PNG**.

TAKE NOTE *

GIF files support 256 colors and are used primarily for Web sites. JPG is the most common picture file format, and it supports over 16 million colors. PNG files are an improvement to the GIF format and support "lossless compression," which means you can enlarge a PNG file to a certain extent without losing clarity and crispness.

8. Click **Save**. The screen capture is saved as a graphics file.

USE THE SNIPPING TOOL TO ANNOTATE AN IMAGE

GET READY. To annotate an image using the Snipping Tool, perform the following steps:

1. In the Snipping Tool editing window, click the down arrow to the right of the pen button on the toolbar. Select a pen color from the list.
2. Write or draw on the image (see Figure 3-16).

Figure 3-16

Annotating an image

Annotation drawn with pen tool

3. Click the **Save Snip** icon to save the annotated image under the current file name or a new file name.

Remember, you can open an image saved with Snipping Tool in any graphics program (including Paint) to make detailed edits.

➕ **MORE INFORMATION**

For more information about the Snipping Tool, visit http://windows.microsoft.com/en-US/windows7/products/features/snipping-tool

---

■ Playing Back and Recording to Media

⬇ **THE BOTTOM LINE**

Windows Media Player and Windows Media Center provide a wealth of media playback, ripping, and recording options. No longer relegated only to home use, both programs can be used in the work place for highly appealing presentations, training, and lobby entertainment.

Digital media is popular for both home and business users of Windows 7. Although many media software packages are available on the market, you should check out the latest versions of Windows Media Player and Windows Media Center to see if third-party tools are even needed. Both programs come bundled with most Windows 7, so home and business users have access to these full-featured programs without spending additional money.

Using Windows Media Player

If you need to simply play back almost any type of multimedia file, Windows Media Player should be the program you use. It's built into Windows 7 (so it's free), and its media burning and ripping features, along with the ability to stream multimedia to other networked computers, makes it a great choice at home and work.

CERTIFICATION READY
What is the name of the main window in Windows Media Player?
1.3

Windows Media Player 12 is a program that allows you to play back music and video files and view photos. Files stored in your Music, Pictures, Videos, and Recorded TV libraries appear in the Windows Media Player file list by default. If you're connected to a network, you can stream digital media files—audio, video, or photos—for playback or viewing from another computer or a server that hosts Windows media files. The main window in Windows Media Player is called the Player Library (see Figure 3-17).

TAKE NOTE ✱

Windows Media Player 12 supports the 3GP, AAC, AVCHD, MPEG-4, WMV, and WMA audio and video formats. It also supports most AVI, DivX, MOV, and Xvid files.

Whether playing digital files on your computer, or from a CD or DVD, Windows Media Player includes common playback controls, such as Play, Shuffle, Repeat, Stop, Next, Previous, and a volume slider. You can switch to a smaller window, referred to as Now Playing mode, by clicking the *Switch to Now Playing* button in the lower-right corner. The Now Playing mode window appears (see Figure 3-18). To return to your library, click the *Switch to Library* button.

With Windows Media Player, you can do the following as well:

- **Create playlists:** Organize your music files into *playlists*, which are simply lists of music composed of songs from different albums, and may even be located on different areas of your computer or attached devices. Whatever appears in the library may be included in a playlist.

Figure 3-17

Windows Media Player main window—the Player Library

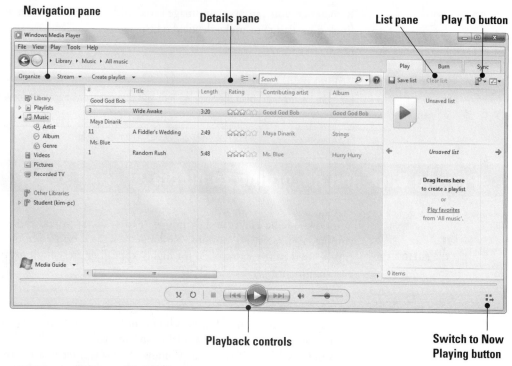

Navigation pane

Details pane

List pane   **Play To button**

Playback controls

Switch to Now Playing button

Figure 3-18

Windows Media Player Now Playing mode

Switch to Library button

- **Rip music from CDs to your computer:** Insert a CD and, when a list of its tracks appears in the Windows Media Player window, click the Rip CD button. Windows Media Player rips the tracks on the CD to your Music library.

- **Burn CDs:** If you have a recordable optical drive on your computer, you can use Windows Media Player to burn a collection of your favorite songs to a CD.

- **Create slide shows:** Use Windows Media Player to create slide shows with playback controls in just a few clicks.

- **Share media across a network:** You can use the *Play to* command to share multimedia files across a network with a homegroup (a personal network, usually set up at home) or across the Internet.

If you pin Windows Media Player 12 to the Windows 7 taskbar, you can take advantage of Jump Lists for previously accessed files. The Jump List also includes playback controls at the bottom of the Jump List window to play music, a video, or view photos without having to open Windows Media Player first.

TAKE NOTE*

Microsoft has made Windows Media Player available in most editions of Windows 7: Starter, Home Premium, Professional, Ultimate, and Enterprise.

+ MORE INFORMATION

For more information about Windows Media Player in Windows 7, visit http://windows.microsoft.com/en-US/windows7/products/features/windows-media-player-12 and http://windows.microsoft.com/en-US/windows7/Getting-started-with-Windows-Media-Player

PLAY BACK MEDIA FILES

GET READY. To listen to music files, watch videos, or view photos in Windows Media Player, perform the steps in this section.

To listen to music files in Windows Media player, perform the following steps:

1. Open Windows Media Player by clicking **Start**, selecting **All Programs**, and then selecting **Windows Media Player** near the top of the programs list. You can also click its icon in the taskbar if it appears there.

2. Click the **Music** library in the navigation pane, click the file you want to hear in the file list, and click the **Play** button along the bottom of the window.

   Another option is to click the **Play** tab in the upper-right corner of the Windows Media Player window, drag the songs you want to hear to the **Play** tab, and then click the **Play** button.

3. After the file has finished playing, Windows Media Player automatically plays the next file in the list.

To watch a video in Windows Media Player, perform the following steps:

1. Click the **Videos** library in the navigation pane, and then double-click the file you want to view in the file list. Windows Media Player launches a special viewing window and plays back the video.

2. Place your mouse pointer over the window to display playback controls (see Figure 3-19).

Figure 3-19

Playback controls appear in the video viewing window when you hover your mouse pointer over the window

Playback controls

To view photos in Windows Media Player, perform the following steps:

1. Click the **Pictures** library in the navigation pane. Thumbnails of the photos in your Pictures library appear.
2. To view all of the photos as a slide show, click the **Play** button. Windows starts the slide show in its own window (see Figure 3-20).

Figure 3-20

A slide show in Windows Media Player

Courtesy of Marion Post Wolcott, Farm Security Administration/Office of War Information

To stop any playback feature, click the Stop button in the playback controls, and then click Go To Library.

CREATE A PLAYLIST

GET READY. To create a playlist of music, perform the following steps:

1. In Windows Media Player, in the Player Library, click the **Create playlist** button on the toolbar.
2. Type a name for the new playlist that appears in the Navigation pane (see Figure 3-21).
3. Drag and drop songs from the file list to the new playlist in the Navigation pane.

An auto playlist gives you more control and options. To create an autoplaylist, click the down arrow on the *Create playlist* button, select *Create auto playlist*, and follow the prompts.

BURN A MUSIC CD

GET READY. To burn a music CD, perform the following steps:

1. Insert a blank CD or DVD into your computer's recordable media drive.
2. In Windows Media Player, in the Player Library, click the **Music** library to display the file list.
3. Click the **Burn** tab.
4. Drag individual songs, playlists, or entire albums to the burn list on the right (see Figure 3-22).
5. Click **Start burn**.

Figure 3-21

Creating a playlist in Windows Media Player

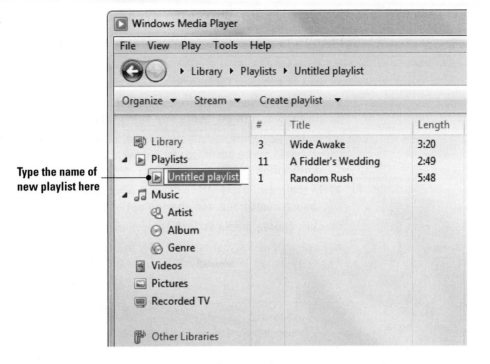

Type the name of new playlist here

Figure 3-22

Creating a list of files to burn to media

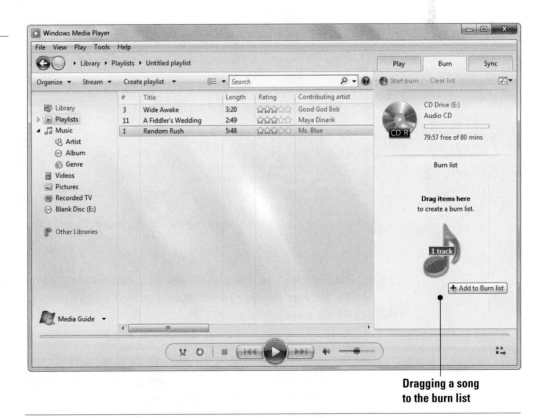

Dragging a song to the burn list

The CD ejects when the burning process completes. The burn process works similarly for other types of media files.

➲ PREPARE YOUR COMPUTER TO STREAM MEDIA FILES

GET READY. To stream media from your home computer, perform the following steps:

1. Ensure your computer is connected to your local network and that you are connected to a homegroup. For information on homegroups, see Lesson 6.

2. In Windows Media Player, in the Player Library, click **Stream** on the menu bar and then select **Turn on media streaming with HomeGroup.**

3. On the Media streaming options page, click **Turn on media streaming.** If you're prompted for an administrator password or confirmation, type the password or provide confirmation and then click **OK.**

4. In the Network and Sharing Center window, click **Advanced sharing settings** (or click **Choose homegroup and sharing options**).

5. Click **Choose media streaming options.**

6. Type a name for your media library in the text box at the top (see Figure 3-23).

Figure 3-23

Configuring streaming media options

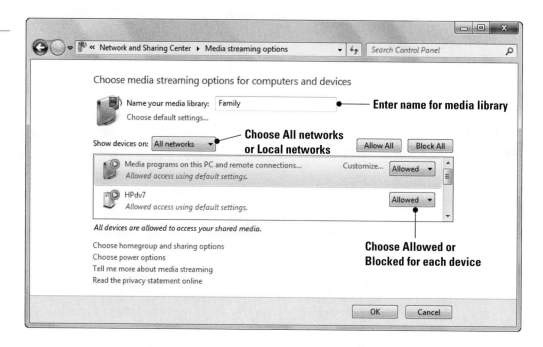

7. Choose to show devices on the local network or on all networks.

8. For each device, choose **Allowed** or **Blocked** to control whether others can see files on those devices.

9. Click **OK** and then close the Network and Sharing Center window.

To stream media files over the Internet, perform the following steps:

1. In Windows Media Player, in the Player Library, click **Stream** and then click **Allow Internet access to my home media.**

2. In the Internet Home Media Access dialog box, click **Link an online ID.**

3. Follow the prompts to link your user account with an online ID, such as your Windows Live ID. When you return to the Internet Home Media Access dialog box, click **Allow Internet access to my home media** again (see Figure 3-24). Click **Yes** in the dialog box that appears, and then click **OK.**

Figure 3-24

The Internet Home Media Access dialog box

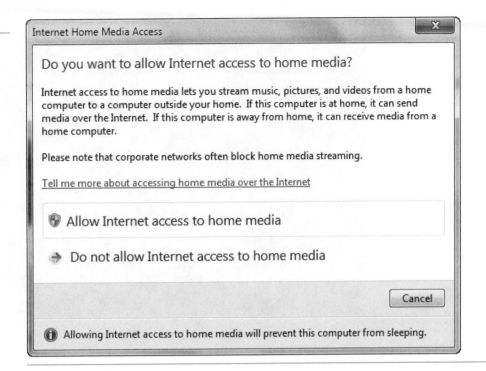

The Play To feature in Windows Media Player allows you to select multimedia you would like to play on a connected device, such as a stereo system at home. Just select the media you want to stream in Windows Media Player, click the Play tab, click the *Play to* button near the upper-right corner of the window, and then select the device on your network that will play back the media. You can use the controls in the Play To dialog box to control playback volume and other settings.

Using Windows Media Center

Windows Media Center is a cut above Windows Media Player, incorporating many of the same types of features but with digital video recorder functionality and built-in access to online entertainment content.

Windows Media Center (see Figure 3-25) is a multi-faceted program that provides a complete entertainment system for your computer. Similar to Windows Media Player, you use Windows Media Center to play music, create playlists, watch videos, play recorded TV programs, and display pictures and slide shows. However, Media Center offers much more. For example, you can watch, pause, and record HDTV, watch live TV and online programming, and listen to radio stations.

CERTIFICATION READY
What Windows 7 program is used to play recorded TV programs?
1.3

Watching TV programming requires a TV tuner and a subscription to a cable service or a similar service. You don't need a digital video recorder (DVR)—your computer acts like a DVR, enabling you to record shows and even schedule shows in advance. If you don't have a TV tuner but do have Internet access, you can still use Internet TV in the latest version of Windows Media Center. Internet TV is a service that allows you to watch some TV shows, movies, and clips streamed from the Internet.

Windows Media Center supports the same audio and video formats as Windows Media Player: 3GP, AAC, AVCHD, MPEG-4, WMV, and WMA, and most AVI, DivX, MOV, and Xvid files.

Figure 3-25

The Windows Media Center
main window

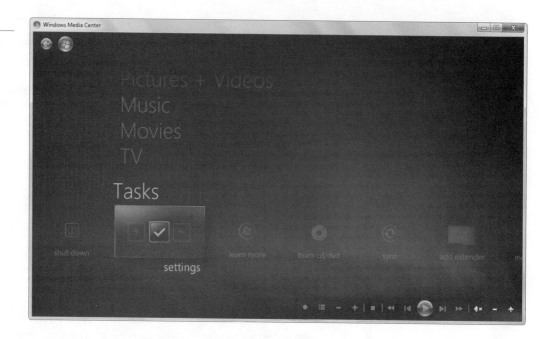

You can also share media over a network from Windows Media Center with the use of a
Windows Media Center Extender. You can buy an actual Extender device or use an Xbox
360 as an Extender. Each device you want to stream media to, such as an HDTV, needs
an Extender. You can stream to up to five Extenders from a single computer running
Windows 7.

 PLAY BACK OR VIEW MULTIMEDIA

GET READY. To use Windows Media Center for multimedia playback and viewing, perform
the following steps:

1. Click the **Start > All Programs > Windows Media Center**.
2. To view photos or videos, click **Pictures + Videos**, and then click **Picture Library** or
   Video Library. Just double-click any pictures or videos you want to view.
3. Click the green Windows Media Center button in the upper-left corner of the Windows
   Media Center to return to the main menu.
4. To listen to music, click **Music Library**. Select music you want to listen to, and then
   click **Add to now playing**.

Use the playback controls at the bottom of the window to stop, pause, play, rewind, and forward the multimedia file that's playing.

 CONFIGURE SETTINGS

GET READY. To configure settings in Windows Media Center, perform the following steps:

1. In the Windows Media Center main window, hover your mouse pointer over the last
   menu item at the bottom. A down arrow displays. Scroll down to the Tasks menu and
   click **Settings**. The Settings window displays (see Figure 3-26).

Figure 3-26

The Windows Media Center Settings window

To add an Extender:

1. Click **Extender**, click **add extender**, and then follow the prompts.

    To add libraries of content to Windows Media Center, return to the Settings window and then perform the following steps:

2. Return to the Settings window and click **Media Libraries**.

3. In the Media Library window, select the type of media you want to add (see Figure 3-27) and then click **Next**.

4. Click **Add folders to the library** and click **Next**.

5. Choose **On this computer** or **On another computer** and then click **Next**.

6. Select the folders to add to the library (see Figure 3-27) and then click **Next**.

Figure 3-27

Adding media to Windows Media Center

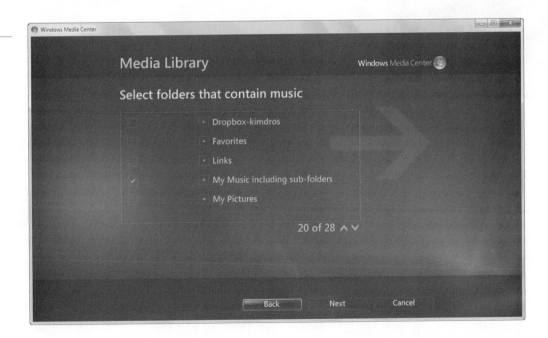

7. Select **Yes, use these locations** and then click **Finish**. Windows Media Center adds the content of the folders to your library.

There are many more settings to be familiar with in Windows Media Center. Take some time to browse all of the options in the Settings window.

➕ **MORE INFORMATION**

To get details about Windows Media Center, visit http://windows.microsoft.com/en-US/windows/products/windows-media-center

---

■ Understanding Sync Center

⬇ **THE BOTTOM LINE**   If you need to frequently switch between network folders and the files on your laptop hard drive, use Sync Center to ensure that you always have the latest files.

CERTIFICATION READY
What Windows 7 feature allows you to sync files between your computer and mobile devices?
1.4

CERTIFICATION READY
What term best describes the type of files you can access without being connected to the resource from which you synchronized?
4.4

Sync Center (see Figure 3-28) is a feature in Windows 7 that allows you to sync files between your computer and a network location or with some mobile devices. Syncing allows you to keep two or more versions of the same file, stored on your computer and on a network folder, identical to the other. For example, if you add, delete, or modify a file in one location, the synchronization process ensures the files match each other.

After syncing is complete, you can access network files without being connected to the resource. These files are referred to as *offline files*. You can also use Sync Center to check the results of a recent sync to ensure the files were synced successfully, or to re-sync if errors occurred.

To get started with Sync Center, you must first set up a sync partnership with the network or external drive you want to use. Then, anytime you want to ensure your files are synced, right-click the network drive and select Always available offline. Once your files are done syncing, a symbol appears next to the network drive so you can see at a glance that the files are synchronized.

The Sync Center allows you to schedule synchronization, resolve errors that occurred during synchronization, change the amount of disk space allocated to offline files, and encrypt your offline files for security.

TAKE NOTE＊   Although you can use Sync Center to sync a mobile device with your computer, Sync Center doesn't work with all devices. Instead, try Device Stage in Windows 7 or use the sync software provided by the mobile device manufacturer.

➕ **MORE INFORMATION**

For more information about Sync Center, visit http://windows.microsoft.com/en-US/windows7/What-is-Sync-Center

Figure 3-28

The Sync Center main window

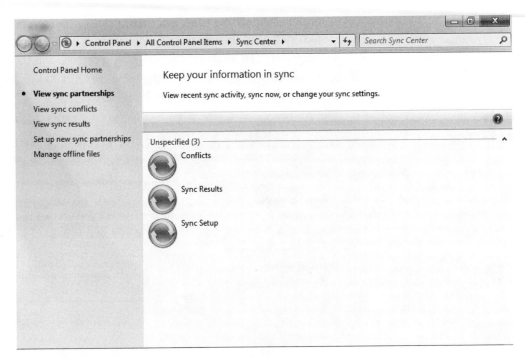

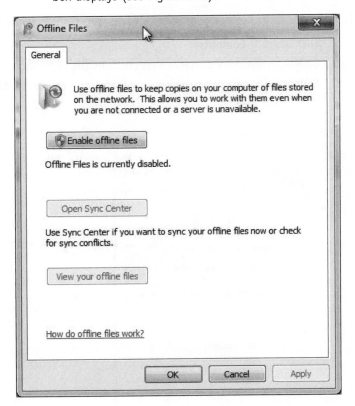

SET UP A SYNCHRONIZATION PARTNERSHIP

GET READY. To set up a synchronization partnership, perform the following steps:

1. Open Sync Center by clicking **Start** > **Control Panel** > **Sync Center**. (Alternately, click **Start**, and in the **Search programs and files** search box, type **sync**. In the results list that displays, select **Sync Center**.)

2. In Sync Center, in the left pane, click **Manage offline files**. The Offline Files dialog box displays (see Figure 3-29).

Figure 3-29

The Offline Files dialog box

3. Click **Enable offline files**, and then click **OK**. If you're prompted for an administrator password or confirmation, type the password or provide confirmation.

4. Close any open windows, shut down all programs, and then restart your computer.

5. Return to Sync Center and, in the left pane, click **Set up new sync partnerships**. The Sync Setup screen displays (see Figure 3-30).

Figure 3-30

The Sync Setup screen

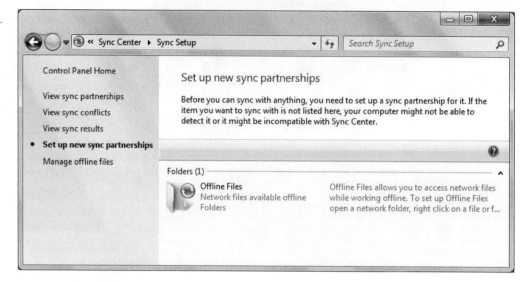

6. Click the name of the drive in the list of available sync partnerships.

7. On the toolbar, click **Set up**.

8. Select the settings and schedule to determine how and when you want to sync your device with your computer.

SYNCHRONIZE FILES

GET READY. To sync files on your computer with a network location, perform the following steps:

1. Click **Start > Computer**.

2. Browse to the drive or folder that contains the files you want to keep synchronized.

3. Right-click the name of the drive or folder, and then click **Always available offline** (see Figure 3-31).

Figure 3-31

Synchronizing files

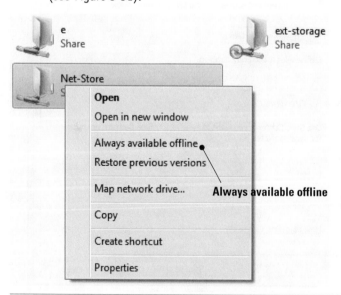

Once the synchronization process is complete, a symbol displays next to the network drive or folder indicating that the files are synchronized.

■ Using Windows Mobility Center

THE BOTTOM LINE

Rather than using different tools to adjust your laptop's screen brightness, wireless settings, and more, just open the Windows Mobility Center, which displays groups of settings all in one interface.

Windows Mobility Center is a control panel of sorts that gives you access to several laptop settings, from volume to screen brightness to power options to WiFi and Bluetooth settings—all in one place. Although the settings can be accessed from various icons and commands within Windows, you can make adjustments from a single window in Windows Mobility Center. Figure 3-32 shows the Windows Mobility Center window.

TAKE NOTE*

Windows Mobility Center is included on laptops running the Windows 7 Home Premium, Professional, Ultimate, and Enterprise editions. Presentation settings, however, are not available in Windows 7 Home Premium.

Figure 3-32

The Windows Mobility Center window

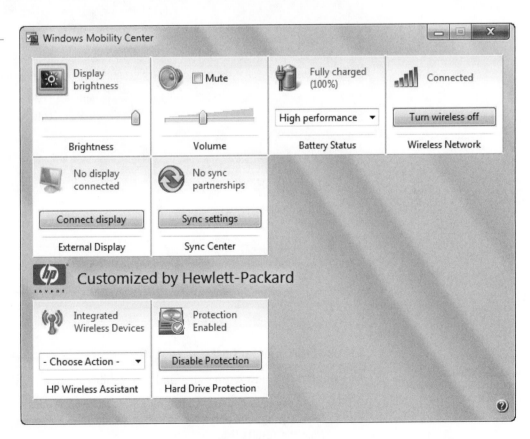

Windows Mobility Center displays settings in boxes, or tiles. The tiles that are displayed depend on your hardware and laptop manufacturer. In addition, a setting that is turned off or disabled might not display, or display with a red X, such as if you turn off your WiFi antenna by pressing the F key.

CERTIFICATION READY
Which settings can be adjusted by using the Mobility Center?
1.4

Table 3-2 describes common Windows Mobility Center settings. Not all settings are available on all laptops, so a few settings in the table are not displayed in Figure 3-32.

Table 3-2

Typical Window Mobility Center Settings

SETTING	DESCRIPTION
Brightness	Allows you to adjust the brightness of your laptop display. Move the slider to the left to decrease brightness, and to the right to increase brightness. Display brightness is related to the power plan for your laptop; those settings are adjusted in the Battery Status tile.
Volume	Allows you to increase or decrease speaker volume, or check the Mute check box to temporarily disable audio.
Battery Status	Allows you to see how much battery charge remains and adjust the power plan for your laptop. Power plans vary but offer two at a minimum: one for running on battery power and another for running on AC power.
Wireless Network	Allows you to turn your wireless network adapter on or off and see the status of your wireless network connection.
Screen Rotation	For tablet PCs, this feature allows you to change the orientation of your screen (portrait or landscape).
External Display	Allows you to connect an external monitor to your laptop.
Sync Center	Allows you to access settings to sync files with a network location, or with a mobile device. Sync Center is covered in more detail in this lesson.
Presentation Settings	Provides you with access to settings for connecting your laptop to a projector for presentations.

+ MORE INFORMATION

For more information about settings in Windows Mobility Center, visit http://windows.microsoft.com/en-US/windows7/products/features/windows-mobility-center

CHANGE MOBILITY CENTER SETTINGS

GET READY. To adjust settings in Windows Mobility Center, perform the following steps:

1. Open Windows Mobility Center by clicking the **Start** button, typing **mobility** in the **Search programs and files** search box, and then selecting **Windows Mobility Center** from the results list.
2. Adjust the screen brightness by moving the **Brightness** slider left or right.
3. Click the **Battery Status** drop-down list (see Figure 3-33) and then select another power plan, such as **Power saver**. Notice how the screen brightness changes again.
4. Click the drop-down list again and select the original power plan.

Figure 3-33

Selecting a different power plan in the Battery Status drop-down list

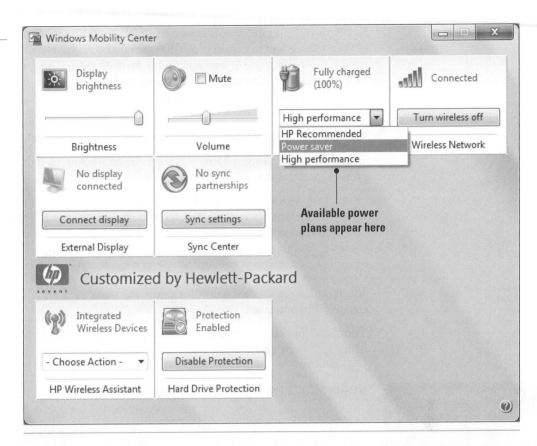

Click the drop-down lists in other tiles of Windows Mobility Center to see which options are available.

■ Understanding Remote Desktop Services

↓
THE BOTTOM LINE

Remote Desktop Services, formerly known as Terminal Services, enables computers to act like mainframe terminals. The processing required to run applications and even use the desktop is performed by the server rather than the client computer.

CERTIFICATION READY
What term best describes the Windows 7 technology that allows a computer to connect to a remote server and then run applications from that server?
2.4

The Remote Desktop Services server must run Windows Server 2008 R2, Windows Server 2008, Windows Server 2003, or Windows 2000 Server.

Windows 7 **Remote Desktop Services** is the technology that allows a computer (the client) to connect to a remote server (also called a host computer) and run applications from the server. Although the client computer may be running Windows 7, it doesn't run the actual application—the server handles all processing. This is the opposite of a typical Windows 7 computer with applications such as Microsoft Office installed on the hard disk. Remote Desktop Services can also provide a virtual user desktop for remote users. When a user accesses the server, the user is provided a virtual desktop interface that looks and responds similarly to the client computer's actual desktop.

A major benefit of Remote Desktop Services is that administrators can manage user desktops and applications from a central place—at the server—rather than at the physical client computer.

A few of the services provided by Remote Desktop Services include the following:

- **RemoteApp:** Enables a remote user to log on to a Remote Desktop Services server via a Web browser and run a single application.
- **Remote Desktop Web Access:** Enables a remote user to log on and run programs and virtual desktops. This feature lets users create a RemoteApp and Desktop Connection using the Start menu on a computer running Windows 7 or via a Web browser.

In a Remote Desktop Services environment, a network administrator must first set up resources for a remote user to connect to. This is referred to as "publishing the resources." The administrator must also send the user a setup file or Web address. The user either runs the setup file or enters the Web address in a Web browser to make the connection to the server. Once a user accesses the remote server, the resources will be available in a folder on the user's computer.

 CONNECT TO A SERVER USING REMOTE DESKTOP WEB ACCESS

GET READY. To connect to a remote server using Remote Desktop Web Access in a Web browser, perform the following steps:

1. In a Web browser, type the Web address provided by the network administrator. The Web address is in the **https://computer name/rdweb** format or the **https://ipaddress/rdweb** format.
2. Type the **User Name** and **Password**, and then click **OK**.

When the user is finished with the session, she should log off and close the Web browser to ensure the connection is closed.

The client application for Remote Desktop Services is called Remote Desktop Connection, which is covered next.

Understanding Remote Desktop Connection

Anyone who's on the go often needs to access a computer at home or at work. Remote Desktop Connection allows you to set up a computer for remote access, and then connect to that computer wherever you may be. All you need is an Internet connection.

Windows 7 *Remote Desktop Connection* allows you to access another computer on a network or over the Internet, and use the computer as if you were sitting in front of it. This feature is handy for people who want to access files on their home computer while at work, for example. Remote Desktop Services is the technology that allows Remote Desktop Connection to work.

When setting up Remote Desktop Connection, you must allow remote connections to the computer you want to access remotely. The remote computer may run any of these operating systems:

- Windows XP Professional edition
- Windows Vista Business, Ultimate, or Enterprise edition
- Windows 7 Professional, Ultimate, or Enterprise edition

Setting up Remote Desktop Connection can take some effort if the remote computer is outside of your network. You might need to configure your firewall to allow Remote Desktop connections. You must also determine the IP address of the remote computer (such as the home computer you want to connect to), and configure the remote computer's router to forward TCP port 3389 to the destination computer's IP address.

CERTIFICATION READY
Which Windows 7 feature allows you to set up a computer for remote access and then connect to that computer regardless of where you might be located?
1.4

CERTIFICATION READY
What does Remote Desktop Connection allow you to do?
2.4

TAKE NOTE*
Remote Desktop comes with all editions of Windows 7; however, you can only connect to computers running the Professional, Ultimate, or Enterprise editions.

TAKE NOTE*
Allowing remote connections between your computer and a remote computer outside your network presents a security risk. The session can be hijacked by a malicious user. Whenever possible, be sure both computers use strong encryption, complex passwords, and strong authentication to minimize the possibility of attack.

To learn how to set up a Remote Desktop connection with a computer outside of your network, visit the Allow Remote Desktop connections from outside your home network Web page at http://windows.microsoft.com/en-US/windows7/allow-remote-desktop-connections-from-outside-your-home-network.

➕ MORE INFORMATION

For more information about how to use Remote Desktop Connection, visit http://windows.microsoft.com/en-US/windows7/products/features/remote-desktop-connection. You can learn about Remote Desktop Services at http://windows.microsoft.com/en-US/windows7/What-is-Remote-Desktop-Services

---

⊙ SET UP REMOTE DESKTOP CONNECTION

GET READY. To set up Remote Desktop Connection, perform the following steps:

1. Click **Start**, right-click **Computer**, and then click **Properties**. The System window displays.

2. In the left pane, click **Remote settings**. If you're prompted for an administrator password or confirmation, type the password or provide confirmation. The System dialog box displays with the Remote tab displayed (see Figure 3-34).

Figure 3-34

The Remote tab

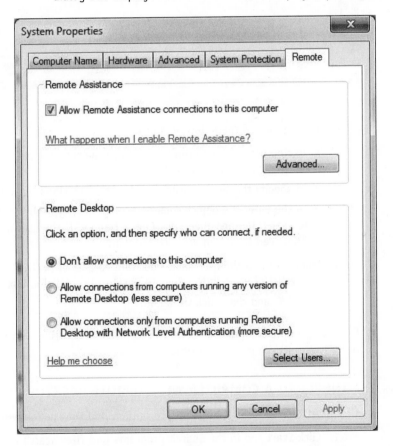

3. In the **Remote Desktop** section, select one of the options to allow connections:

   - **Don't allow connections to this computer:** Selecting this option prevents anyone from connecting to your computer using Remote Desktop or RemoteApp.

   - **Allow connections from computers running any version of Remote Desktop:** This option allows users running Windows XP, Windows Vista, or Windows 7 to connect to your computer using Remote Desktop or RemoteApp. If you aren't sure which operating system is running on the remote computer, use this option.

- **Select Allow connections only from computers running Remote Desktop with Network Level Authentication:** This option allows Windows 7 users to connect to your computer if they're running Remote Desktop or RemoteApp with Network Level Authentication. This option offers the most security.

4. Click **Select Users**.

5. In the Remote Desktop Users dialog box, click **Add**. The Select Users dialog box displays (which might be named Select Users or Groups). See Figure 3-35.

Figure 3-35

The Select Users dialog box

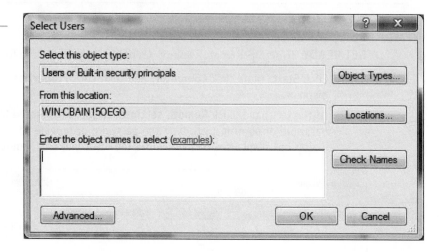

6. Perform one of the following steps:

   - To find users, specify the types of user names (objects) you want to search for by clicking the **Object Types** button.
   - To specify the search location, click the **Locations** button.
   - In the Enter the object names to select box, type the user name that you want to search for, and then click **Check Names**. If the user name isn't found, click **Advanced** to run an advanced search.

7. When you find the user name you want to add, click **OK**. The name will be displayed in the list of users in the Remote Desktop Users dialog box.

8. Click **OK**, and then click **OK** again.

Once the remote computer is set up to accept connections, leave the computer running in order to connect to it at a later time.

 CONNECT TO A COMPUTER WITH REMOTE DESKTOP CONNECTION

GET READY. To connect to a remote computer, perform the following steps:

1. Click **Start** and in the **Search programs and files** search box, type **remote connect**. In the results list that displays, select **Remote Desktop Connection**. The Remote Desktop Connection window displays (see Figure 3-36).

2. In the **Computer** field, type the IP address or name of the remote computer if both computers are on the same private network. If the remote computer is on a different network, type the router's public IP address followed by a colon and the port number (for example, **XXX.XXX.XX.XXX:3389**). Replace the Xs with your actual public IP address.

3. Log on to the remote computer.

Figure 3-36

The Remote Desktop
Connection window

Once you connect, you can access resources on the remote computer as if you were sitting in front of it.

+ MORE INFORMATION

For more information about Remote Desktop Connection, visit http://windows.microsoft.com/en-US/windows7/products/features/remote-desktop-connection

■ Understanding Remote Management and Assistance

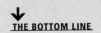

THE BOTTOM LINE

When you're asked to help a friend or co-worker with a computer problem, being able to see the person's computer can make all the difference in resolving the problem. Windows Remote Assistance allows you to see the desktop of another user even though that user (and his computer) is located remotely. You can even take control of the remote computer if necessary.

Windows Remote Assistance is similar to Remote Desktop Connection, but the purpose of Remote Assistance is to allow one person to connect to another user's computer to provide "hands-on" help. For example, Albert is a traveling salesperson who is having trouble formatting a document in Microsoft Word. Maria, a technical support specialist at the main office, can set up a Remote Assistance connection with Albert's laptop, and then take control of his computer and show him how to fix the formatting issues.

Windows Remote Assistance sessions are encrypted for safety. They're also password protected, so only a person who is invited to the Remote Assistance session can connect to the computer.

To request remote help and initiate a Remote Assistance session, you send an invitation to the person who will be assisting you. That person accepts the invitation and connects to your computer.

+ MORE INFORMATION

For more information about Windows Remote Assistance, visit http://windows.microsoft.com/en-US/windows7/What-is-Windows-Remote-Assistance

⊙ **SET UP A WINDOWS REMOTE ASSISTANCE SESSION**

GET READY. To set up a Windows Remote Assistance session, perform the following steps:

1. Click **Start** and in the **Search programs and files** search box, type **remote assist**. In the results list that displays, select **Windows Remote Assistance**. The Windows Remote Assistance window displays.

2. Click **Invite someone you trust to help you.**

TAKE NOTE *

If an error message appears stating that your computer is not set up to send invitations, click Repair. The problem may be related to your firewall, which needs to be disabled temporarily. Start Windows Remote Assistance again after the problem is resolved.

3. In the screen that displays (see Figure 3-37), either create an invitation as a file and send it via e-mail automatically (if the option is available) or click **Save this invitation as a file**. If you chose to save the file, the file is named Invitation.msrc. Send it via e-mail to the support person.

Figure 3-37

The Windows Remote Assistance window

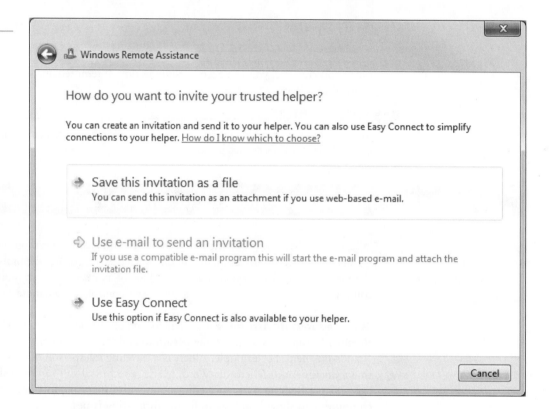

4. A dialog box displays with a password (see Figure 3-38). Give this password to the support person over the phone.

Figure 3-38

The Windows Remote Assistance password dialog box

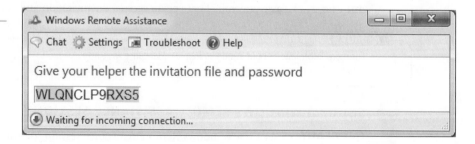

5. Leave the session open and wait for the support person to connect to your computer.
6. The support person receives the invitation and opens it. A Remote Assistance dialog box displays, prompting for the password (see Figure 3-39).

Figure 3-39

The Remote Assistance dialog box appears on the support person's desktop

7. After typing the password, Windows Remote Assistance attempts to connect to the client's computer.

8. The client must click **OK** in the dialog box that displays, asking if it is OK for the support person to connect.

9. The Windows Remote Assistance window displays on both the client's desktop (see Figure 3-40) and the support person's desktop.

Figure 3-40

The Windows Remote Assistance window on the client's computer

Any actions the client performs are displayed to the support person. The support person can click *Request control* to take control of the client's desktop through the Windows Remote Assistance window. For security purposes, a dialog box is displayed on the client's desktop, prompting for permission. At any time, either user can click *Stop sharing* to prevent the support person from controlling the client's desktop. While a Remote Assistance session is live, both the support person and the client can open a chat window to communicate rather than communicate using a telephone. To end the session, simply close the Windows Remote Assistance window.

Using the MMC

When assisting users with computer problems or maintaining systems, a support person often needs to check computer events, look at computer resource usage, or examine a disk's partition, among other tasks. You may use Microsoft Management Console (MMC) tools and utilities for this purpose.

Lesson 2 introduced the ***Microsoft Management Console (MMC)***, a collection of administrative tools called ***snap-ins***. An MMC snap-in is a utility provided by Microsoft or a third party that's accessible through a common interface. Administrators use MMC tools for managing hardware, software, and network components on a computer.

Administrative Tools is a popular collection of tools that use the MMC. You can access Administrative Tools by typing **admin tools** in the *Search programs and files* search box and selecting Administrative Tools from the results list. The Administrative Tools window (see Figure 3-41) lists several tools.

Figure 3-41

The Administrative Tools window

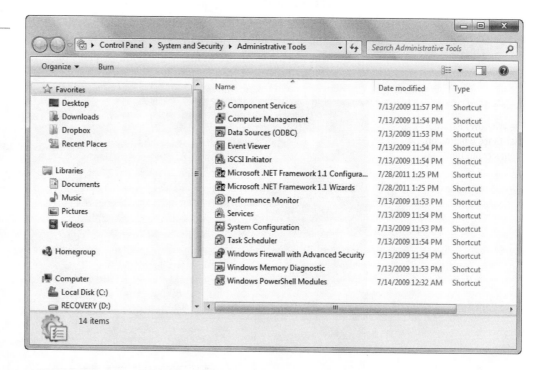

TAKE NOTE* To show Administrative Tools in the Start menu, right-click Start, click Properties, and then click Customize. Scroll down to the System administrative tools heading, select *Display on the All Programs menu,* and then click OK.

Computer Management is a popular snap-in that includes several tools such as Disk Management for configuring hard disks and their partitions and Event Viewer, which allows you to view computer event information such as program starting and stopping (including program crashes) and security problems. (See Figure 3-42.) You can manage system performance and resources using Performance Monitor, which is under Performance > Monitoring Tools.

Some administrators and power users create a custom MMC that includes only the tools they use regularly, creating a toolkit of sorts.

Figure 3-42

The Computer Management window

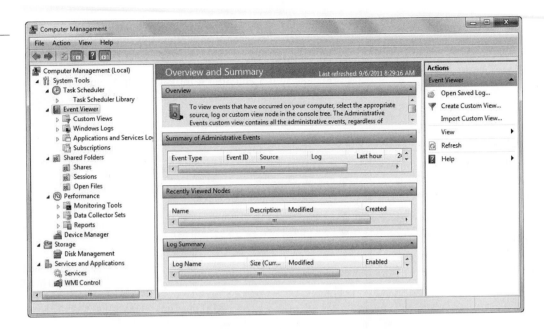

CREATE A CUSTOM MMC

GET READY. To create a custom MMC, perform the following steps:

1. Click **Start**, type **MMC** in the Start menu and in the **Search programs and files** search box, type **mmc**. In the results list that displays, select **mmc.exe**.

2. In the MMC Console window that displays, click **File > Add/Remove Snap-in**. The Add or Remove Snap-ins dialog box displays.

3. In the Available snap-ins on the left, select a snap-in of your choice, such as **Computer Management** (see Figure 3-43). In the middle of the dialog box, click the **Add** button.

Figure 3-43

Selecting snap-ins for a custom MMC

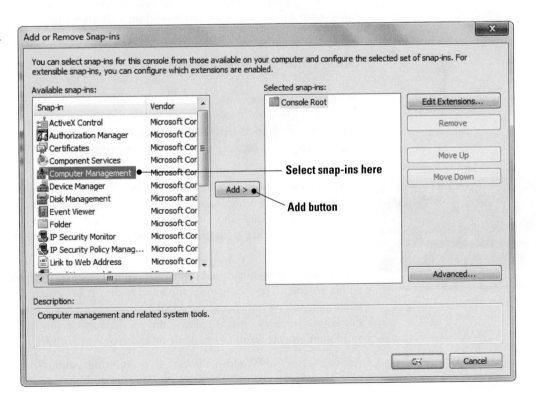

In the dialog box that displays, leave **Local computer** selected (unless the computer you want to manage is one other than the current computer).

4. Click **Finish**. The snap-in is added to the Selected snap-ins pane on the right.

5. Repeat Step 3 and Step 4 for each snap-in you want to include in the custom MMC. Figure 3-44 shows the Console window with a few snap-ins added.

Figure 3-44

A custom MMC

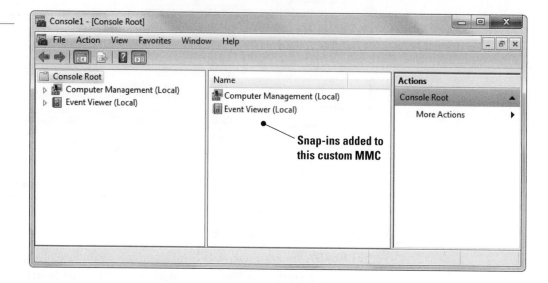

6. Click **OK**.

7. Click **File > Save As**. In the **File name** text box, type a name for the custom MMC and then click **Save**.

To avoid exposing a computer to malicious attacks, Microsoft recommends that you use MMC snap-ins when you are not logged on as Administrator.

Using Windows PowerShell

The MS-DOS command window—accessed by clicking Start and typing **cmd** in the *Search programs and files* search box and selecting cmd.exe in the resulting list—doesn't provide all of the commands you might need. For scripting and other administrative tasks, you must use Windows PowerShell.

CERTIFICATION READY
What term describes the command-line interface used mainly by IT professionals to run scripts?
1.5

Windows PowerShell is a command-line interface used mainly by IT professionals to run cmdlets (pronounced *command-lets*), complete background jobs (processes or programs that run in the background without a user interface), and run scripts to perform administrative tasks. If you're familiar with the UNIX shell, Windows PowerShell commands should seem highly familiar.

The Windows PowerShell environment is built on the .NET Framework, which allows administrators to use many more tools and commands than the MS-DOS command window environment. PowerShell and the MS-DOS command environment are compatible, however. For example, you can run Windows command-line programs in Windows PowerShell and also start Windows programs like Calculator and Notepad at the Windows PowerShell prompt.

Another feature of Windows PowerShell is remoting. Administrators can use cmdlets to access remote computers or use the Windows PowerShell Remoting service to run commands on remote computers or even many remote machines. Windows PowerShell Remoting can require substantial setup, which is not within the scope of this book.

➕ MORE INFORMATION

For more information about Windows PowerShell, visit the Windows PowerShell Getting Started Guide at http://msdn.microsoft.com/en-us/library/aa973757%28v=vs.85%29.aspx. Windows PowerShell Remoting commands can be found at http://msdn.microsoft.com/en-us/library/ee706585(v=vs.85).aspx

---

⊙ RUN A CMDLET IN WINDOWS POWERSHELL

GET READY. To run a cmdlet in Windows PowerShell, perform the following steps:

1. Click **Start > All Programs > Accessories**, click the **Windows PowerShell** folder, and then click **Windows PowerShell**. (Alternately, click **Start**, and in the **Search programs and files** search box, type **powershell**. In the results list that displays, select Windows PowerShell. The **Windows PowerShell** window displays.

2. A commonly used command is ps (or get-process). The ps command lists the currently running processes and their details, such as the process ID, process name, and percentage of processor usage (CPU). Type **ps** and press Enter. (See Figure 3-45.)

Figure 3-45

Running the ps command in Windows PowerShell

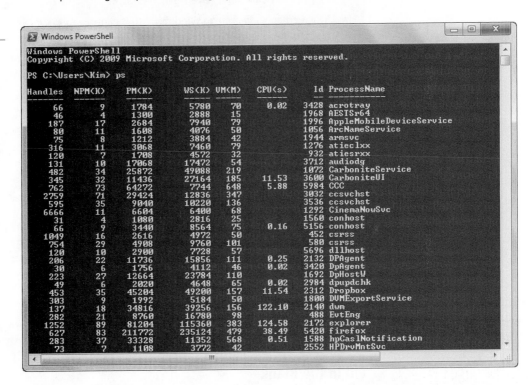

3. To get help with the ps command, type **get-help ps** and press **Enter**.

4. To view running services, type **get-service** and then press **Enter**. A list of services displays, along with their status (Running or Stopped).

TAKE NOTE*

You'll learn about managing services in Lesson 4 using the MMC; for now, know that you can use the PowerShell commands Stop-Service *servicename* and Start-Service *servicename* to accomplish the same tasks.

---

5. To exit the Window PowerShell window, type **exit** and then press **Enter**.

SKILL SUMMARY

IN THIS LESSON YOU LEARNED:

- Internet Explorer 9 is the latest Web browser from Microsoft. The Internet Explorer 9 interface includes enhanced user features, such as a large Back button, a combined Address bar and search box, One Box, the New Page tab, and the ability to pin sites to the Windows 7 taskbar.

- Internet Explorer 9 security and privacy features include ActiveX Filtering, SmartScreen Filter, a Cross-Site Scripting (XSS) Filter, InPrivate Browsing, Tracking Protection, and domain highlighting.

- Windows 7 native applications include accessory programs such as Calculator, Notepad, and Paint, plus much more. The Snipping Tool allows you to capture, save, an annotate screen shots. Windows Media Player is a versatile music and video player, with the ability to view slide shows of photos, share media across a network, and burn and rip CDs.

- Windows Media Center turns your computer into a digital video recorder, allowing you to record and play back TV programs, including HDTV. You need a TV tuner and a subscription to a TV programming service (such as cable).

- Sync Center is a feature in Windows 7 that allows you to sync files between a computer and a network location, and between a computer and some mobile devices.

- Windows Mobility Center is a control panel of sorts that gives you access to several laptop settings, from volume to screen brightness to power options to WiFi and Bluetooth settings—all in one place.

- Windows 7 Remote Desktop Connection allows you to access another computer on a network or over the Internet and use the computer as if you were sitting in front of it.

- Windows Remote Assistance is similar to Remote Desktop Connection. Remote Assistance allows one person to connect to another user's computer to provide "hands-on" help.

- You can access Administrative Tools from the Microsoft Management Console (MMC) and even create your own custom MMCs.

- Windows PowerShell is a command-line utility that enables administrators to perform many administrative tasks, similar to MS-DOS and UNIX commands.

■ Knowledge Assessment

Fill in the Blank

Complete the following sentences by writing the correct word or words in the blanks provided.

1. _____ is a feature in Internet Explorer 9 that incorporates search functionality into the Address bar.

2. A _____ is an Internet Explorer 9 Web site you "attach" to the Windows 7 taskbar.

3. _____ helps prevent personal information and browsing history from being stored by Internet Explorer 9.

4. The _____ detects threats on Web sites, such as phishing attacks and malware downloads, and prevents them from running.

5. _____ is an accessory program that comes with Windows 7 that allows you to take screen shots, annotate them, and save them.

6. _____ is a feature of Internet Explorer 9 that helps you control which Web sites can track your online browsing activity and receive that information.

7. After you synchronize files between your computer and a network location, the files you use on your computer are referred to as _____.

8. _____ allows you to set up a computer for remote access and then connect to that computer wherever you may be.

9. An MMC _____ is a utility provided by Microsoft or a third party that's accessible through a common interface, such as Administrative Tools.

10. _____ is a command-line interface used mainly by IT professionals to run cmdlets, background jobs, and scripts to perform administrative tasks.

Multiple Choice

Circle the letter that corresponds to the best answer.

1. Which of the following is not a security or privacy feature of Internet Explorer 9?
   a. InPrivate Browsing
   b. Pinned site
   c. ActiveX Filtering
   d. Domain highlighting

2. Which of the following can you do with the Snipping Tool?
   a. Annotate an image with the pen tool
   b. Change the color of a captured image
   c. Add typed callouts
   d. Save in PDF format

3. You want to use the Run command, however, the program requires elevated or administrative privileges. When you right-click the program to run it, which command do you select from the shortcut menu?
   a. Run elevated
   b. Run protected
   c. Run with permission
   d. Run as administrator

4. Which of the following can you do with Windows Media Player 12? (Choose all that apply.)
   a. Stream video files over the Internet
   b. Rip music from a CD
   c. Play a slide show
   d. Create playlists

5. Where do you configure security zones in Internet Explorer 9?
   a. Internet Options Security tab
   b. Internet Options Privacy tab
   c. Safety menu
   d. Tracking Protection window

6. You want to run the ps cmdlet. Which utility do you use?
   a. MS-DOS command window
   b. Windows Remote Assistance
   c. Windows PowerShell
   d. Computer Management

7. Which of the following are accessible from the Computer Management window? (Choose all that apply.)
   a. Event Viewer
   b. Performance Monitor
   c. Remote Desktop Connection
   d. Disk Management

8. You want to access your home computer from work to get a file you worked on last night. Which program can you use?
   a. Disk Management
   b. Remote Desktop Connection
   c. Windows Remote Assistance
   d. Sync Center

9. Which of the following is an option in Windows Media Center but not in Windows Media Player?
   a. Record TV programming
   b. Watch recorded TV
   c. Share files over a network
   d. Create playlists

10. Where can you find the program to help you use a projector connected to your computer?
    a. The All Programs Accessories folder
    b. Computer Management console
    c. Administrative Tools folder
    d. Windows Media Player

True / False

Circle T if the statement is true or F if the statement is false.

T F 1. You can click and drag a Web site's thumbnail that appears on the Internet Explorer 9 New Tab page to the taskbar to pin it.

T F 2. Remote Desktop Connection and Windows Remote Assistance are the same program used in different ways.

T F 3. Windows Remote Assistance sessions are encrypted for safety.

T F 4. Remote Desktop comes with all editions of Windows 7; however, you can only connect to computers running the Professional, Ultimate, or Enterprise editions.

T F 5. Windows Mobility Center includes access to power plans and screen brightness.

■ Competency Assessment

Scenario 3-1: Securing Internet Explorer 9

Your co-worker Preena is finalizing a big project for a medical client and has many sensitive client files on her computer. She asks you to help her make her computer as safe as possible while accessing the Internet. What do you do?

Scenario 3-2: Offering Remote Assistance

Your sales people travel extensively and often need technical assistance with configuration settings on their laptops running Windows 7. Which feature or program do you use to provide remote support for these employees?

■ Proficiency Assessment

Scenario 3-3: Pinning Multiple Web Sites

Roberta is a high-tech researcher who uses the Bing search site and the Microsoft Web site daily. She wants to access the sites quickly whenever she uses Internet Explorer. How do you advise her on how she can access sites quickly?

Scenario 3-4: Creating a Playlist

You provide technical support to a small dental practice. The office manager, Shanice, hands you several company-owned music CDs. She wants the music piped to the lobby area where patients wait to be seen for their appointments. The computer used at the receptionist's desk is running Windows 7 and has wireless speakers that can be set up in the waiting area. What is one method of providing the requested music without spending additional money?

Managing Applications, Services, Folders, and Libraries

EXAM OBJECTIVE MATRIX

SKILLS/CONCEPTS	EXAM OBJECTIVE DESCRIPTION	EXAM OBJECTIVE NUMBER
Installing and Managing Applications	Understand application installations.	3.1
Understanding Services	Understand services.	3.4
Using MSCONFIG (System Configuration utility)	Understand native applications and tools.	1.3
Understanding File Systems	Understand file systems.	4.1
Exploring and Managing Libraries	Understand libraries.	4.4
Encrypting and Compressing Files and Folders	Understand encryption. Understand storage.	4.3 5.2

KEY TERMS

Active Directory

application

assign

BitLocker Drive Encryption

compression

EFS certificate

Encrypting File System (EFS)

encryption

encryption key

FAT

FAT32

file system

Group Policy

Group Policy object (GPO)

install application

library

local application

MSCONFIG

multi-booting

NTFS

Programs and Features

publish

services

System Configuration utility

uninstall application

At Interstate Snacks, Inc., management wants to maximize the return on their investment in Windows 7. The IT group has requested that you prepare user training materials to teach employees how to make best use of Windows 7 files, applications, libraries, and file encryption. You need to learn as much as possible about these technologies to provide accurate materials and in-depth training.

■ Installing and Managing Applications

↓ THE BOTTOM LINE

You *install applications*, or programs, either at the local level or the network level. A local installation results in the software files running directly from a computer. Installing over a network generally means the software files are made available from an application server on a network. The network method, along with Group Policy, gives an administrator more efficient control over who can use the software and who can remove it.

TAKE NOTE *

The terms "application" and "program" are used interchangeably in this book.

CERTIFICATION READY
What are the differences between local and networked applications?
3.1

An *application* is a program that runs "on top" of the operating system or from a server, and helps a user perform a specific task, such as word processing, appointment scheduling, or accounting. Some applications are included with Windows—such as Notepad for simple text editing or Internet Explorer for browsing the Web. Other applications must be licensed from a software publisher, such as Microsoft, Adobe, and Intuit, and then installed on your computer locally or on a server.

This section explores application installation and management in Windows 7. Installing a single application on one computer is easy, although the installation process varies a bit depending on the application. Installing applications on many Windows 7 computers is more efficiently tackled using a network. For example, you can use Group Policy to install and control access to applications. *Uninstalling applications* is a breeze, whether local or over a network.

In Windows 7, users might access applications in a variety of ways. For applications that users must be able to run with or without network or Internet access, you should install those applications directly on individual computers. This involves running setup.exe or a Microsoft Installer (which usually has an .msi file extension) in Windows 7, or building a custom installation image that includes one or more pre-installed applications. In this case, you install the application directly onto a computer running Windows 7; it's considered to be a *local application* because it stays with that computer.

X REF

In Lesson 2, you learned about Microsoft Application Virtualization (App-V), which represents one way to deliver applications over a network. However, it requires a supporting virtualization infrastructure.

If you're working in a networked environment with a domain, it's more efficient to store the application's installation files in a network location; they are installed on the client computer or are available to run from the server when users log on. Many IT administrators want to maintain tight control over specific applications, so administrators require that all users access applications from a network rather than locally. As you'll learn in this lesson, Group Policy gives administrators control over which users, computers, or groups can have access to applications.

 INSTALL AN APPLICATION LOCALLY

GET READY. To install an application in Windows 7, perform the following steps:

1. Start the application's installation program.

   • If installing from a CD/DVD, insert the application's installation media into your computer's CD/DVD drive. The installer program should run automatically.

- If installing an application you downloaded from the Web, or if the installer program doesn't start automatically when inserting a CD/DVD, open Windows Explorer, browse to the location of the application's installer program (such as **setup.exe**), and then double-click it.

2. Follow the prompts to install the application.

Every program is different, but most programs prompt you to accept the license agreement, select a location on your computer in which to install the software files, and then enter a product ID or key.

Removing or Uninstalling an Application

A user or administrator might need to remove, or uninstall, a local application for a variety of reasons. Windows 7 provides the Programs and Features applet in Control Panel for this purpose.

CERTIFICATION READY
How are applications removed or uninstalled?
3.1

Application removal means uninstalling a program from your computer. In the process, the program's files are removed, but not the data created while using the program. Some applications come with a utility for uninstalling the program when it's no longer needed (see Figure 4-1). However, many programs written to run in Windows 7 make use of the Programs and Features applet in Control Panel (see Figure 4-2).

Figure 4-1

Some applications provide uninstall utilities to remove the application from your computer

Figure 4-2

The Programs and Features applet in Control Panel

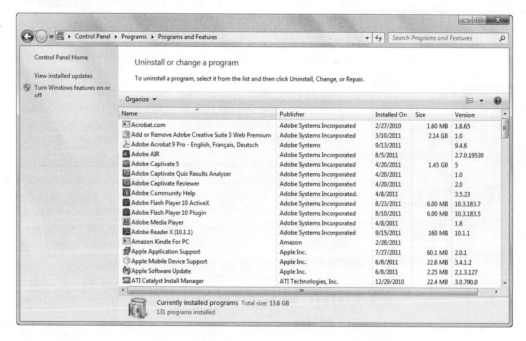

Using *Programs and Features*, simply browse the list of programs, click the program you want to uninstall, and then click Uninstall on the toolbar. Follow the prompts that display until the program is removed. You might be prompted to restart your computer.

You'll learn about the Windows registry later in this lesson and in Lesson 7. You'll learn about Safe Mode, other boot options, and System Restore in Lesson 8.

If the program does not uninstall properly, try running the uninstall process again. You can also try uninstalling the program in Safe Mode. Rolling back (or returning) to a previous system state using System Restore might also resolve the problem. Doing so, however, will also "uninstall" other programs that were installed since the last system restore point was saved. As a last resort, contact the software publisher to find out how to manually remove the application from your computer. (A manual removal involves editing the registry and deleting files and folders.)

Sometimes you simply need to change or repair a program rather than uninstall it. Some programs provide those options, which will display on the Programs and Features toolbar when you select the program in the list.

In addition, you can turn Windows features on and off—no installation/uninstall is required. In the Programs and Features window, in the left pane, click *Turn Windows features on or off*. In the Windows Features dialog box (see Figure 4-3), select the check boxes of features you want to turn on and deselect those you want to turn off.

Figure 4-3

The Windows Features dialog box

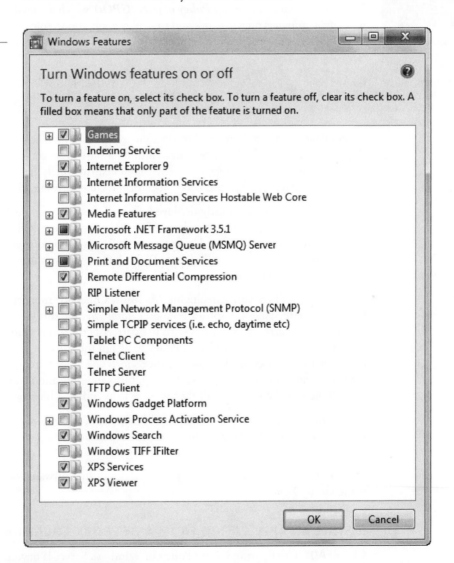

MORE INFORMATION

For more information about installing and uninstalling applications in Windows 7, visit http://windows.microsoft.com/en-US/windows7/Install-a-program and http://windows.microsoft.com/en-US/windows7/Uninstall-or-change-a-program, respectively.

Understanding Group Policy and Network Application Installation

In a Windows network in a domain environment, administrators can use Group Policy to ease the burden of administering and managing many users and client computers. Group Policy lets you control who may install software, and on which computers, and helps you push software updates and security configurations across the network. Group policies also exist in Windows 7 and other Windows operating systems. They are referred to as Local Group Policies and affect only the users who log on to a particular computer. This section focuses on Group Policy at the network domain level.

CERTIFICATION READY
How are network applications installed using Group Policy?
3.1

Group Policy is a collection of settings (policies) stored in Active Directory on a Windows network. *Active Directory* is an infrastructure (directory) that stores information and objects. An object can be a file, a printer, a computer, a user account, or other entities. Objects in Active Directory are linked to *Group Policy objects (GPOs)*, which are used by administrators to control users and computers on a network and to deploy applications, software updates, and security. Group Policy affects users and computers contained in sites, domains, and organizational units.

TAKE NOTE *Group Policy is supported in Windows 7 Professional, Ultimate, and Enterprise editions. Active Directory was renamed Active Directory Domain Services in Windows Server 2008.*

Group Policy works well in small to large environments whether an organization is located in a single area or has multiple offices spread around a state or several states, for example. It's easiest to manage in mostly "heterogeneous environments," in which many of the client computers use the same hardware and users use much of the same software with the same configurations.

If your organization has already deployed Active Directory, such as Microsoft Windows 2008 R2 Active Directory Domain Services (AD DS), using Group Policy to push applications to users or computers is efficient. Using Group Policy, you can *assign* or *publish* an application to all users or computers in a designated site, domain, organizational unit (OU), or to a local, individual user or computer.

For example, let's say you're deploying Microsoft Office for more than 20 users. If you set up Group Policy to assign the software on each *computer*, the software is installed the next time the computer starts and any users with the correct permissions who log on to the computer run the software. If you use Group Policy to assign the software to *users*, the next time an authorized user clicks the Microsoft Office shortcut or menu item, the software installs on the user's computer and Office opens. If you publish an application to users, the next time a user logs on, he can choose to install the software from a dialog box that appears.

With Group Policy, you can control which users can use the software. If a user logs on who isn't authorized to run the software (considered "out of scope"), the software can be uninstalled automatically.

Once software is installed, you can push updates to the software and even upgrade programs using Group Policy.

 INSTALL AN APPLICATION FROM A NETWORK LOCATION

GET READY. Configuring Group Policy in Windows Server is beyond the scope of this book, but this exercise shows you how to install an application from a network location in a domain, from the user's perspective. Perform the following steps:

1. Click **Start > Control Panel > Programs > Programs and Features**. In the left pane, click **Install a program from the network**.

TAKE NOTE *

These steps work if you set the GPO to install an application to a *user* versus a *computer*.

2. Browse the list of programs, click a program you want to install, and then click **Install**.

Follow the prompts to move through the installation. You might be prompted for an administrator password or confirmation during the installation.

 MORE INFORMATION

For more information about Group Policy in Windows 7, visit http://windows.microsoft.com/en-US/windows7/Group-Policy-management-for-IT-pros. To learn how to use Group Policy to remotely install software in Windows Server 2003 and in Windows Server 2008, visit http://support.microsoft.com/kb/816102

■ Understanding Services

↓
THE BOTTOM LINE

Services run in the background on a Windows system to help the operating system run other programs. The Services console is the central management point of services in Windows Vista and Windows 7.

X REF

You learned about the MMC in Lesson 3.

Windows uses services to handle requests for print spooling, file indexing, task scheduling, the Windows Firewall, and much more. Services run in the background, essentially helping the operating system work with other programs. Although services do not usually have user interfaces, you can manage services through the Microsoft Management Console (MMC) Services snap-in (see Figure 4-4).

Figure 4-4

The Services console in Windows 7

Export List button

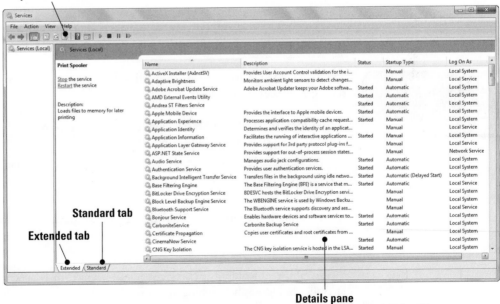

Standard tab

Extended tab

Details pane

A Windows 7 system can have more than 100 services running at any one time. Each computer can have different services running, depending on the version of Windows in use, the computer manufacturer, and the applications installed, but Windows 7 generally uses many of the same services across its editions.

To use the Services snap-in and configure services, you must be a member of the Account Operators group, the Domain Admins group, or the Enterprise Admins group, or you must have received the appropriate authority. Using the **Run as** command to open the Services console ensures you have the proper level of authority.

You can access Windows services in many different ways:

- Click Start, type **services** in the *Search programs and files* search box, and then click Services or services.msc in the resulting list. (Or right-click Services or services.msc and select *Run as administrator*. You must provide an administrative password or confirm to continue.) The Services console displays.
- In Computer Management, expand the Services and Applications node and click Services.
- In Administrative Tools, double-click Services or double-click Component Services and then click Services.
- Open Task Manager and click the Services tab.
- Open MSCONFIG and click the Services tab. (MSCONFIG is covered in the next section in this lesson.)

The Extended and Standard tabs (at the bottom of the Services console) both display all of the services in the system; however, the Extended tab provides descriptive information for a selected service in the space to the left of the details pane. Sometimes a link is displayed for you to get more information about a particular service.

The Services console enables you to view all services and their status; add, start, stop, or disable services; select user accounts that might run the service (for security purposes); define how a service recovers from failures; or view a list of service, program, and driver dependencies. To use any of these options, double-click the service to open its Properties dialog box.

> **TAKE NOTE***
>
> You can export service information to a .txt or .csv file.

Understanding Service Startup Types

> **CERTIFICATION READY**
> What are the four service startup types?
> 3.4

The General tab in the service's Properties dialog box (see Figure 4-5) provides options for setting a service's startup type:

- **Automatic (Delayed Start):** The service starts approximately two minutes after the operating system is up and running.
- **Automatic:** The service starts as the operating system starts.
- **Manual:** The service must be started manually, by a user, a dependent service, or a program.
- **Disabled:** The service is disabled and will not start.

> **TAKE NOTE***
>
> Be careful when disabling any services. Some services, such as Security Center and Windows Firewall, should not be disabled unless the computer is behind a hardware firewall. Many computer users disable unnecessary services to optimize the speed of their computers. You should create a system restore point (covered in Lesson 8) before disabling services. And although it's time consuming, you should disable one service at a time, reboot your computer, and check for side effects of disabling that service before disabling any other services.

Figure 4-5

The General tab

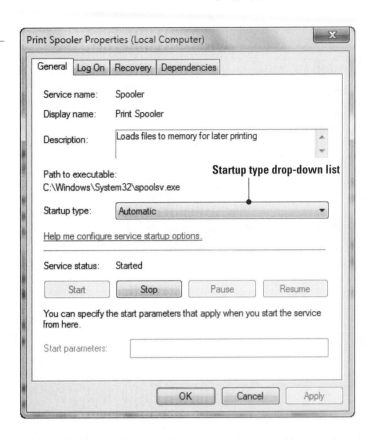

You can also start, stop, pause, or resume a service using the buttons in the Service status section. For example, let's say a printer has several duplicate (unnecessary) print jobs and the queue is not responding. You've restarted the printer a few times but that didn't work. To fix the problem, just restart the Print Spooler service in the Services console to clear the print queues.

TAKE NOTE * While troubleshooting a service, try pausing the service (if it's an option) and then unpausing the service before stopping and restarting the service. By pausing and then continuing, you might be able to resolve the problem without having to reset connections or cancel jobs.

CERTIFICATION READY
Which service or user accounts can you specify a service to use?
3.4

The Log On tab (see Figure 4-6) allows you to specify the user account the service can use, which might be different from the logged-on user or the default computer account. Your options are:

• **Local Service account:** Click *This account* and then type **NT AUTHORITY\ LocalService**. The Local Service account is a built-in account (it's already created in the operating system). It can run services in the background but has limited access to resources and objects, which helps protect the system if individual services are compromised. No password is required.

• **Network Service account:** Click *This account* and then type **NT AUTHORITY\ NetworkService**. The Network Service is similar to the Local Service account but is geared for networking services. Like the Local Service account, the Network Service account can run services in the background but it helps to protect the computer from compromise.

• **Another account:** Click *This account*, click Browse, browse for a different user account, select it, and then click OK. Type the password for the user account you selected and then click OK.

The service will run in the security context of the account you choose.

Figure 4-6

The Log On tab

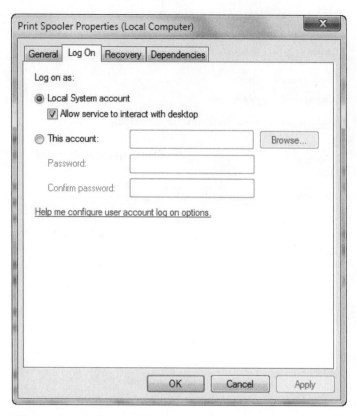

The Recovery tab (see Figure 4-7) lets you choose recovery actions the computer will take if a service fails. For example, if a service fails, the computer might first try restarting the service. If that doesn't work, you can instruct the computer to restart the service again or you can restart the computer to clear memory and refresh connections.

Figure 4-7

The Recovery tab

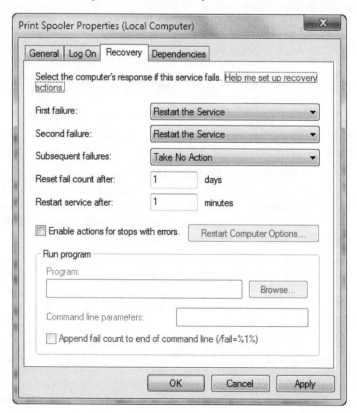

CERTIFICATION READY
What is a service
dependency?
3.4

The Dependencies tab (see Figure 4-8) shows you which services depend on other services to run. A dependent service starts after the service upon which it depends starts. Stopping a service also stops any other service that depends on it. There are no options available on this tab—it's informational only. However, before you stop or disable a service on the General tab, you should view the information on the Dependences tab to know which other services might be affected by your change.

Figure 4-8

The Dependencies tab

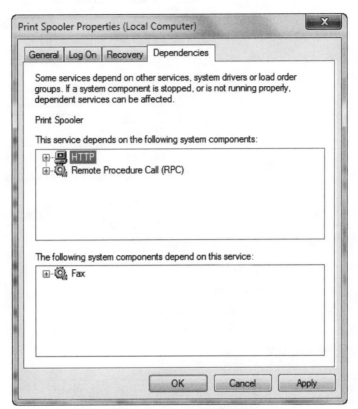

CONFIGURE A SERVICE

GET READY. To configure a service in the Services console, perform the following steps:

1. Click **Start** and in the **Search programs and files** search box, type **services**, right-click **services.msc** in the resulting list, select **Run as administrator**, click **Yes** to continue (or type a password), and then press **Enter**.

2. In the details pane, double-click the service that you want to configure, such as **Print Spooler** (see Figure 4-9). The service's Properties dialog box displays.

3. On the General tab, click the **Startup type** drop-down list (see Figure 4-10). Select **Automatic (Delayed Start)**, **Automatic**, **Manual**, or **Disabled**.

4. Click the **Log On** tab. To specify the user account that the service can use to log on, perform one of the following steps:

   - To use the Local System account, click **Local System** account.
   - To use the Local Service account, click **This account** and then type **NT AUTHORITY\LocalService**.
   - To use the Network Service account, click **This account** and then type **NT AUTHORITY\NetworkService**.
   - To specify another account, click **This account**, click the **Browse** button, and then specify a user account in the Select User dialog box that displays. Click **OK** to save your changes and close the dialog box.

Figure 4-9

The Print Spooler service in the Services console

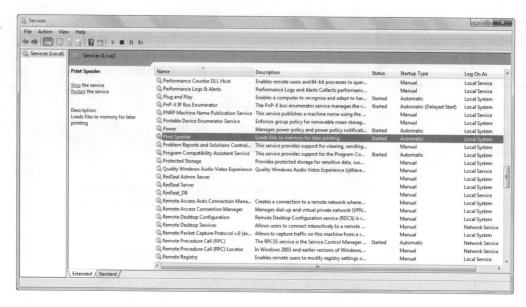

Figure 4-10

Selecting a startup type

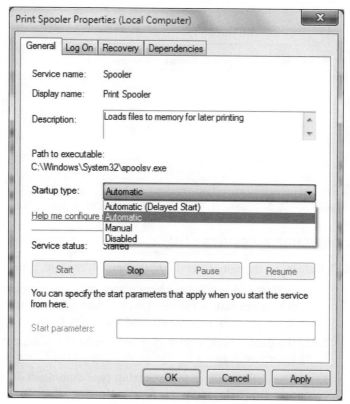

5. Type the password for the user account in the **Password text box** and the **Confirm password** text box, and then click **OK**. You do not have to type a password if you selected the Local Service account or Network Service account.

+ MORE INFORMATION

For more information about Windows 7 services, visit http://msdn.microsoft.com/en-us/library/windows/desktop/ms685141(v=vs.85).aspx

■ Using MSCONFIG (System Configuration utility)

THE BOTTOM LINE

Use MSCONFIG, also known as the System Configuration utility, to troubleshoot and diagnose startup problems.

MSCONFIG, also known as the ***System Configuration utility***, lets you enable or disable startup services, set boot options such as booting into Safe Mode, access tools like Action Center and Event Viewer, and more. You'll use this utility mainly to troubleshoot startup problems with Windows.

Understanding MSCONFIG

To open System Configuration, click Start, type **msconfig** in the *Search programs and files* search box, and then click msconfig.exe from the resulting list. The System Configuration window displays, showing the General tab (see Figure 4-11). Normal startup is selected by default (unless you've previously changed startup settings). A normal startup runs all device drivers and services. Other options include the following:

- **Diagnostic startup:** Runs basic devices and services only; equivalent to starting the computer in Safe Mode.
- **Selective startup:** Starts the system with some or all system services and startup items disabled.

CERTIFICATION READY
What is the purpose of MSCONFIG?
1.3

Figure 4-11

The General tab

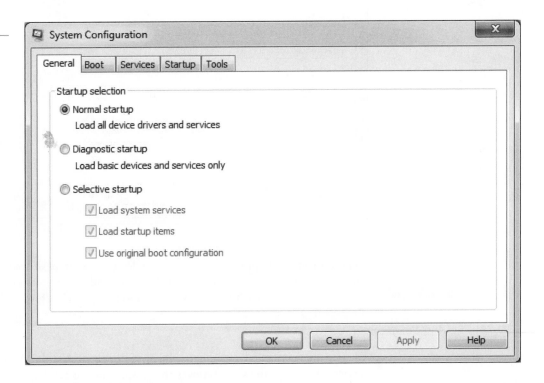

The options on the Boot tab (see Figure 4-12) enable you to adjust boot options, usually for diagnostic purposes. The Boot tab options match the options in the Advanced boot configuration menu that displays when you press F8 at startup. To boot the system into Safe Mode, select the

Safe boot check box. When you do this, the Minimal option is selected by default. The other safe boot options are:

- **Alternate shell:** Boots to the command prompt without network support.
- **Active Directory repair:** Boots to the Windows GUI and runs critical system services and Active Directory.
- **Network:** Boots into Safe Mode with network services enabled.

The options in the right column are as follows:

- **No GUI boot**: Disables the Windows Welcome screen.
- **Boot log**: Creates a boot log of startup activity in a file named ntbtlog.txt.
- **Base video**: Starts the Windows graphical user interface using standard VGA drivers.
- **OS boot information**: Displays driver names as drivers are installed during the startup process.

Figure 4-12

The Boot tab

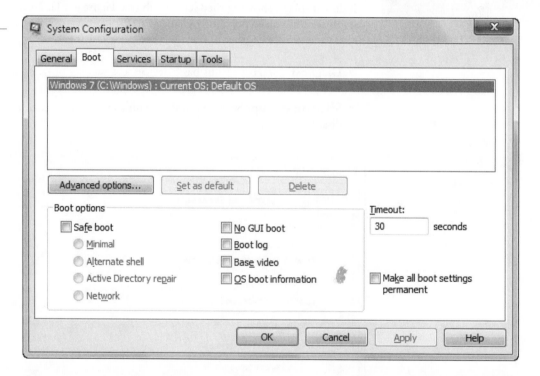

You can make boot options permanent by selecting the *Make all boot settings permanent* check box, clicking Apply, and then clicking OK. Administrators often do this on test computers that they use to test new programs and updates before rolling them out to ordinary users.

TAKE NOTE*

You use the Services tab (see Figure 4-13) to enable or disable Microsoft and third-party services. These are the same services that display in the Services console covered earlier in this lesson.

The Startup tab (see Figure 4-14) allows you to enable or disable startup programs by selecting or deselecting the check boxes. The Startup tab lists the name of the startup item, its manufacturer, the path to and the name of its executable file, its location in the Windows registry, and the date it was disabled (if applicable).

Figure 4-13

The Services tab

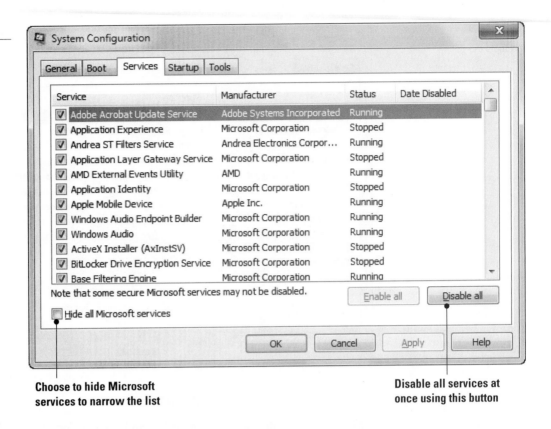

Choose to hide Microsoft
services to narrow the list

Disable all services at
once using this button

Figure 4-14

The Startup tab

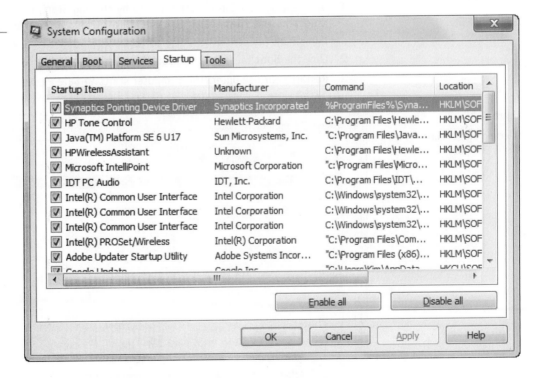

Finally, the Tools tab (see Figure 4-15) lists many programs you can start for reporting and
diagnostic purposes. Some of the tools are Change UAC Settings, Event Viewer, Performance
Monitor, and Task Manager.

Figure 4-15

The Tools tab

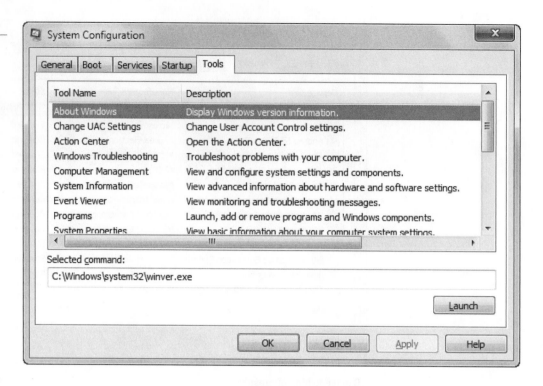

CHANGE SYSTEM CONFIGURATION SETTINGS

GET READY. To configure settings in the System Configuration utility, perform the following steps:

1. Open the System Configuration utility by clicking **Start**, typing **msconfig** in the **Search programs and files** search box, and then clicking **msconfig.exe** in the resulting list. Provide an administrative password or confirm to continue, when prompted.

2. Click the **Boot** tab, select the **Safe boot** check box (see Figure 4-16), and then click **OK**.

3. Restart your computer. The computer starts in Safe Mode.

Figure 4-16

Selecting the Safe boot option on the Boot tab

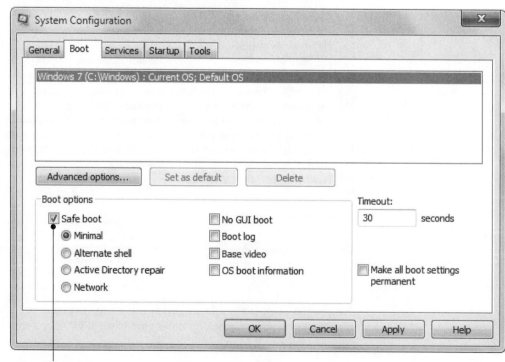

Safe boot option

TAKE NOTE *

Clicking a column heading arranges the entries in alphabetical order.

4. Open the System Configuration utility, click the **Boot** tab, deselect the **Safe boot** check box, click **OK**, restart your computer, and then return to the System Configuration utility.

5. Click the **Services** tab. Browse the list of services and select a service that is not needed on your PC. In this example, we use the LightscribeService Direct Disc Labeling Service because it's seldom, if ever, used. Deselect the check box to the left of the service name (see Figure 4-17). Click **Apply**.

Figure 4-17

Disabling an unneeded service

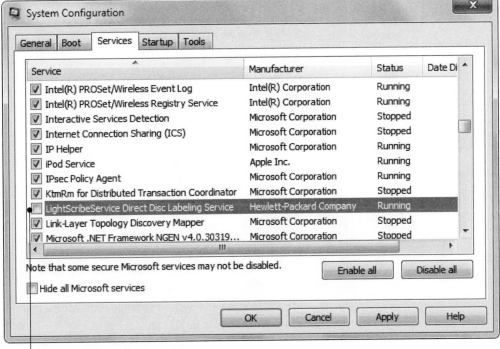

Deselect a service to disable it

6. Click the **Startup** tab. Browse the list of startup items and deselect an item that you don't want to start when your computer starts. In our example (see Figure 4-18), we deselected the Lightscribe program. Click **Apply**.

Figure 4-18

Disabling an unneeded startup item

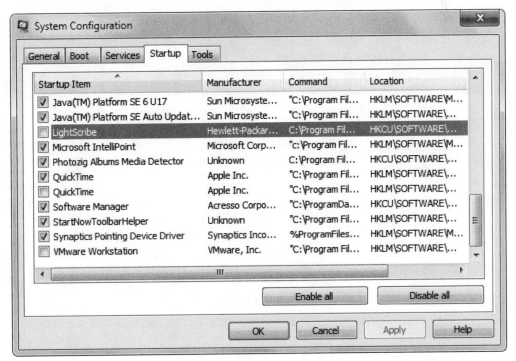

7. Click the **General** tab and notice (see Figure 4-19) that **Selective startup** is now selected (instead of the Normal startupsetting).

Figure 4-19

Selective startup enabled

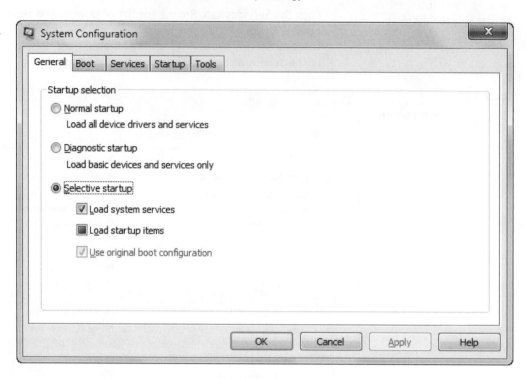

8. Click **OK** to close the System Configuration utility.

If you have any problems with your system after disabling a service or startup item, return to the System Configuration utility and enable the service or startup item.

➕ **MORE INFORMATION**

For more information about System Configuration, visit http://windows.microsoft.com/en-US/windows-vista/Using-System-Configuration

■ Understanding File Systems

THE BOTTOM LINE

The three primary types of file systems for Windows are FAT, FAT32, and NTFS. It's best to use NTFS-formatted disks for Windows Vista and Windows 7 because NTFS handles small to very large hard disks, provides better security, and is the most reliable.

A *file system* is the overall structure your computer uses to name, store, and organize files and folders on a hard disk or partition. The file system provides a map of the clusters (the basic units of logical storage on a hard disk) that a file has been stored in. When you install a hard disk in a computer, you must format it with a file system. Today, the primary file system choices for a computer that will run Windows are NTFS, FAT32, and FAT. In Windows 7, you can view file systems in use on your computer from the Disk Management MMC snap-in (see Figure 4-20).

Figure 4-20

The Disk Management MMC snap-in displays disks and partitions as well as the file system in use

Drive (volume) label and drive letter

File system(s) listed here

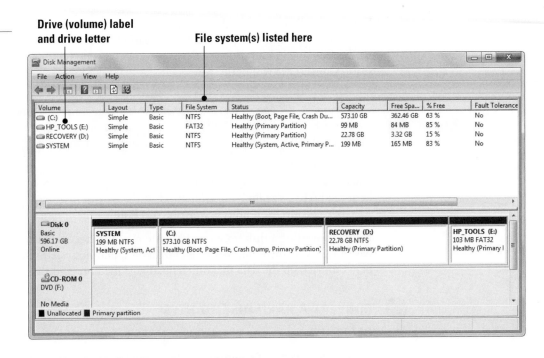

CERTIFICATION READY
What are the differences between FAT, FAT32, and NTFS?
4.1

TAKE NOTE*

You can view all available disks in the Windows Computer folder in the Hard Disk Drives section.

Understanding FAT, FAT32, and NTFS

Most Windows Vista and Windows 7 users use *NTFS* because it supports larger disks (up to 256 terabytes [TB]!) than FAT32 or FAT, and NTFS-formatted files and folders provide better security. It's also more reliable, with built-in features for recovering from disk errors automatically. Microsoft recommends NTFS for its security features: You can use encryption and permissions to restrict file access to specific users.

FAT32 and *FAT* (which is seldom used today) were popular in earlier versions of Windows (such as Windows 95, Windows 98, Windows Millenium Edition, Windows NT, and Windows 2000). The limitations of FAT32 make it less desirable than NTFS:

- A FAT32 partition is limited to a maximum size of 32 gigabytes (GB).
- The maximum size of a file that can be stored on a FAT32 volume is 4 GB.

So why use FAT32? Many universal serial bus (USB) flash drives come formatted as FAT32 to be compatible with a large variety of operating systems. If you plan to configure your computer for *multi-booting*, where you choose at startup which operating system you want to load, you might need to format a partition with FAT32 if that partition will run Windows 95, Windows 98, or Windows Millenium Edition.

Table 4-1 compares attributes of FAT, FAT32, and NTFS.

Table 4-1

Comparing FAT, FAT32, and NTFS

FILE SYSTEM	MAXIMUM PARTITION SIZE	MAXIMUM FILE SIZE
FAT	2 GB	2 GB
FAT32	32 GB	4 GB
NTFS	256 TB	Limited by size of volume on which it resides

You can usually convert a FAT or FAT32 partition to NTFS with few to no problems. One hitch you might run into is if the disk is nearly full. The conversion process (Convert.exe) needs a certain amount of free disk space to work properly. If there is insufficient free disk space, Convert.exe will notify you.

TAKE NOTE *

Converting to NTFS is a one-way process. After you convert a drive to NTFS, you cannot convert it back to FAT or FAT32. You can reformat an NTFS drive to FAT32, but you would need to back up all of your data first and then copy it back.

You can also convert to FAT32 from a different type of file system, although you need to keep the FAT32 size limitations in mind. If the partition you want to format is larger than 32 GB, the conversion process won't be successful.

Before converting a disk from one file system to another, back up your data, if possible. If you have a relatively small number of files on a disk, and no system files or programs installed, it's better to back up the data to a different storage medium and then format the disk.

CONVERT A HARD DISK TO NTFS

GET READY. To convert a hard disk to NTFS format, perform the following steps:

1. Click **Start > Computer**. In the Computer window (see Figure 4-21), note the name of the drive you want to convert and the volume label. You can also get this information from the Disk Management snap-in.

Figure 4-21

The Computer window

Drive (volume) label and drive letter

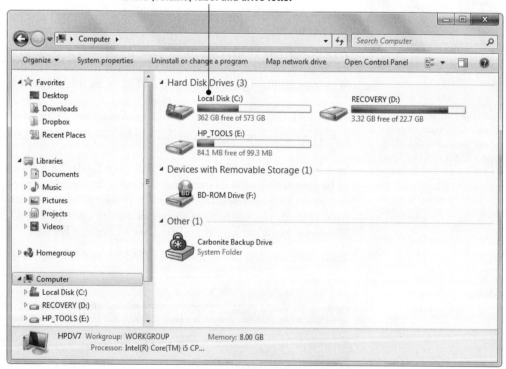

2. Close the Computer window and make sure no programs are running, including anti-virus and firewall programs. You should disconnect your computer from the Internet as a safety precaution.

3. Click **Start**, type **cmd** in the **Search programs and files** search box, right-click **cmd.exe** in the resulting list, and then select **Run as administrator**. If you're prompted for an administrator password or confirmation, type the password or provide confirmation.

4. At the command prompt, type **convert** *drive_letter***: /fs:ntfs**, where *drive_letter* is the letter of the drive you want to convert. (See Figure 4-22.) Press **Enter**. For example, typing **convert G: /fs:ntfs** and pressing Enter converts drive G to NTFS.

Figure 4-22

The convert command in a command-prompt window

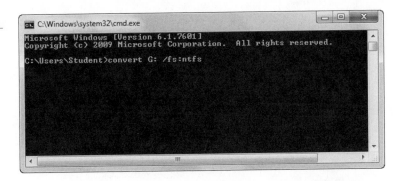

5. A message displays, prompting you for the volume label. Type the volume label of the drive you're converting and press **Enter**.

The conversion begins and might take several minutes to more than an hour, depending on the size of the disk and the amount of data stored on it. A message displays when the conversion is finished. If the drive contains system files, you'll need to restart your computer before use.

+ MORE INFORMATION

To compare FAT32 and NTFS, go to http://windows.microsoft.com/en-US/windows7/Comparing-NTFS-and-FAT32-file-systems. To learn how to convert a hard disk or partition to NTFS, see http://windows.microsoft.com/en-US/windows7/Convert-a-hard-disk-or-partition-to-NTFS-format. For considerations when converting to FAT32 from a different file system, read http://windows.microsoft.com/en-US/windows7/Convert-a-hard-disk-or-partition-to-FAT32-format

■ Exploring and Managing Libraries

THE BOTTOM LINE

Libraries were introduced in Windows 7. A library looks like an ordinary folder, but it is a virtual folder that simply points to files and folders in different locations on a hard disk, network drive, or external drive.

In Windows 7, a *library* is a virtual folder that can display content from different locations (folders, for example) on your computer or an external drive. A library looks like an ordinary folder but simply points to files and folders that are located elsewhere. You access libraries in Windows Explorer, just like you do files and folders.

Windows 7 includes several default libraries (see Figure 4-23):

- **Documents library:** Stores word-processing documents, spreadsheets, and similar files
- **Music library:** Stores audio files, such as those you've downloaded from the Web, transferred from a portable device (music player), or ripped from a CD
- **Pictures library:** Stores digital image files
- **Videos library:** Stores video files

Figure 4-23

Default libraries in Windows 7

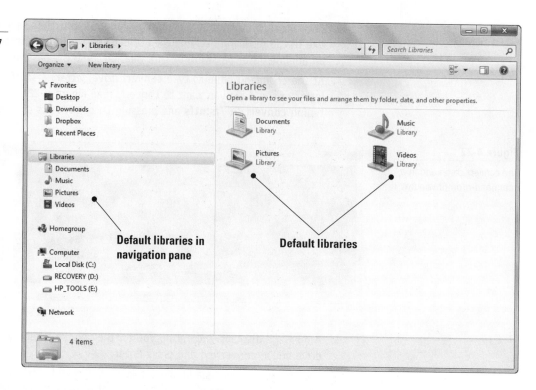

Each default library contains a "My" folder that matches the library name. For example, the Documents library contains a My Documents folder, the Music library contains a My Music folder, and so on. Libraries and folders are unique for each Windows user account on a computer. For example, if three users share the same computer and each user has a user account, each has separate libraries and folders. Windows 7 stores data files in C:\ Users*username*.

Adding Local and Networked Locations to a Library

Want to create a new library, add local locations to a library, or add a networked location to a library? All of these tasks are easy to do.

When creating a new library, you must include at least one folder within the library for organizational purposes. You can then copy, move, or save files to the folder in the library.

You can add a location such as a folder on your C: drive, a second hard drive in your computer, or an external drive to an existing library. Just navigate to the folder in Windows Explorer, select it, click *Include in library* on the toolbar, and select the library to which you want to add the folder. You can also add multiple folders to a single library.

The same principal applies to networked locations. The only caveat with a networked location is that it must be added to the search index or be available offline before you can add it to a library.

 ADD A FOLDER TO A LIBRARY

GET READY. To add a folder to a library, perform the following steps:

1. Click **Start > Computer**. Windows Explorer opens. (You can also open Windows Explorer by clicking **Start** and then clicking **Documents**.)

CERTIFICATION READY
How are multiple local locations added to a library?
4.4

CERTIFICATION READY
How is a networked location added to a library?
4.4

X REF

Offline Files were covered in Lesson 3. The Windows 7 libraries FAQ, mentioned in the More Information bar at the end of this section, offers a pointer for getting help with search indexing.

2. In Windows Explorer, use the navigation pane on the left to locate the folder you want to include in a library and click to select it. The folder cannot already be included in another library.

3. On the toolbar, click **Include in library** (see Figure 4-24), and then click a library (such as Documents, Music, Pictures, or Videos).

Figure 4-24

Selecting a library in which to include a folder

Include in library command

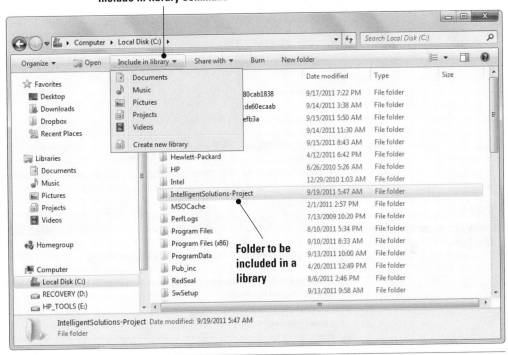

To include a folder on an external drive in a library, follow the previous steps but navigate to the folder on your external hard drive that you want to include. Make sure the external hard drive is connected to your computer and that your computer recognizes the device—it should be listed in Windows Explorer near your C: drive. You can't include content on removable media, such as a CD or DVD, in a library. Some USB flash drives devices don't work with libraries either.

ADD A FOLDER TO THE PICTURES LIBRARY

GET READY. Adding photos from various locations to the Pictures library requires a few different steps. To add photos in a folder that's already in another library (such as Documents) to the Pictures library, perform the following steps:

1. In Windows Explorer, navigate to and click the **Pictures** library to open it.

2. Click the locations hyperlink at the top of the main pane (see Figure 4-25).

3. The Pictures Library Locations dialog box displays (see Figure 4-26). Click **Add**.

Figure 4-25

The locations hyperlink is located at the top of the main pane

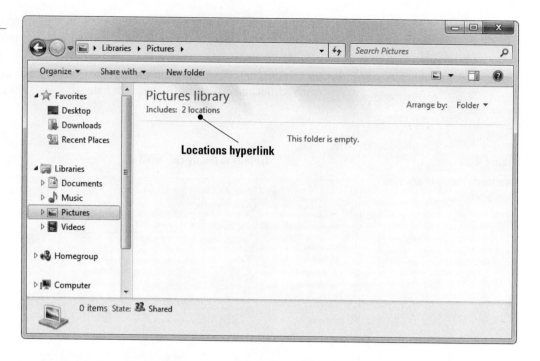

Figure 4-26

Pictures Library Locations dialog box

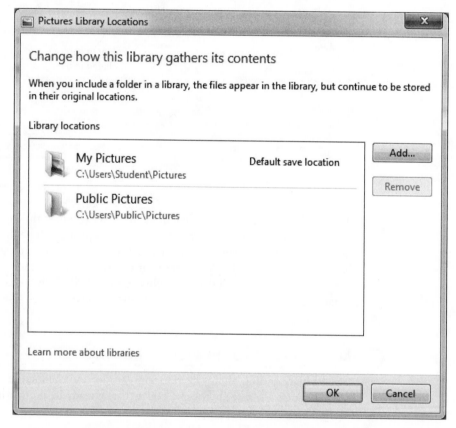

4. Navigate to the folder that contains the images you want to include in the Pictures library (in this example, a folder named "Report images"), click the folder, and then click **Include folder**.

5. The Pictures Library Locations dialog box displays the newly added folder (see Figure 4-27). Click **OK**.

Figure 4-27

Pictures Library Locations
dialog box displaying a newly
added folder

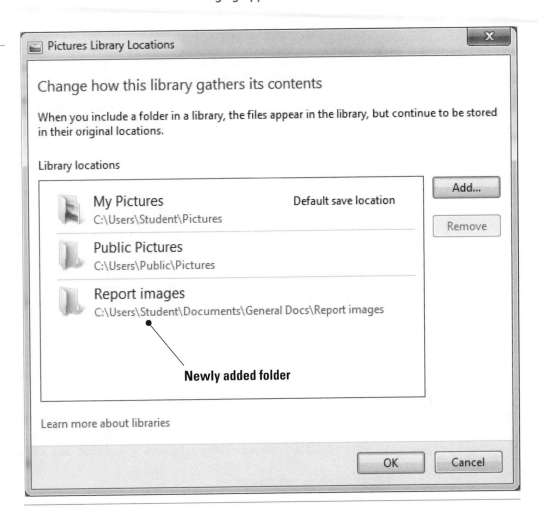

Newly added folder

The photos remain in the original location, but can now be accessed from the Pictures library.

ADD A NETWORKED LOCATION TO A LIBRARY

GET READY. To add a networked location to a library, perform the following steps:

1. In Windows Explorer, in the navigation pane, click **Network**.
2. Navigate to the folder on your network that you want to include in a library on your computer.
3. On the toolbar, click **Include in library**, and then click a library.

Remember, content in a network location must be indexed for search or available offline in order to include it in a library.

CREATE A NEW LIBRARY

GET READY. To create a new library, perform the following steps:

1. In Windows Explorer, in the navigation pane, click **Libraries** (unless Libraries is already displayed).
2. On the toolbar, click **New library**.
3. Type a name for the library (see Figure 4-28) and then press **Enter**.

Figure 4-28

Creating a new library

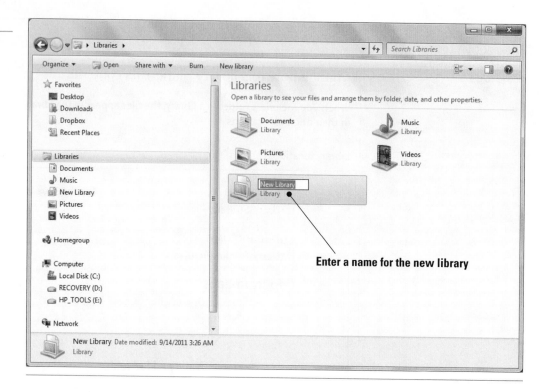

Enter a name for the new library

The newly created library has the same functionality as the default libraries. After double-clicking the new library to open it, click the *Include a folder* button, use the navigation pane to find a folder you want to include, click it, and then click *Include folder*.

> **➕ MORE INFORMATION**
>
> For more information about Windows 7 libraries, visit http://windows.microsoft.com/en-US/windows7/products/features/libraries. You might also want to read the Windows 7 libraries FAQ at http://windows.microsoft.com/en-US/windows7/Libraries-frequently-asked-questions

■ Encrypting and Compressing Files and Folders

THE BOTTOM LINE

Encrypting files and folders protects them from unwanted access. Microsoft uses the Encrypting File System (EFS) to encrypt individual files and folders in Windows Vista and Windows 7.

TAKE NOTE ✱

Windows 7 Starter, Home Basic, and Home Premium do not fully support EFS.

Encryption protects the contents of files and folders from unauthorized access. Windows uses *Encrypting File System (EFS)* to allow users to encrypt information on hard disks, external flash disks, CDs, DVDs, backup tapes, and other types of physical media. Files and folders are not encrypted in Windows 7 by default; however, users can enforce encryption on data files, folders, and entire drives. Encrypted (EFS) files and folders are displayed in green in Windows Explorer.

CERTIFICATION READY

How are files and folders encrypted using Encrypting File System (EFS)?

4.3

Understanding Encrypting File System (EFS)

The data in an encrypted file is "scrambled" but still readable and usable by the user who encrypted the file; that user—and any other authorized users—can open and change the file as necessary. However, an unauthorized user who tries to open the file or copy it receives an

"Access Denied" message. Only the original owner and the computer's designated recovery agent can access encrypted files. The designated recovery agent is the Administrator account, by default, on a local computer or in a domain.

A file created in or moved to an encrypted folder is automatically encrypted. The folder itself isn't encrypted; however, a user with appropriate file access permissions can see the names of the files in the folder.

When you mark a file for encryption, Windows generates a large, random number—a unique **encryption key**. The key is used to scramble the contents of the file. This encryption key is also encrypted with a personal file encryption certificate, which is stored in the Windows Certificate database. The file's encryption key is stored along with the file.

When you're logged on to Windows and attempt to open an encrypted file, Windows retrieves your personal **EFS certificate**, decodes the file's unique encryption key, and uses that key to decode the contents of the file.

If you lose an encryption key or your EFS certificate, or one of them becomes damaged, you could lose your data. It's important to back up your encryption key(s) and certificate and keep them in a safe place. You should also consider creating a file recovery certificate.

 ENCRYPT A FILE OR FOLDER

GET READY. To encrypt and decrypt a file or folder, perform the following steps:

1. In Windows Explorer, right-click the file or folder you want to encrypt, and then click **Properties**. The Properties dialog box displays.

2. On the **General** tab, click **Advanced**. The Advanced Attributes dialog box displays (see Figure 4-29).

Figure 4-29

The Advanced Attributes dialog box

3. Select the **Encrypt contents to secure data** check box, and then click **OK**.

4. Click **OK** to accept your settings and close the Properties dialog box.

5. The Confirm Attribute Changes dialog box displays (see Figure 4-30). Choose either **Apply changes to this folder only** or **Apply changes to this folder, subfolders and files**.

Figure 4-30

The Confirm Attribute Changes dialog box

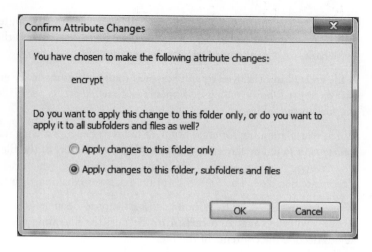

6. Click **OK**.

As Windows encrypts the folder, you are reminded to back up your encryption key. Microsoft recommends that you back up the encryption key immediately. Click the balloon reminder and follow the prompts.

An encrypted folder displays in green in the Windows Explorer file list (see the Books folder in Figure 4-31) so you can see at a glance that it's encrypted.

Figure 4-31

An encrypted folder displays in green in the file list

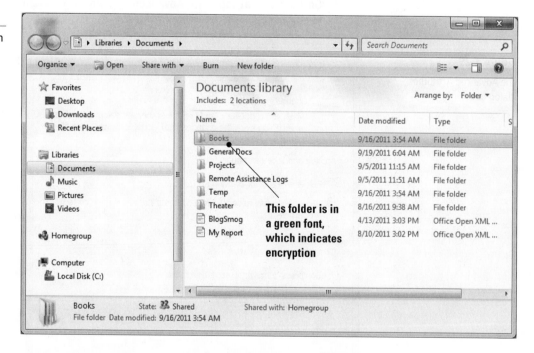

DECRYPT A FILE OR FOLDER

GET READY. To decrypt a file or folder, perform the following steps:

1. Right-click the file or folder you want to decrypt, and then click **Properties**.
2. Click the **General** tab, and then click **Advanced**.
3. Deselect the **Encrypt contents to secure data** check box, and then click **OK**.

BACK UP YOUR EFS CERTIFICATE

GET READY. To back up your EFS certificate, perform the following steps:

1. Click **Start** and in the **Search programs and files** search box, type **certmgr.msc** then click **certmgr** in the resulting list. The Certificate Manager displays.

2. Expand the **Personal** folder by clicking its arrow.

3. Click **Certificates**. The user's personal certificates are listed (see Figure 4-32).

Figure 4-32

Personal certificates in
Certificate Manager

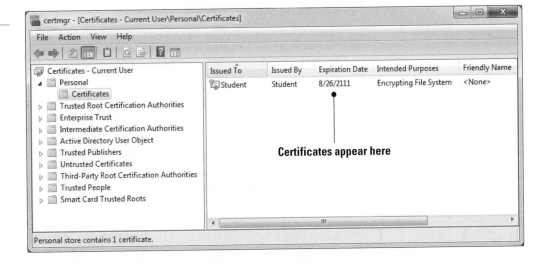

4. Click the certificate that lists Encrypting File System in the **Intended Purposes** column. If there is more than one EFS certificate, select all of them.

5. Click the **Action** menu, point to **All Tasks**, and then click **Export**. The Export wizard starts.

6. Click **Next**.

7. Leave the **Yes, export the private key** option selected (see Figure 4-33) and then click **Next**.

8. Click **Personal Information Exchange**, and then click **Next**.

9. Type the password you want to use, confirm it, and then click **Next**.

10. The wizard creates a file to store the certificate. Click **Browse** and navigate to the location where you want to save the file, and then enter a name for the file. Click **Save**.

11. In the next screen, click **Next**.

12. Click **Finish**, and then click **OK**.

Be sure to back up the certificate file to a location that is different from where it's saved. For example, if you saved the file on your computer's hard disk, copy the file to removable media or a network location.

➕ MORE INFORMATION

For details about EFS, visit http://windows.microsoft.com/en-US/windows7/What-is-Encrypting-File-System-EFS. To learn more about backing up an EFS certificate, go to http://windows.microsoft.com/en-US/windows7/Back-up-Encrypting-File-System-EFS-certificate

Figure 4-33

Using the Certificate Export Wizard

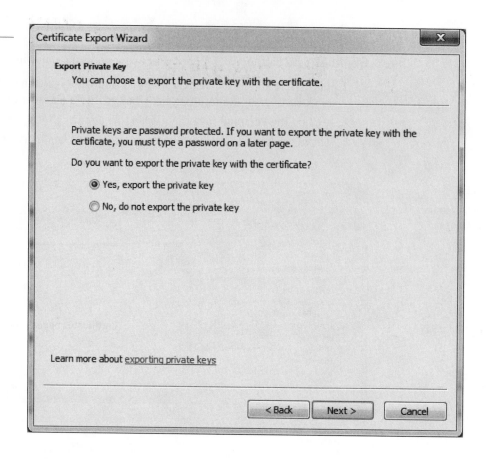

Understanding Compression

> Compression allows you to save disk space by reducing the size of files and folders without affecting their content.

Compression is the process of decreasing the size of files or folders without affecting the files' content. The purpose of compression is to decrease large files that would otherwise use a lot of storage space. Because files often include a lot of redundant, repeated data, compressing them replaces repeated data with pointers to the data. The pointers take up much less space than the repeated data, so the size of the file is reduced.

 TAKE NOTE * You cannot encrypt files or folders that are compressed. If you want to encrypt a compressed file or folder, you must decompress it first.

⊙ COMPRESS A FILE OR FOLDER

GET READY. To compress a file or folder, perform the following steps:

1. In Windows Explorer, right-click the file or folder you want to compress, and then click **Properties**. The Properties dialog box displays.
2. On the **General** tab, click **Advanced**. The Advanced Attributes dialog box displays (see Figure 4-34).
3. Select the **Compress contents to save disk space** check box, and then click **OK**.

Figure 4-34

The Advanced Attributes
dialog box

The compressed file or folder displays in blue in Windows Explorer. To uncompress the file or folder, select it, return to the Advanced Attributes dialog box, and deselect the *Compress contents to save disk space* check box.

Understanding BitLocker

CERTIFICATION READY
What is the purpose of BitLocker?
4.3

BitLocker Drive Encryption encrypts an entire fixed disk to prevent access by unauthorized users. BitLocker To Go protects removable drives, such as external flash drives. You can encrypt drives with BitLocker in Windows Ultimate and Enterprise editions only.

CERTIFICATION READY
How does BitLocker encrypt and protect a hard drive?
5.2

BitLocker Drive Encryption is another method of protecting data stored on a fixed drive in a Windows computer. BitLocker encrypts the entire drive, rather than individual files and folders. The complementary BitLocker To Go protects data on removable data drives, such as an external flash drive.

TAKE NOTE*

BitLocker encryption is available in Windows 7 Ultimate and Enterprise editions, not in Professional, Home Premium, or Starter.

When you add new files to a BitLocker-encrypted disk, the files are encrypted automatically. If you copy the files to another drive, BitLocker automatically decrypts the files, which means they're no longer protected.

Anytime you start a computer on which the operating system disk is BitLocker-encrypted, BitLocker scans the drive for security risks. If BitLocker detects a potential security risk such as a change to the startup files, it locks Windows (prevents it from running) and requires the user to provide the BitLocker recovery key to unlock Windows. This ensures that unauthorized users cannot access the system to steal files or somehow damage the system or data.

Some computers have a Trusted Platform Module (TPM) chip on the motherboard. If the chip is present, BitLocker uses the TPM chip to protect the BitLocker keys. When a user starts a computer with a TPM chip and with BitLocker enabled, BitLocker requests the keys from the TPM and unlocks the system.

TAKE NOTE * BitLocker Drive Encryption encrypts an entire drive. EFS protects individual files and folders on any drive on a per-user basis.

You can turn off BitLocker at any time by suspending it temporarily or decrypting the drive.

TURN ON BITLOCKER DRIVE ENCRYPTION

GET READY. To turn on BitLocker Drive Encryption, perform the following steps:

1. Click **Start > Control Panel > System and Security > BitLocker Drive Encryption**.
2. Click **Turn On BitLocker** for the operating system drive (see Figure 4-35). Provide an administrative password or confirm to continue, when prompted.

Figure 4-35

Turning on BitLocker

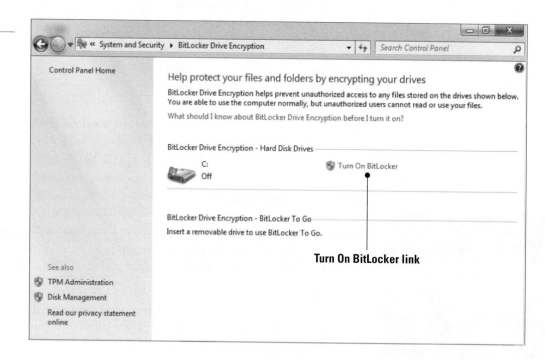

BitLocker scans your computer to ensure that it meets the BitLocker system requirements.

3. When the BitLocker Setup Wizard starts, follow the prompts to choose how to store the recovery key.
4. When prompted, confirm that the **Run BitLocker system check** check box is selected and then click **Continue** to encrypt the drive.
5. Restart the computer by clicking **Restart now**.

The encryption process might take several minutes to more than an hour. Windows displays a completion message when the encryption process is finished.

 **+ MORE INFORMATION**

For more information about BitLocker Drive Encryption, visit http://windows.microsoft.com/en-US/windows7/products/features/bitlocker. For step-by-step deployment instructions, see http://technet.microsoft.com/en-us/library/dd835565(WS.10).aspx

SKILL SUMMARY

IN THIS LESSON YOU LEARNED:

- You install applications, or programs, either at the local level or the network level. A local installation results in the software files running directly from a computer. Installing over a network generally means the software files are made available from an application server on a network. The network method, along with Group Policy, gives an administrator more efficient control over who can use the software and who can remove it.

- Use the Programs and Features applet in Control Panel to uninstall a local application from a Windows 7 computer.

- In a Windows network in a domain environment, administrators can use Group Policy to ease the burden of administering and managing many users and client computers. Group Policy lets you control who can install software, and on which computers, and helps you push software updates and security configurations across the network.

- Services run in the background on a Windows system to help the operating system run other programs. The Services console is the central management point of services in Windows Vista and Windows 7.

- Use MSCONFIG (also known as the System Configuration utility) to troubleshoot and diagnose startup problems.

- The three primary types of file systems for Windows are FAT, FAT32, and NTFS. It's best to use NTFS-formatted disks for Windows Vista and Windows 7. NTFS handles small to very large hard disks, provides better security, and is the most reliable.

- Libraries were introduced in Windows 7. A library looks like an ordinary folder, but it is a virtual folder that simply points to files and folders in different locations on a hard disk, network drive, or external drive.

- Encrypting files and folders protects them from unwanted access. Microsoft uses the Encrypting File System (EFS) to encrypt individual files and folders in Windows Vista and Windows 7.

- Compression allows you to save disk space by reducing the size of files and folders without affecting their content.

- BitLocker Drive Encryption encrypts an entire fixed disk to prevent access by unauthorized users. BitLocker To Go protects removable drives, such as external flash drives. You can encrypt drives with BitLocker in Windows Ultimate and Enterprise editions only.

■ Knowledge Assessment

Fill in the Blank

Complete the following sentences by writing the correct word or words in the blanks provided.

1. An _____ is a program that runs "on top" of the operating system and helps a user perform a specific task, such as word processing, appointment scheduling, or accounting.

2. _____ is a collection of settings (policies) stored in Active Directory on a Windows network.

3. Windows uses _____ to handle requests for print spooling, file indexing, task scheduling, the Windows Firewall, and much more.

4. _____ allows you to enable or disable startup services, set boot options such as booting into Safe Mode, access tools like Action Center and Event Viewer, and more.

5. Most Windows Vista and Windows 7 users use the _____ file system because it supports larger disks than FAT32 or FAT.

6. Using Group Policy, you can _____ (or publish) an application to all users or computers in a designated group.

7. In Windows 7, a _____ is a virtual folder that can display content from different locations (folders, for example) on your computer or an external drive.

8. Windows uses _____ to allow users to encrypt information on hard disks, external flash disks, CDs, DVDs, backup tapes, and other types of physical media.

9. _____ is the process of decreasing the size of files or folders without affecting the files' content.

10. _____ encrypts an entire drive, rather than individual files and folders on a disk.

Multiple Choice

Circle the letter that corresponds to the best answer.

1. Which of the following can you do in the Programs and Features applet in Control Panel?
   a. Install an application
   b. Uninstall an application
   c. Encrypt an application's files
   d. Compress an application's files

2. Which of the following can you perform using Group Policy? (Choose all that apply.)
   a. Restrict user access to an application
   b. Encrypt a user's files
   c. Update an application
   d. Install applications from a network location

3. Which of the following do you access to enter Safe Mode the next time the computer starts?
   a. The General tab
   b. The Boot tab
   c. The Startup tab
   d. Services console

4. You are in the System Configuration utility and want to run Performance Monitor. Which tab do you select to start Performance Monitor?
   a. General
   b. Startup
   c. Services
   d. Tools

5. What is the maximum disk size NTFS can handle?
   a. 32 GB
   b. 256 GB
   c. 32 TB
   d. 256 TB

6. Which of the following are default libraries in Windows 7? (Choose all that apply.)
   a. Documents
   b. Photos
   c. Audio
   d. Videos

7. Which of the following settings is not configurable from the Screen Resolution window?
   a. Orientation
   b. Font color
   c. Display
   d. Windows theme

8. Where are EFS certificates stored?
   a. EFS Certificate database
   b. Windows Certificate database
   c. Certificate library
   d. Documents library

9. After you compress a folder, in what color does it display in Windows Explorer?
   a. Blue
   b. Green
   c. Black
   d. Red

10. BitLocker can use a chip, found on some computers, to protect BitLocker encryption keys. What is the name of the chip?
    a. Trusted Platform Module
    b. Trusted Protection Module
    c. Encryption Platform Module
    d. Trusted Hard Drive Module

True / False

Circle T if the statement is true or F if the statement is false.

T | F 1. Use Programs and Features to install applications in Windows 7.

T | F 2. Objects in Active Directory are linked to Group Policy objects (GPOs).

T | F 3. A Windows 7 system can have more than 100 services running at any one time.

T | F 4. Use the Tools tab in System Configuration to enable or disable services.

T | F 5. EFS and BitLocker Drive Encryption are the same thing.

■ Competency Assessment

Scenario 4-1: Resolving Technical Problems

One of your co-workers reports that the network printer won't print. She says she has sent a print job at least 10 times but nothing prints, and she's sure the printer has paper and toner. As an IT technician, what do you do to resolve this problem?

Scenario 4-2: Protecting Laptop Computers

Henry, a traveling salesperson at your company, left his laptop at the airport on his last trip. The laptop was never recovered. His new laptop arrived yesterday and you installed Windows 7 Enterprise and productivity applications and restored data from a backup. What should you do to the laptop to protect all programs and data on the computer in the event of loss or theft?

■ Proficiency Assessment

Scenario 4-3: Uninstalling Local Software

Henry, the salesperson, left on an extended business trip to Asia. He called you one day and asked if the voice transcription software could be deleted from his computer. He doesn't use it after all and doesn't want it taking up space. What do you tell Henry to help him remove the software on his own?

Scenario 4-4: Adding Locations to a Library

Maria has two folders named AP and AR at the root of her hard disk (located at C:\). She wants to access them when she opens the Documents library. How do you advise Maria?

Managing Devices

EXAM OBJECTIVE MATRIX

SKILLS/CONCEPTS	EXAM OBJECTIVE DESCRIPTION	EXAM OBJECTIVE NUMBER
Understanding Storage	Understand storage.	5.2
Understanding Printing Devices	Connect devices.	5.1
	Understand printing devices.	5.3
Understanding System Devices	Connect devices.	5.1
	Understand system devices.	5.4

KEY TERMS

audio device

basic disk

cloud storage

Computer Management

Device Manager

Disk Management

driver

dual-boot environment

dynamic disk

External Serial Advanced Technology
  Attachment (eSATA)

fill and spill

FireWire

IEEE 1394

input device

infrared technology

Internet Small Computer System Interface (iSCSI)

isochronous data transfer

local printer

mirrored volume

network printer

partition

plug-and-play (PnP) technology

print queue

spanned volume

striped volume

universal serial bus (USB)

video device

volume

Windows Live Mesh

Windows Live SkyDrive

Some of the computers you support at Interstate Snacks have two or more disks. To make the most of the storage space, you plan to span, stripe, or mirror the volumes, depending on the needs of each user. You also plan to run a pilot project using cloud storage and services such as Windows Live SkyDrive, Windows Live Mesh, and OneNote to SkyDrive.

Understanding Storage

↓ THE BOTTOM LINE
Storage in Windows 7 refers to storing data as well as an operating system on disks. There are a number of different types of storage: internal, external, network, and cloud.

When it comes to Windows storage, there's more to it than just saving data on a disk. There are different types of disks (basic and dynamic) you need to know about, along with choices of partition styles such as master boot record (MBR) and GUID partition table (GPT), which determine the number of partitions you are allowed to create along with the size limitations of those partitions.

Understanding Disk and Drive Types

Windows 7 supports two primary types of disks: basic and dynamic. In addition, the operating system supports simple, spanned, striped, and mirrored volumes. Use the Disk Management tool in the Computer Management snap-in to manage disks, partitions, and volumes.

CERTIFICATION READY
What are common types of drives supported by Windows 7?
5.2

In Windows 7, a physical hard drive can be designated as a basic disk or a dynamic disk. *Basic disks* contain only simple volumes. *Dynamic disks* can contain simple, spanned, striped, and mirrored volumes.

Traditionally, basic disks use *partitions* and logical drives. The MBR partition style has been around for quite a while and all Windows operating systems support MBR partitions. But as with most legacy technologies, MBR partitions have their limitations. MBR partitions are limited to four basic partitions and each partition is limited to 2 terabytes (TB) in size. The four basic partitions can be either four primary partitions or three primary partitions with one extended partition, which can be further divided into multiple logical partitions.

TAKE NOTE*

One zeta byte is equal to one billion terabytes.

A GPT partition style allows for more partitions and larger volume sizes. A disk initialized as a GPT partition style may contain up to 128 primary partitions and each can be larger than 2 TB; in fact, they can be as large as 9.4 zetabytes (ZB).

With dynamic disks, free space on a hard drive is divided into *volumes* instead of partitions. Dynamic disks are not limited by partition styles as are basic disks. You can configure dynamic disk volumes as simple, spanned, mirrored, striped, or RAID-5:

- **Simple volume:** This type of volume uses free space available on a single disk.
- **Spanned volume:** This type of volume extends a simple volume across multiple disks, up to a maximum of 32.
- **Mirrored volume:** This type of volume duplicates data from one disk to a second disk for redundancy and fault tolerance; if one disk fails, data can be accessed from the second

disk. You cannot span a mirrored volume; a mirrored volume must reside on a single disk. Mirroring is also referred to as RAID-1.

- **Striped volume:** This type of volume stores data across two or more physical disks. Data on a striped volume is written evenly to each of the physical disks in the volume. You cannot mirror or span a striped volume. Striping is often referred to as RAID-0.

- **RAID-5 volume:** This type of volume is a type of striped volume that also provides fault tolerance. Data is written to three or more disks; if one disk fails, the remaining drives re-create the data.

You can typically convert a basic disk to a dynamic disk without losing any data, but it's a best practice to back up all data before attempting the conversion. You might need to convert a hard disk from dynamic to basic at some point. For example, a user's computer runs Windows 7 and the single hard disk is configured as a dynamic disk. However, he needs access to both Windows 7 and Windows XP on the same computer. This is called a *dual-boot environment*. When the user starts the computer, he can choose one or the other operating system to run. Because Windows XP does not support dynamic disks, you would need to convert the hard disk from dynamic to basic. This conversion requires you to delete all volumes first, which deletes the data, so you must back up the data before you begin the conversion.

Recall from Lesson 4 that the three primary types of file systems for Windows are FAT, FAT32, and NTFS. It's best to use NTFS-formatted disks for Windows 7 because NTFS handles small to very large hard disks, provides better security, and is the most reliable. Both basic and dynamic disks can contain any combination of FAT, FAT32, and NTFS partitions or volumes.

CERTIFICATION READY
What types of disks and file systems does Windows 7 support?
5.2

Using Disk Management

When you add a new hard drive to a computer, there a few steps you need to take to introduce a new drive to the operating system. You need to initialize the disk, and then choose a drive type and a partition style (for basic disks). You can perform all of these steps in the Disk Management tool, which is part of the *Computer Management* MMC snap-in.

To open Computer Management, click Start, type computer in the Search programs and files search box, and then select Computer Management from the resulting list. Alternately, you can use the menus: Click Start, right-click Computer, and then click Manage. Figure 5-1 shows the tools in the Computer Management snap-in. The tool you use to work with disks is the *Disk Management* tool.

Figure 5-1

The Computer Management snap-in

Disk Management

Click the Disk Management node. If you just installed a new hard disk, Disk Manager prompts you to initialize the new disk by displaying the Initialize Disk dialog box (Figure 5-2).

Figure 5-2

The Initialize Disk dialog box

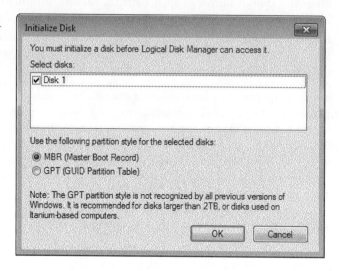

The first choice you need to make is the partition style of the disk. You need to be sure you select the correct partition style because this is not something easily changed later. The two partition styles are master boot record (MBR) and GUID partition table (GPT).

You can change your partition style as long as you have not created any partitions. If you have created partitions that contain data and wish to change the partition style, you need to back up your data, delete all partitions, and then right-click the disk number and choose to convert to the new partition style.

Next you need to choose the type of disk: basic or dynamic. Basic disks contain only simple volumes. The partition style you choose dictates the number of partitions you can create and their sizes. Dynamic disks can contain simple, spanned, striped, and mirrored volumes.

 CONVERT A DISK FROM BASIC TO DYNAMIC

GET READY. To convert a disk from basic to dynamic, perform the following steps:

1. Back up all data on the disk you want to convert.
2. Open Disk Management in the Computer Management console.
3. Right-click the basic disk you want to convert and select **Convert to Dynamic Disk**.
4. If the disk is currently MBR, the Convert to GPT Disk option displays on the menu. If the disk is GPT, the Convert to MBR Disk option displays. Select the appropriate option.

After you convert the partition style, you can create partitions again and restore the data that you previously backed up.

TAKE NOTE*

The conversion from basic to dynamic can occur automatically based on the type of volume you create. You'll see this in action in the step-by-step exercise named "Create a Spanned Volume."

In the next example, a second disk is added to the computer, so two disks have been initialized as MBR. However, you will create a simple volume on only one of the dynamic disks. Spanning, striping, and mirroring, which you will do in subsequent step-by-step exercises, involve two or more disks.

 CREATE A SIMPLE VOLUME

GET READY. To create a simple volume, perform the following steps:

1. Open Disk Management from the Computer Management console. (Click **Start**, type **computer** in the **Search programs and files** search box, select **Computer Management** from the resulting list, and then click the **Disk Management** node.)

2. Right-click an empty area (unallocated space) of a dynamic disk. The New Volume menu displays, similar to Figure 5-3. Click **New Simple Volume**.

Figure 5-3

The New Volume menu

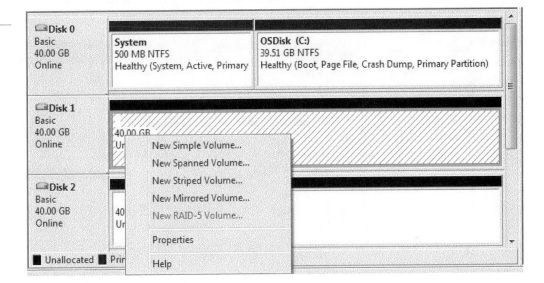

3. The New Simple Volume Wizard starts. Click **Next** on the welcome screen.

4. On the Assign Drive Letter or Path screen, specify your volume size, assign a drive letter or path, and choose a file system such as FAT, FAT32, or NTFS.

5. On the Format Partition screen, you may choose an allocation unit size and a name for the volume label. (If you're not familiar with allocation unit sizes, accept the default.) There are also two options you can set: **Perform a quick format** (selected by default, which is a good idea) and **Enable file and folder compression**, which is not selected by default.

6. On the Completing the New Simple Volume Wizard screen, click **Finish**.

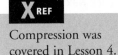

Compression was covered in Lesson 4.

You will now have a new partition on the dynamic disk where you can store data. All the other volume types—spanned, striped, and mirrored—require two or more disks. Therefore, if you have only one disk, the options to create spanned volumes, striped volumes, or mirrored volumes are grayed out and thus cannot be selected.

Spanned Volumes

If you have an additional disk with unused space, you can create a **spanned volume**. Spanned volumes include two or more disks (up to 32 may be included) that are represented in Windows Explorer as a single drive letter. They are sometimes referred to as **fill and spill** because all storage space on the first disk must be filled before data is stored on the second and subsequent disks.

 CREATE A SPANNED VOLUME

GET READY. To create a spanned volume, perform the following steps:

1. Open Disk Management from the Computer Management console. (Click **Start**, type **computer** in the **Search programs and files** search box, select **Computer Management** from the resulting list, and then click the **Disk Management** node.)

2. Right-click an empty area of a dynamic disk and then click **New Spanned Volume**.

3. Click **Next** on the Welcome to the New Spanned Volume Wizard screen.

4. Highlight the desired disk in the Available box, shown in Figure 5-4. Click **Add**. (You can also double-click the available disk to add it to the selected box).

Figure 5-4

The Select Disks page

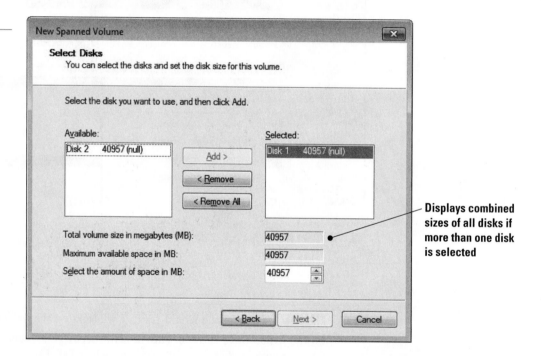

5. When you add disks to the **Selected** box, the **Total volume size in megabytes (MB)** box displays the combined sizes of all disks, yet when you highlight one of the disks in the **Selected** box, the **Maximum available space in MB** box and **Select the amount of space in MB** box show what you have selected from that specific disk. You can select different amount of space from each disk you add. You can continue to add as many disks as you would like included in your spanned volume. When you have selected the disks, click **Next**.

6. On the Assign Drive Letter or Path screen, select a drive letter and click **Next**.

7. The Format Volume screen is the same as creating a simple volume. Set your format volume options and click **Next**.

8. Click **Finish** on the Completing the New Spanned Volume Wizard page.

9. A warning message displays (see Figure 5-5), letting you know that in order to create a spanned volume, the basic disk will be converted to a dynamic disk. If you convert the disk to dynamic, you will not be able to start installed operating systems from any volume on the disk. Click **Yes** to continue or **No** to cancel the operation.

Figure 5-5

The convert basic disk to dynamic disk warning message

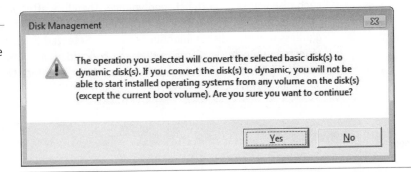

Do not plan to use spanned volumes for fault tolerance. If one disk in the spanned volume fails, all data in the spanned volume is lost unless you have a backup.

Striped Volumes

Creating a *striped volume* is similar to creating a spanned volume in that almost all the steps are the same. However, the way data is stored on a striped volume is different than a spanned volume. As with a spanned volume, striped volumes must contain at least two disks and can contain up to 32. But when the data is stored, it is separated into 64 kilobyte (KB) chunks. The first 64 KB is stored on Disk 1 in the striped volume, the second 64 KB chunk is stored on Disk 2, and so on. (See Figure 5-6.) The data is literally striped across multiple drives.

Figure 5-6

A striped volume

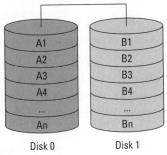

Accessing data on a striped volume is faster than accessing data on a spanned volume because a striped volume has multiple sets of read/write heads working simultaneously when reading and writing data. In this regard, spanned volumes are good for high capacity, whereas striped volumes are better for performance.

 CREATE A STRIPED VOLUME

GET READY. To create a striped volume, perform the following steps:

1. In Disk Management, right-click an empty disk and choose **New Striped Volume**. Click **Next** on the Welcome to the New Striped Volume Wizard screen.

2. Highlight the second disk from the **Available** box (same dialog box as Figure 5-4) and then click **Add**.

When you add disks to the **Selected** box, the **Total volume size in megabytes (MB)** box displays the combined sizes of all disks. This is where one of the big differences between spanned volumes and striped volumes takes place: On spanned volumes you can take different amounts of hard drive space from each disk—you cannot do this with striped volumes. Striped volumes must use the same amount of disk space from each disk you take to the striped volume. Therefore after you add two or more disks to the Selected box, if you change the **Select the amount of space in MB** setting (regardless of which disk is highlighted in the **Selected** box), the size difference will be reflected on both (or all) disks that you had added, as shown in Figure 5-7. Both disks have 40957 MB of space but we have changed the **Select the amount of space in MB** value to 39975.

Figure 5-7

Selecting disks for a striped volume

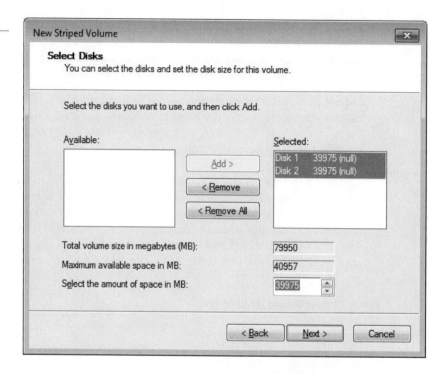

3. When you have selected the disks, click **Next**.

4. On the Assign Drive Letter or Path screen, select your drive letter and then click **Next**. The Format Volume screen displays. Set your format volume options and then click **Next**. Click **Finish**.

5. The same warning message from Figure 5-5 displays: To create a striped volume, the basic disk will be converted to a dynamic disk. If you convert the disk to dynamic, you will not be able to start installed operating systems from any volume on the disk. Click **Yes** to continue or **No** to cancel.

Striped volumes do not offer fault tolerance. Just as with spanned volumes, if one disk in the striped volume fails, all data from the entire striped volume is lost. You'll have to retrieve the data from a previous backup.

Mirrored Volumes

Mirrored volumes require only two disks. You cannot mirror to a third or fourth disk. Mirrored volumes store an exact copy of data from the first member of the mirrored volume to the second member. Because the data is written across both drives, you do get fault tolerance with mirrored volumes. Figure 5-8 shows an example of a mirrored volume.

Figure 5-8

A mirrored volume

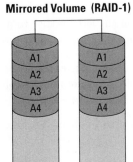

Mirrored Volume (RAID-1)

Disk 0   Disk 1

CREATE A MIRRORED VOLUME

GET READY. To create a mirrored volume, perform the following steps:

1. In Disk Management, right-click an empty disk and then click **New Mirrored Volume**. Click **Next** on the Welcome to the New Mirrored Volume Wizard screen.

2. Highlight the second disk from the **Available** box. Mirrored volumes require the same amount of disk space from each disk. When you add a disk to the **Selected** box, the **Total volume size in megabytes (MB)** box displays the most available free space from the disk with the smallest amount (see Figure 5-9).

Figure 5-9

Adding disks to a mirrored volume

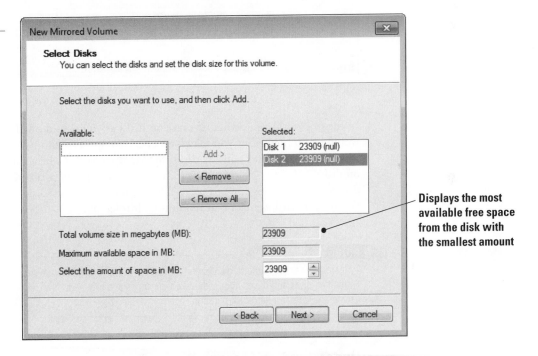

Displays the most available free space from the disk with the smallest amount

Notice that Disk 1 has 24.35 GB available and Disk 2 has only 23.35. On the Select Disks screen, the most that can be added is 23909 because that's the amount of available space from Disk 2. You can reduce the amount of space, but it will be reduced on both disks. This makes sense because you're creating an exact copy of data stored on the source disk, so you don't need the destination disk to have additional free space that will never be used. When you have selected the disks, click **Next**.

3. On the Assign Drive Letter or Path screen, select a drive letter and then click **Next**. The Format Volume screen is the same as the previous Format Volume screens. Set your format volume options and then click **Next**. Click **Finish**.

4. A warning message displays (see Figure 5-5), informing you that the basic disk will be converted to a dynamic disk. If you convert the disk to dynamic, you will not be able to start installed operating systems from any volume on the disk. Click **Yes**.

After you create a few different types of volumes, it's easy to figure out which volume is which—they're identified by a strip of color at the top of the volume. Figure 5-10 shows the default legend colors for the different types of volumes:

- Simple volumes (volume C) are identified by their dark blue strips
- Spanned volumes display purple strips (volume E)
- Striped volumes display aqua marine strips (volume F)
- Mirrored volumes display burgundy red strips (volume G)

Figure 5-10

What the different volumes look like

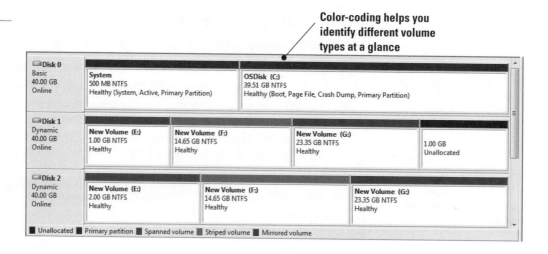

In the real world, you wouldn't carve up disks as you would on client computers—there would be no point. But you may have client computers with two, three, four, or even six disks. On a computer with six disks, for example, you might want to create a spanned volume on disks 2, 3, and 4 so they appear in Windows Explorer as a single drive (such as drive E). It can be less confusing for end users. Then you could mirror disks 5 and 6 to create a mirrored volume for sensitive data that requires fault tolerance.

+ MORE INFORMATION

To learn more about formatting disks and disk types, visit http://windows.microsoft.com/en-GB/windows7/ Formatting-disks-and-drives-frequently-asked-questions and http://windows.microsoft.com/en-GB/windows7/ Create-and-format-a-hard-disk-partition

Understanding Storage Device Types

Windows 7 supports many different types of storage devices in addition to ordinary hard disks. Other storage device types include eSATA, USB and USB 2.0, IEEE 1394 (FireWire), and iSCSI.

There are many different types of storage devices supported in Windows 7. This section explains eSATA, USB and USB 2.0, IEEE 1394 (FireWire), and iSCSI.

External Serial Advanced Technology Attachment (eSATA)

External Serial Advanced Technology Attachment (eSATA) is an external interface for SATA technologies. eSATA competes with IEEE 1394 (also called FireWire 400) and universal serial bus (USB) 2.0. eSATA is very fast, with read access times of 12.7 milliseconds (ms), read throughput of 93.5 MB/s, and a write throughput of 94 MB/s. In a nutshell, eSATA has a maximum speed of 300 MB/s for 3 Gb/s SATA connections, which is three times faster than either USB 2.0 or FireWire 400. eSATA cables can be up to 6.56 feet or 2 meters in length and are narrow. An eSATA cable is shown in Figure 5-11.

Figure 5-11

An eSATA cable

© Vicente Barcelo Varona/iStockphoto

However, there is one negative aspect—eSATA requires its own power connector (USB 2.0 and FireWire 400 do not). The reason eSATA can transfer data so quickly is because eSATA requires no translation between the interface and computer. This also helps save computer processing resources.

Universal Serial Bus (USB) and USB 2.0

Universal serial bus (USB) was a standard developed in the mid-1990s that defines cable connectors and protocols used to connect external devices to a computer. The devices include keyboards, digital cameras, portable media players, and external hard drives, to name a few. One type of USB cable is shown in Figure 5-12.

Figure 5-12

A USB cable

© Lev Mel/iStockphoto

USB version 1.0 had data transfer rates of 1.5 megabits per second (Mbp/s) at low speed and 12 Mbps at full speed.

USB 2.0 increased this speed to 480 Mpbs, which is 40 times faster. USB 2.0 has a read access time of 13.3 milliseconds (ms), a read throughput time of 40.1 megabytes per second (Mbps), and a write throughput of 30.9 Mbps. USB cables can be up to 16.4 feet (5 meters) in length.

USB 3.0 is the newest version and boasts transfer speeds up to 5 gigabits per second (Gbps). For this reason it has acquired the nickname SuperSpeed. USB 3.0 ports don't need as much power and are backward compatible with USB 2.0 ports.

IEEE 1394 (also known as FireWire)

IEEE 1394, also known as *FireWire* and i.link, has been around for many years and has undergone several revisions. One of the original reasons behind the creation of IEEE 1394 was to serve as an interface between the computer and a digital video camera so that video could be imported for editing. Today, IEEE 1394 is used for many different types of high-speed data transfers, including video, and serves the same purpose as USB. Several types of IEEE 1394 cables are shown in Figure 5-13.

Figure 5-13

IEEE 1394 cables

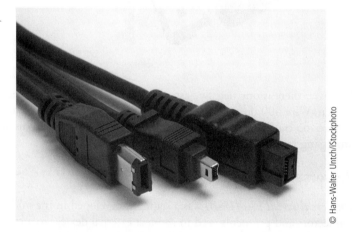

© Hans-Walter Untch/iStockphoto

IEEE 1394 supports plug-and-play technology, hot swapping, multiple speeds on the same bus, *isochronous data transfer* (which means a constant data rate), as well as providing power to peripheral devices.

The original standard, FireWire 400 (1394a), provides 400 Mbps throughput and isochronous transfer with read access times of 13.3 ms, read throughput of 40.1 Mbps, and a write throughput of 30.9 Mbps. FireWire 800 (1394b) doubled the throughput to 800 Mbps. IEEE 1394 supports cable lengths up to 14.76 feet (4.5m).

Internet Small Computer System Interface (iSCSI)

While all other storage devices covered in this lesson are mainly for consumer products to connect peripheral devices to laptops and desktop computers, *Internet Small Computer System Interface (iSCSI)* connects enterprise network storage devices such as a storage area network (SAN). iSCSI is used to transfer data over local area networks (LANs), wide area networks (WANs), and even the Internet.

Understanding Cloud Storage

Cloud services are becoming highly popular, and they provide convenient storage and application hosting for consumers and businesses alike.

If you've been in the IT industry for any length of time, you've probably seen outsourcing of data storage. Generally, when a company outsources the storage of its data, another company assumes the burden of maintaining all the storage devices and data backups. ***Cloud storage*** is remote data storage with backups, but can also include application hosting. You can use applications like Microsoft Word and Outlook, along with many other applications, over the Internet. Client machines can run applications from the cloud and access data; in fact, they can maintain complete control of their data and security.

Windows Live SkyDrive

Windows Live SkyDrive is a great way to experience the touch and feel of cloud services, and you can't beat the price—it's free. Originally named Windows Online Folder, Window's SkyDrive is a reliable password-protected online service offering file storage that enables people to share files and photos. Each person receives 25 GB of free online storage.

All you need to get started is a Windows Live login ID—no installation is necessary.

 EXPLORE WINDOWS LIVE SKYDRIVE

GET READY. To explore Windows Live SkyDrive, perform the following steps:

1. Launch Internet Explorer and go to ***https://Skydrive.live.com***. The sign in page appears.

2. Sign in using your Windows Live ID. If you don't have a Windows Live ID, you can sign up for one on this page by clicking the **Sign up** button and typing the answers to a few questions; it takes just a few minutes.

3. After you sign in, the SkyDrive home page looks similar to Figure 5-14. Starting in the upper-left corner, there are five top-level menus: Windows Live, Hotmail, Messenger, SkyDrive, and MSN.

Figure 5-14

The SkyDrive home page

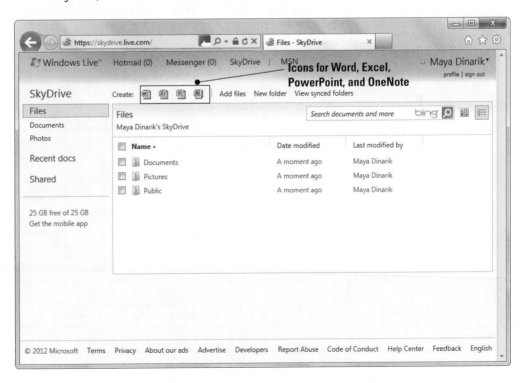

4. Hover your mouse pointer over the **Windows Live** menu to see its submenu items: Home, Devices, Mobile, Downloads, and All services.

The menu items are described as follows:

- **Home:** Takes you to the Windows Live home where you can perform tasks such as: check your Hotmail account or sync up your social media with Messenger social, which links your Facebook, MySpace, and LinkedIn to a central console.
- **Devices:** Allows you to add computers and mobile phones that you want to link together. (Phones must use the AT&T cellular service.)
- **Mobile:** Allows you to get Windows Live for your phone, set up SMS services, and set 5 GB of SkyDrive synced storage.
- **Downloads:** Takes you to a page to download Windows Live Essentials.
- **All Services:** Lists a wealth of services you can set up from calendaring options to Hotmail to setting up computer security for your family. Family Safety software creates activity reports to monitor your kids' computer activity; you can choose Web sites, games, and programs that are accessible and you can even specify time periods when they can use the computer.

The Hotmail menu provides the following links: Inbox, Calendar, Contacts, and Send email. These commands allow you to use your Hotmail e-mail account to view e-mail in your inbox, set up calendar events, and create a list of contacts that can be used to send e-mails, instant messages and many other things. The Send email link allows you to send an e-mail from your Hotmail account.

The Messenger menu allows you to instant message friends who are currently online and that you have previously added as a contact.

The SkyDrive menu has links to Files, Documents, Photos, Recent docs, Shared, Groups, and Photos of you. You can also create new Office documents like Word, Excel, PowerPoint, and OneNote.

The MSN menu provides links to MSN Home, Autos, Games, Money, Movies, Music, News, Sports, and Weather.

As shown in Figure 5-15, the SkyDrive section on the left displays Files, which is a top-level folder. The Documents and Photos folders are nested under the Files folder. There are two Quick views:

- Recent docs, which shows the documents you have recently opened.
- Shared, which are documents that other people have shared with you.

Figure 5-15

Creating a Word document

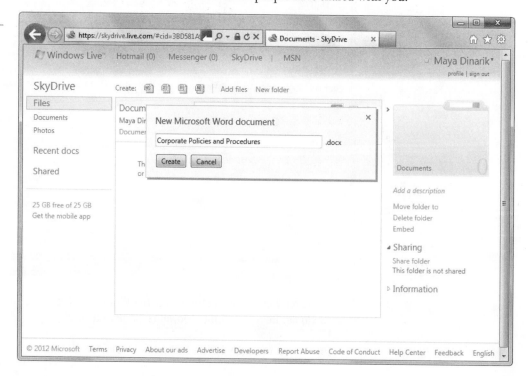

The main section of Figure 5-14 is where you can create your own Office documents and additional folders to help organize your documents. The maximum size of each file is 100 MB. Each file or folder on SkyDrive has a unique Web address (URL), which makes it easy to paste that link into e-mail messages or other documents for direct access. There are also quick-start icons to create Word, Excel, PowerPoint, and OneNote documents.

 CREATE A DOCUMENT IN SKYDRIVE

GET READY. To create a new document in SkyDrive, perform the following steps:

1. Open the folder you want to store the new document in, such as Documents.

2. Click the appropriate icon near the top of the window (click the **Word** icon to create a Word document, for example), and type a name for the file.

3. Figure 5-15 shows a new Word document being created named **Corporate Policies and Procedures**. Click **Create**. The document opens so you can begin typing. When you are finished, close and save the document.

4. You are returned to the Documents folder. If this is the first document you created or added to the Documents folder, your view should look similar to Figure 5-16.

Figure 5-16

The contents of Documents after adding a Word document

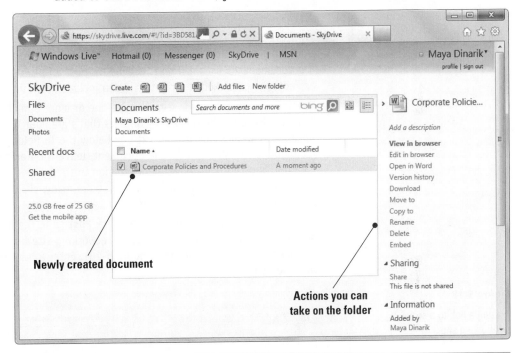

To open any files listed in Documents, just click the file name.

With a file selected (make sure the check box to the left of the file name is checked), notice the menu on the right side of the window. You can view the document in the browser, open it in Word on your computer if you have Word installed, view the document's version history (which shows when changes were made and by whom), download the document to your computer or device, move the file to another folder, copy the file, rename the file, delete the file, or generate HTML code to embed in a blog or Web page that allows users to view the document.

The Sharing section provides a Share link, which you click to share the document with other users. Next, you'll learn how to share a document in SkyDrive.

 SHARE A DOCUMENT IN SKYDRIVE

GET READY. To share a document in SkyDrive, perform the following steps:

1. With the document selected in folder view in SkyDrive, click the **Share** link on the right side of the screen. A Share window appears, as shown in Figure 5-17. You can share

Figure 5-17

A share window

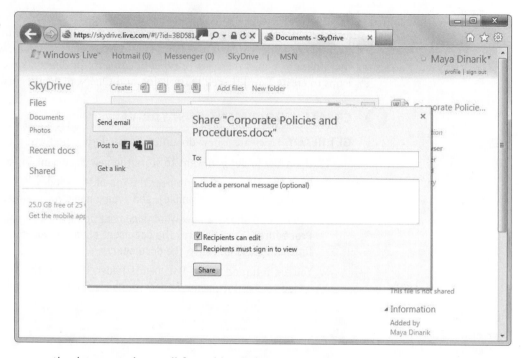

the document via e-mail from this window, post a link to a social networking site such as Facebook or LinkedIn, or get a link to include in a different e-mail or document.

2. To share the document via e-mail, type one or more e-mail addresses in the To field. You can also type the names of contacts that's are your Windows Live contact list. Enter a personal message in the text box below the To field, if you want. If you want the recipients to be able to edit the document, leave the **Recipients can edit** check box checked. You can require recipients to sign in to SkyDrive by checking the **Recipients must sign in to view** check box. When you're ready, click **Share**. The recipients receive an e-mail with a link to the document.

3. To share via a social networking site, click **Post to** in the left pane. Click the **add services** link, and then select a social networking site from the list or click **Find more services** to add a new site (see Figure 5-18). Enter a brief message in the text box, and then click **Post**.

Figure 5-18

Posting a link to a social networking site

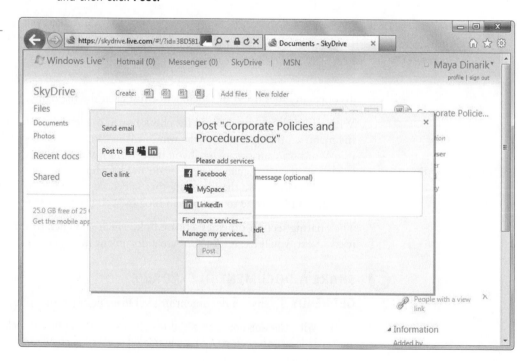

4. Another way to share the document is to click the **Get a link** option in the right pane. Three options appears: View only, View and edit, and Make it public! (see Figure 5-19). Click the **Get a link** button that's appropriate to how you want to share the document. Doing so displays a link you can copy and paste into an e-mail or document for direct access, as shown in Figure 5-20.

Figure 5-19

Get a link options

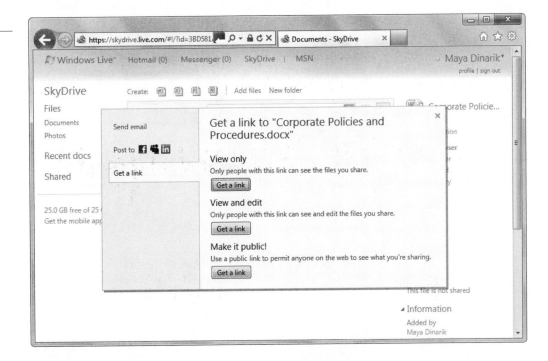

Figure 5-20

A unique link is generated for sharing

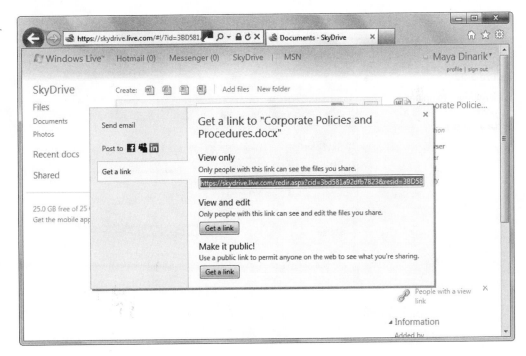

5. Click the X in the upper-right corner of the link dialog box to close it, if necessary.

Click Documents near the upper-left part of the window. The Create menu enables you to create new files and folders. You've already seen how the Word, Excel, and other file icons work. Now you'll learn how to create a folder in SkyDrive.

CREATE A FOLDER IN SKYDRIVE

GET READY. To create a new folder in SkyDrive, perform the following steps:

1. In SkyDrive, click the **New folder** link on the toolbar.
2. Type a name for the new folder (see Figure 5-21). If you decide to share the folder, the process is the same as sharing documents, described in the "Share a File in SkyDrive."

Figure 5-21

Creating a new folder

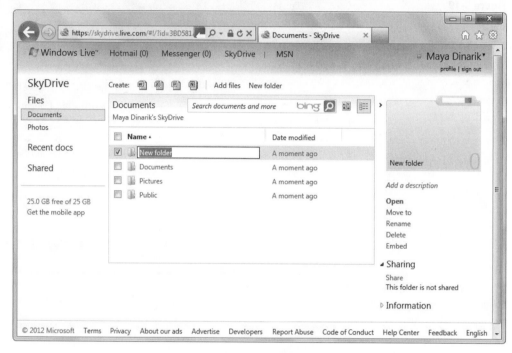

3. Click the new folder to open it. You can drag and drop documents into the folder or click-select documents from your computer and browse to the files you would like to add. You can also click **Add files** to upload files from your computer (Figure 5-22).

Figure 5-22

Click Add files to upload files from your computer to a SkyDrive folder

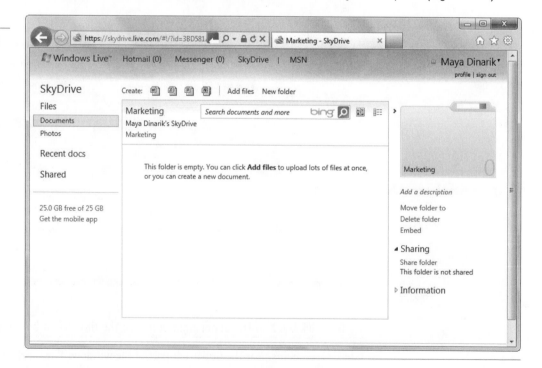

OneNote to SkyDrive

OneNote is an application that allows multiple users access to a shared set of notes all at the same time. Everyone's changes are automatically synchronized to the notebook, so the notebook is current. OneNote saves an offline copy on each user's computer so she can edit the notes even when she's not connected to the network. When she connects, OneNote automatically merges her changes with the Notebook along with everyone else's changes. When a user adds new sections, pages, and links in OneNote, the program displays the name of the user (author) who added them.

There are four views to choose from in OneNote:

- **Editing View:** Allows the notebook to be edited
- **Reading View:** Removes extra information like author names and dates of changes
- **Show Authors:** Displays the authors of sections, pages, and notebooks
- **Page Versions:** Shows various versions of a page

 CREATE A ONENOTE NOTEBOOK

GET READY. To create a new notebook in OneNote, perform the following steps:

1. Sign in to SkyDrive by opening Internet Explorer, going to ***https://Skydrive.live.com***, and signing in.
2. Create a new notebook by clicking the **OneNote** icon near the top of the window.
3. Type a name for the new notebook.

To share a OneNote notebook, follow the same steps you followed for sharing the SkyDrive My Documents folder covered in the previous section.

Windows Live Mesh

Windows Live Mesh is a part of the Windows Live Essentials suite. Windows Live Mesh enables you to keep data synchronized between computers (and some devices such as mobile phones) as well as some program settings. Data is synced using the online service, and there are some limitations to the amount of storage space you get: You can sync up to 200 folders, which can each grow as large as 50 GB in size and can contain up to 100,000 files. Like SkyDrive, Windows Live Mesh is a free service.

You need to install Windows Live Mesh on each computer for which you want keep the data synchronized. As you sync folders between computers, the changes that you make on one computer are automatically changed on the other computer when they are online at the same time. The contents of the synced folders are saved locally on each computer so you still have access to the data even if you are not connected to the Internet. Data transfers are encrypted via the Transport Layer Security (TLS) or Secure Sockets Layer (SSL) protocols.

 INSTALL WINDOWS LIVE MESH

GET READY. To install Windows Live Mesh, perform the following steps:

1. Launch Internet Explorer and go to ***http://explore.live.com/windows-live-mesh***.
2. Click the **Download now** button.

3. Save the **wlsetup-web.exe** file to your computer (such as in the Downloads folder).

4. Locate and double-click **wlsetup-web.exe**.

5. On the What do you want to install? screen of the installation wizard, you can choose to install all of Windows Live Essentials or you can install individual programs. For this example, choose to install individual programs. The screen shown in Figure 5-23 displays.

Figure 5-23

Installing Windows Live Mesh

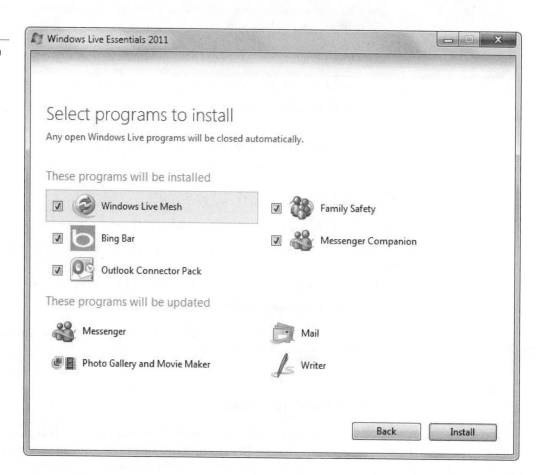

6. Uncheck all programs other than **Windows Live Mesh** and then click **Install**. Follow the prompts to install the software.

7. Restart your computer.

To use the program, click Start > All Programs > Windows Live > Windows Live Mesh. Sign in using your Windows Live ID and password.

From the Windows Live Mesh Status page shown in Figure 5-24, you can synchronize folders, your Internet Explorer favorites, and Microsoft Office settings (such as styles, templates, custom dictionary, and e-mail signatures). You can also go to Windows Live Devices to add more devices, such as computers with which you want to synchronize.

Click Go to Windows Live Devices to open the Windows Live Devices page (Figure 5-25). If you add devices using SkyDrive, you'll see the same devices here because all Windows Live products are linked. Choose to add a computer or phone and then answer a few short questions.

A computer in the syncing pair might show a status of *Remote connections aren't available.* The remote connections feature allows you to connect to a machine across the Internet

Figure 5-24

The Windows Live Mesh Status page

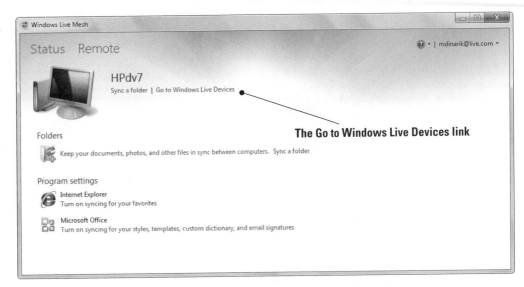

The Go to Windows Live Devices link

Figure 5-25

The Windows Live Devices page

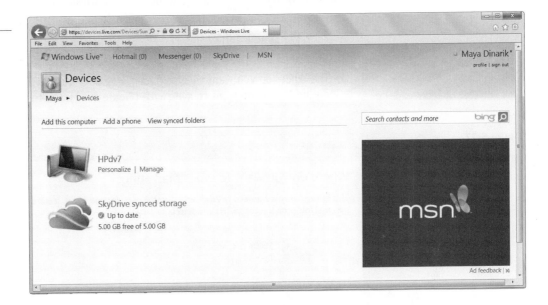

and access the data as if you were physically on that machine. Windows Live Mesh requires computers to allow remote connections. Remote connections are encrypted using Secure Sockets Layer (SSL), so they are safe to use.

To enable remote connections from the Windows Live Mesh Status page, click Remote in the upper-left corner. Figure 5-26 shows the Windows Live Mesh Remote page.

In the Remote connections to this computer section, the default setting is *You don't allow remote connections to <computer name>*. If you're not sure if you want to allow remote connections to this computer, click the *What happens when I allow them?* link. The Windows Live Mesh and Devices Help Center displays, where you can review some of the most commonly asked questions about remote connections.

When you're ready to allow remote connections, click *Allow remote connections to this computer*. The *Allow remote connections to this computer link* changes to *Block remote connections*. Just click *Block remote connections* if you want to stop allowing remote connections to this machine.

Figure 5-26

The Windows Live Mesh
Remote page

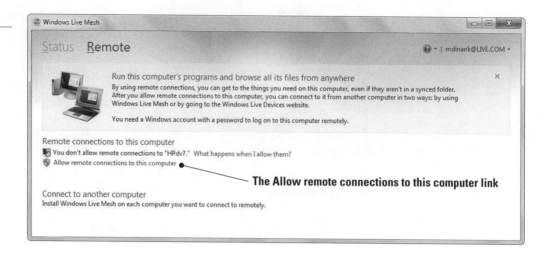

The Allow remote connections to this computer link

➔ **USE WINDOWS LIVE MESH TO SYNC A FOLDER**

GET READY. To sync a folder using Windows Live Mesh, perform the following steps:

1. Click the icon in the taskbar to display the Windows Live Mesh Status page and then click the **Sync a folder** link.

2. Browse to the folder you'd like to sync, select it, and then click the **Sync** button.

3. The Where do you want to sync *foldername* page displays. Select the computer or online folder you want to sync with (Figure 5-27) and then click **OK**.

Figure 5-27

Syncing a folder

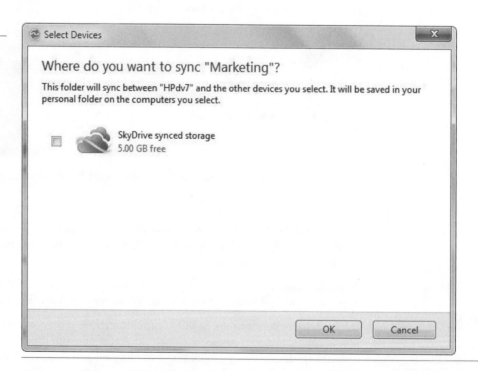

On the Windows Live Mesh Status page, you should see a green circle with a white check mark and text that reads *Your synced folders are up to date on this computer* (see Figure 5-28).

To enable synchronization of your Internet Explorer favorites on the same page, in the Program settings/Internet Explorer section, click *Turn on syncing for your favorites.* To synchronize your Microsoft Office settings, click *Turn on syncing for your styles, templates, custom*

Figure 5-28

The Windows Live Mesh Status page showing that folders are synced

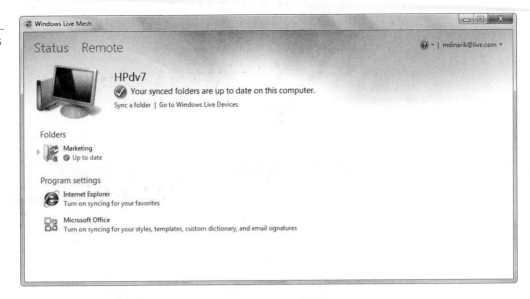

dictionary, and email signatures. Once they are successfully synced, you will see *Syncing turned on.*

If you ever need to turn syncing off, you can click the icon (either Internet Explorer or Microsoft Office) to open the details and then click *Turn off syncing.*

➕ MORE INFORMATION

To learn more about Windows Live Mesh, visit http://explore.live.com/windows-live-mesh

---

▪ Understanding Printing Devices

↓ THE BOTTOM LINE Printing devices can be local or networked; they can even be available over the Internet. You can perform most printer support from the Devices and Printers applet.

Printers can be either local or networked. Microsoft has historically used the term "print device" to refer to the actual hardware, but is now using the term "printer" in most consumer-level documentation. You will see both "printer" and "print device" in Microsoft documentation and in this lesson.

Understanding Local Printers

CERTIFICATION READY
What is a local printer?
5.3

A *local printer* is connected directly to your computer via a cable, such as serial, parallel, USB, infrared, or other port type. Most printers come with a manufacturer's CD containing the printer software that must be installed for your operating system to talk to the printer. A good rule of thumb is if your printer ships with a manufacturer CD, use the setup program on the CD to install the driver. A *driver* is a small program that enables hardware to interact with the operating system.

CERTIFICATION READY
How can you add or remove a printer?
5.1

If you do not have a CD from the manufacturer, you can use the built-in printer drivers in Windows 7. However, it is almost always preferable to use the printer setup program on the CD or download the latest print driver setup installation file from the manufacturer's Web site than to use the built-in Windows 7 driver. The built-in driver typically provides access to a minimal subset of the printer's features.

ADD A LOCAL PRINTER

GET READY. To add a local printer, perform the following steps:

1. Physically connect the printer to a computer with the appropriate cable.

2. Click **Start > Devices and Printers**. The Devices and Printers page displays (see Figure 5-29).

Figure 5-29

The Devices and Printers window

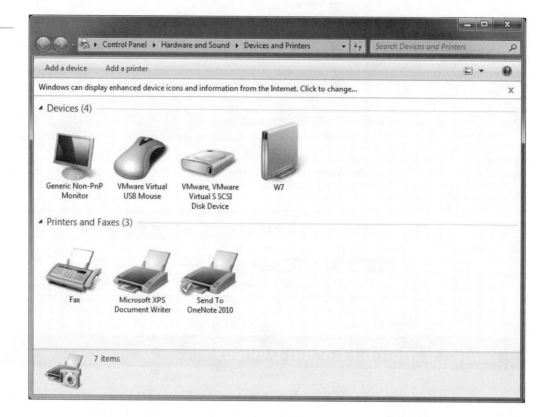

3. Select **Add a printer** from the menu bar or right-click in the white space on the page and select **Add a printer** from the shortcut menu. The Add Printer Wizard starts.

4. On the What type of printer do you want to install? page (see Figure 5-30), select **Add a local printer**.

5. For a local printer, on the Choose a printer port page, select the port that your printer is currently connected to: **Use an existing port** or **Create a new port**. Figure 5-31 shows the default existing ports. Your choices for creating a new port are local port or TCP/IP port (whereby you enter the IP address or name of a printer).

6. The Install the printer driver page asks for a printer driver and displays a list of manufacturers and printers. Select the manufacturer of the printer and then the printer displayed in Figure 5-32. If you do not see your printer, click the **Windows Update** button to get a more extensive list of printers to choose from.

7. When you've found your printer, click the **Have Disk** button. Ensure the CD is in the CD/DVD drive, browse to the appropriate printer model, and then click **OK**.

8. Type a name for your printer and then click **Next**.

Figure 5-30

The What type of printer do you want to install? screen

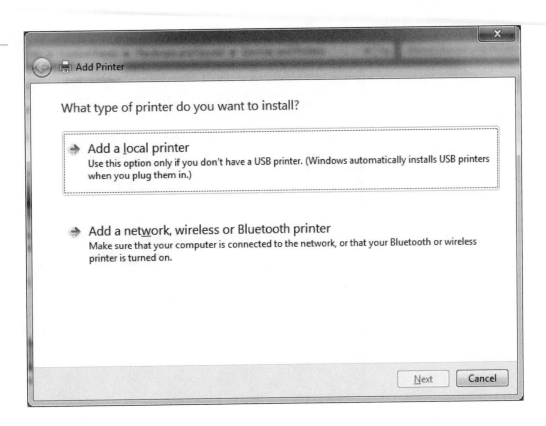

Figure 5-31

The Choose a printer port screen

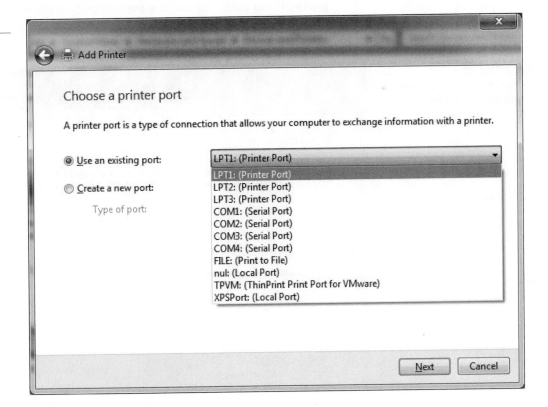

Figure 5-32

Selecting your printer

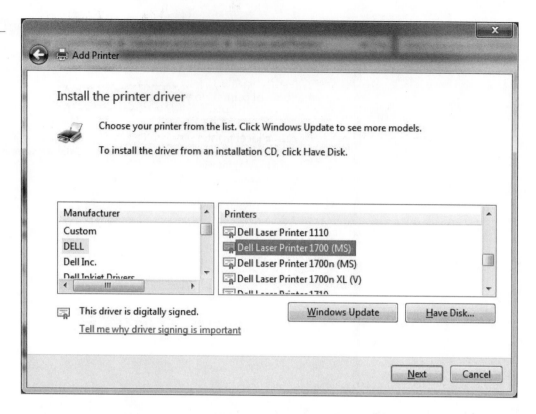

9. The Printer sharing screen displayed in Figure 5-33 allows you to share the printer so other people can connect to and use the printer across the network. The printer is local for you, but for all others connecting across the network, it's a networked printer. If you would like to share the printer, type the respective information for the **Share name**, **Location**, and **Comment** text boxes. If you do not want to share the printer, select the **Do not share this printer** option.

Figure 5-33

Sharing your printer (or not sharing your printer)

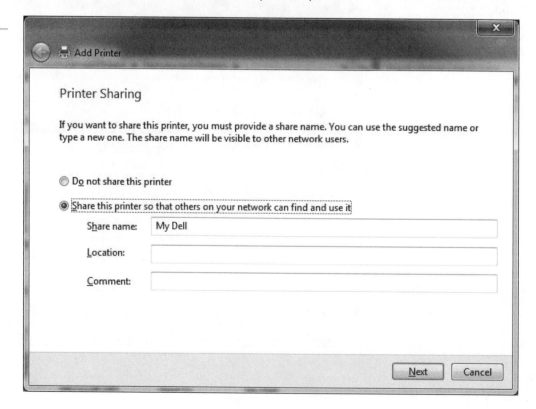

10. Click **Next**.

11. The message **You've successfully added** *printername* should display (see Figure 5-34). To ensure that your computer and printer are communicating properly, click the **Print a test page** button.

Figure 5-34

Successfully adding your printer

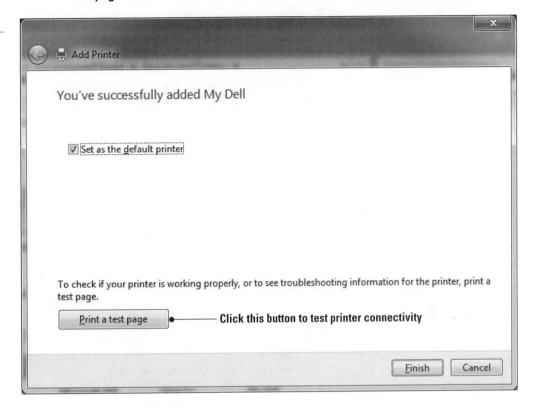

12. If a page prints properly, click **Finish**.

Your newly added printer should display in the Devices and Printers window with a green circle and a white check mark, indicating that it is your default printer. From this point forward, whenever you tell the computer to print, it automatically prints to your default printer. You can always choose to print to a different printer by selecting a different printer from the list of printers when you print a document.

 REMOVE A LOCAL PRINTER

GET READY. To remove a local printer, perform the following steps:

1. Open Devices and Printers.

2. Right-click the printer that you want to remove and then click **Remove device**.

You can't remove a printer that has print jobs in the queue.

Understanding Network Printers

A *network printer* generally has a network adapter and is connected to a network. The printer receives an IP address and is a node on the network much like a networked computer. You can share a local (directly connected) printer with others on a network; in this case, the printer is considered to be both local (to the computer to which it is connected) and networked.

However, a true network printer is most commonly connected to and shared from a network server. Connecting to a network printer requires different steps than setting up a local printer.

INSTALL A NETWORK PRINTER

GET READY. To install a network printer, perform the following steps:

1. Click **Start > Devices and Printers.**

2. Select **Add a printer** from the top menu or right-click a blank area on the page and select **Add a printer.**

3. On the Add Printer page, click **Add network, wireless or Bluetooth printer.** The Add Printer wizard searches for shared printers. If a list of shared printers does not display (or if the printer you are looking for doesn't display), on the Add Printer page, click **The printer that I want isn't listed.**

4. Figure 5-35 shows how you can find a printer by name or by a TCP/IP address. You can browse for a printer (chances are, however, that if it didn't show up before, it won't show up by browsing). Type the Universal Naming Convention (UNC) path to the computer name and shared printer name or add a printer using a TCP/IP address or hostname.

Figure 5-35

Adding a network printer

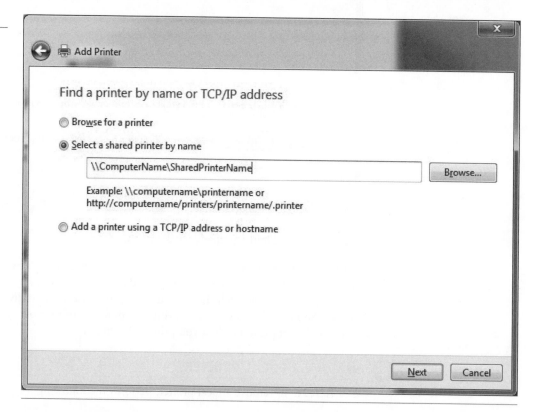

Some network printers on the market today use proprietary connectivity methods and can only be accessed by installing a driver that is supplied by the manufacturer.

Printing a Document

Figure 5-36 shows a document that is ready to be printed in Word 2010. You can access this page by clicking the File menu and then choosing Print. (You can alternately press Ctrl+P.)

The first option at the top of the page is the number of copies; the default is to print 1 copy but you can change this by typing a number or clicking the up and down arrows to increase or decrease the number.

The print device displays directly under the Printer heading. A status message indicates whether the printer is ready to print or not. If the printer is not ready to print, because

Figure 5-36

Printing a Word 2010 document

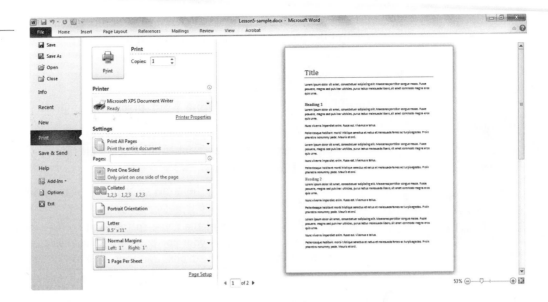

it's out of paper or offline, the status message indicates the problem so you can fix the issue before attempting to print. You can click the arrow to the right of the printer name and select a different printer if others are available.

The Settings section includes many print options:

- **Print All Pages:** The default setting prints the entire document; however, you can click the arrow at the right side of the option box and specify to print the current page or a custom page range. You can also use the Pages text box to print a range of pages. For example, if you have a 100-page document but want to print only pages 5 through 10, type 5-10 in the Pages text box.

- **Print One Sided:** The default is to print on one side of the paper. You can change the setting to manually print on both sides of the paper. Printers with built-in duplexers can print on both sides of the paper automatically.

- **Collated:** This setting applies to multiple copies of a document. It affects whether multiple copies are printed in order (one complete set, and then another, and so on) or all copies of page 1 first, and then all copies of page 2, and so on.

- **Orientation:** Select to print the document in portrait (upright) or landscape (lengthwise) format.

- **Size:** This option enables you to select the size of paper you are printing to. Letter 8.5 x 11 is the default for most printers.

- **Margins:** This setting enables you to change the document margins.

- **Pages Per Sheet:** This setting enables you to select the number of pages you want to print on one sheet of paper. You can typically choose from 1 to 16. The larger the number, the smaller the text will be on the printed page.

After making your selections, click the large Print button above the printer name to send the print job to the printer.

Understanding Print to File

You can also choose to print a document to a file rather than to a print device. Why? Let's say you need to send a Word file to a coworker but he doesn't have Word installed on his computer. He doesn't need to modify the file you send to him, he just needs to view the file's

CERTIFICATION READY
How do you print to a file?
5.3

contents. You can print the Word document to a file, which adds a .prn extension. When he receives the file, he can print the file to a printer.

 PRINT TO A FILE

GET READY. To print to a file from Word, perform the following steps:

1. Launch Word.
2. Open the document you want to print to a PRN file.
3. Select **File > Print.**
4. On the Print page, click the arrow to the right of the printer name and select **Print to File** at the bottom of the list.
5. Click **Print** at the top of the page. In the Print to file dialog box that displays, navigate to the location on your computer where you want to save the file, type a file name in the File name text box, and then click **OK.**

 PRINT A PRN FILE

GET READY. To print a PRN file to a local printer, perform the following steps:

1. Open a command prompt window by clicking **Start**, typing **cmd** in the **Search programs and files** search box, and then selecting **cmd.exe** from the resulting list.
2. Use the cd command to navigate to the location of the file. For example, if the file is named doc.prn and you saved it to the root of drive C, type **cd c:** and press **Enter** to execute the command.
3. Execute the following command to send the file to the directly connected printer: **copy /B doc.prn ***computername******printer_sharename*

   This command sends a binary (/B) copy of doc.prn to the device PRN, which is the system name for the default printer. A binary copy prevents anything in the file from changing during the process.

Understanding Print Queues

Some printers can accept multiple pages of data at one time but larger documents can take a while to print. You can think of a *print queue* as a holding area until the printer is finished printing the entire document. Consider a document that's over 200 pages in length. Most printers cannot actually print a job that large because they don't have enough memory to hold that many pages and print them at the same time. This is where printer queues come into play. Your print job is sent to a print queue, which stores it until the printer can accept it. The printer then prints page by page until the entire document has been printed.

 EXPLORE A PRINT QUEUE

GET READY. To explore a print queue, perform the following steps:

1. Click **Start > Devices and Printers.**
2. Double-click your printer. A page similar to Figure 5-37 displays. The printer information displayed on this screen includes:
   - The printer name
   - The printer's status (in this example the printer status = error)
   - The orientation of the printout (such as Letter)
   - The number of documents in the queue (3)

Figure 5-37

Viewing printer information

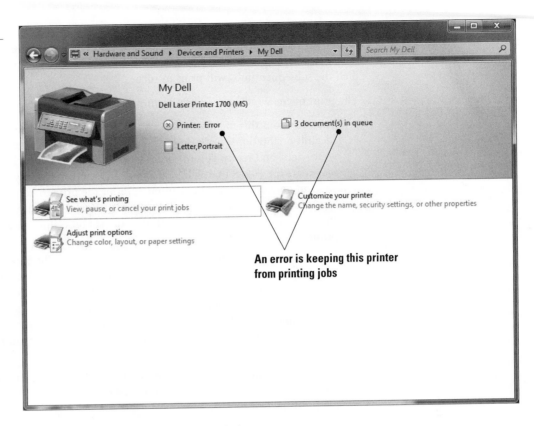

Other options on this page include:

- **See what's printing:** This is the actual print queue.
- **Adjust print options:** This includes changing color, layout, or paper settings.
- **Customize your printer:** This includes changing the printer name, security setting (who has permission to print to your printer), and other properties.

> **TAKE NOTE***
>
> For network printing, it's recommended that you configure the printer to send a separator page between print jobs. This helps users easily determine where their print job ended and the next one began. You must first create a page, such as in Word, and save it to your computer or the server. The page can be blank or have the word "Separator" on it, for example. Then double-click the printer in Devices and Printers, double-click *Customize your printer*, and in the Properties dialog box that displays, click the Advanced tab, click *Separator Page*, browse to select the separator page, and click OK.

3. To open the print queue, click **See what's printing**. Figure 5-38 shows the print queue. You can view the document name, status, owner (person who sent the print job), number of pages to be printed, size of the document, date and time submitted, and the port to which the print job was submitted.

Figure 5-38

The printer queue

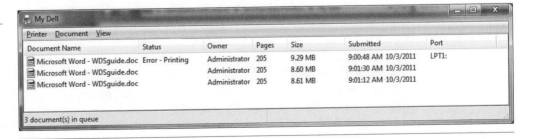

In this example, the first document in the print queue is in an error status. No other jobs can print until the error is resolved or the job is cancelled. If you have checked that your printer is turned on, has paper, and the ready lamp is lit, chances are you can get that job to print and then the subsequent jobs will print in turn.

The print queue window has three menus at the top: Printer, Document, and View:

- **Printer:** From this menu you can choose a default printer, set printing preferences (default orientation), print on both sides of paper, select page order, add a watermark to your pages, and set up color profiles so you can ensure that the colors you see on your screen are the colors that will be printed. Most printers today come with color profiles you can download from the manufacturer of the printer. You can also pause printing, cancel all documents (deletes all documents from the queue), share a printer (or stop sharing if it was previously shared), use the printer offline, and open the properties of the printer to make changes.

- **Document:** This menu is grayed out and thus cannot be accessed unless a document is highlighted. In the previous example, where the first print job has an error status, you could highlight that document and from the Document menu choose to restart the printing of the document or cancel the printing of the document. If you cancel the printing of the document, the next document in the queue begins printing. Other options from the Document folder include: pause, resume, and viewing properties of the document.

- **View:** This menu has two selections: Status Bar shows the number of documents in the queue on the status bar and Refresh refreshes the screen to show the most current view of the print queue.

Understanding Internet Printing

If you run Windows Server 2008 R2, you can create a Web site hosted by Internet Information Services (IIS) using the Internet Printing role service. Clients can then use a Web browser to connect and print to shared printers on the server using the Internet Printing Protocol (IPP). Users must have the Internet Printing Client installed on their computers to use IPP.

 INSTALL THE INTERNET PRINTING CLIENT

GET READY. To install the Internet Printing client, perform the following steps:

1. Click **Start > Control Panel > Programs**.
2. Under Programs and Features, click **Turn Windows features on or off**. Provide an administrative password or confirm to continue.
3. In the Windows Features dialog box, scroll down and expand the **Print and Document Services** option (see Figure 5-39).
4. Select the **Internet Printing Client** check box and then click **OK**.

You should restart the print queue at this point to ensure that print jobs reach the printer. Just restart the Print Spooler service in the Services console to clear the print queues. (You learned about services in Lesson 4.)

+ MORE INFORMATION

To learn more about printing in Windows 7 and installing printers, visit http://windows.microsoft.com/en-US/windows7/Getting-started-with-printing and http://windows.microsoft.com/en-US/windows7/Install-a-printer. You can get more details about Internet printing from http://technet.microsoft.com/en-us/library/cc731857.aspx

Figure 5-39

Expanding the Print and Document Services option

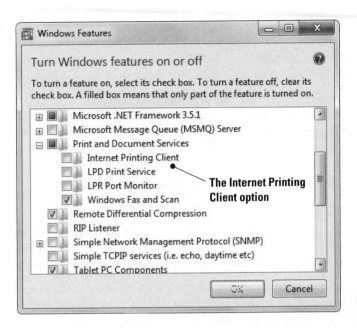

Understanding System Devices

THE BOTTOM LINE

A computer requires many different devices (such as video, audio, and input and output devices) to enable interactivity with a user. Although the Devices and Printers feature is used to manage printers and other peripherals in Windows 7, Device Manager is the main tool for managing other devices (such as internal components, pointing devices, and so on).

Today's computers have several external devices that you can connect and use. In this section, you'll learn about installing and connecting video, audio, and infrared input devices as well as how to update drivers and uninstall devices.

Understanding Video, Audio, and Input Devices

CERTIFICATION READY
What type of video devices does Windows 7 support?
5.4

The main *video device* on a computer is the video adapter or card. This is an internal circuit board that's either in the form of a physical card inserted into a slot on the motherboard or is manufactured as part of the motherboard. Other types of video devices include webcams, video capture cards, and TV tuners, to name a few.

CERTIFICATION READY
What type of audio devices does Windows 7 support?
5.4

The main *audio device* in a computer is a sound card. Like a video card or adapter, it is either in the form of a circuit board that's inserted into a motherboard slot or hard-wired into the motherboard. Additional audio devices include microphones, headsets, and speakers. Headsets are always external devices, but microphones and speakers can be either internal or external.

Input devices are items such as keyboards, mice, trackballs, touchpads, digital pens, and joysticks (for gaming). On desktop computers, input devices are almost always external devices that plug into different ports on the computer. On a laptop computer, keyboards and touchpads are built in, although you can connect external input devices as well.

CERTIFICATION READY
What type of infrared input devices does Windows 7 support?
5.4

Many external devices, such as headsets and input devices, connect to a computer using wireless technology. A wireless keyboard or mouse, for example, comes with a small Bluetooth receiver that you plug into a USB port on the computer. The mouse contains a

Bluetooth transmitter that communicates with the receiver. As you move the mouse around, it transmits signals using Bluetooth radio signals rather than a wire. If your computer already has Bluetooth technology built in, you may be able to set up Bluetooth to communicate directly with the external Bluetooth device without the need for the USB receiver.

Many wireless mice use *infrared technology* and are referred to as optical mice. These mice have an infrared light-emitting diode (LED) inside the mouse that detects the surface over which it is moved. This technology lets you use the mouse on a wider variety of surfaces compared to legacy trackball mice that required a mouse pad to operate.

Understanding Plug-and-Play Technology

Nearly all modern devices that you attach to a computer port are automatically detected by the operating system. This is part of *plug-and-play (PnP) technology*. As long as a PnP device is plugged into your computer and powered on (if the device requires power, like a printer), Windows detects the device and automatically installs the drivers.

The first time you connect a device, you should see a bubble message on the status bar that states *Installing device driver software*. When it installs the device driver successfully, you'll see *Your device is ready to use*. The device has now been added to Device Manager. You can unplug the device and plug it in again, but the device driver installs only one time.

Understanding Device Manager

You can manage most devices in the snap-in called *Device Manager*. Device Manager displays a list of all devices currently installed on the computer and their status. Not just anyone can make changes in Device Manager—you must be an administrator or have administrative credentials to offer when the UAC prompts for them.

 EXPLORE DEVICE MANAGER

GET READY. To explore Device Manager, perform the following steps:

1. Click **Start**, type **device man** in the **Search programs and files** search box, and then select **Device Manager** from the resulting list. (Alternately, click the **Start** button, right-click **Computer**, click **Manage**, and then lick the **Device Manager** node in the left pane.) Provide an administrative password or confirm to continue. The Device Manager page is shown in Figure 5-40.

2. The top line displays the name of the computer. Each of the nodes beneath are types of devices, such as battery, disk drive(s), display adapter, and so on. Within each device type are the various devices that are installed. To view the devices, expand the device type node (click the clear, right-facing triangle next to a node).

> **TAKE NOTE***
>
> If there is a problem with a device, you will see a node expanded and a device listed beneath it that contains either a yellow yield sign (warning there is something wrong with the device) or a red circle with a white X to show that a device is not working at all.

3. To refresh Device Manager, click the **Scan for hardware changes** icon on the toolbar. Device Manager scans the computer looking for new devices to install or to remove devices that have been uninstalled but still display in Device Manager.

Figure 5-40

The Device Manager page

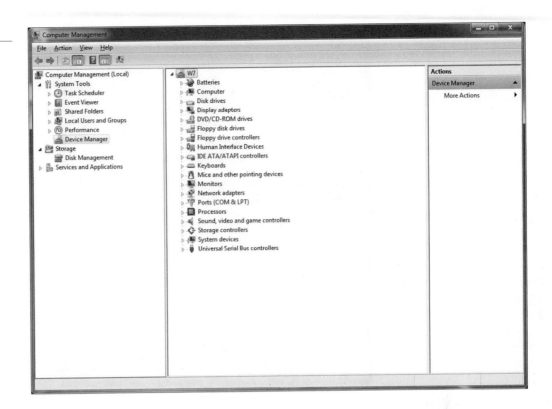

Let's look at an example of a newly added device. A Sennheiser headset was plugged into a computer named W7. The operating system detected the device and used PnP technology to automatically install the appropriate device driver. The device is ready to use. That means the headset is now listed in Device Manager, in the Sound, video and game controllers node. If you right-click the device (Sennheiser USB Headset) and select Properties, the options on the shortcut menu are as follows:

- **Update Driver Software:** This option enables you to instruct Windows to search the computer and Internet for an updated driver, or to walk through manual installation of an updated driver you have on CD or downloaded from the manufacturer's Web site.

- **Disable:** This option disables access to the device but leaves the driver installed.

- **Uninstall:** This option disables access to the device and removes the device driver.

- **Scan for hardware changes:** This option scans the computer, looking for new devices to display or missing devices to remove from Device Manager.

The last option is Properties. Clicking this option displays the Properties dialog box for the device. For example, Figure 5-41 displays the properties of the Sennheiser USB headset that was just added.

The Properties dialog box features three tabs:

- **General:** This tab displays the device type, manufacturer, and the device status. You should see *This device is working properly.* If the device status indicates a problem, the message typically provides some information as to the nature of the problem and how to resolve it.

- **Driver:** This tab displays the source of the driver (Microsoft or the manufacturer), the driver date, the driver version, and the digital signer. (Windows 7 64-bit versions require that all drivers are signed or they will not be installed.) See Figure 5-42.

Figure 5-41

The properties of a newly added device

Figure 5-42

The Driver tab

The Driver tab includes five buttons: Driver Details, Update Driver, Roll Back Driver, Disable, and Uninstall. Clicking each button results in the following:

- **Driver Details:** Shows the actual files installed by the driver and their paths (see Figure 5-43). Clicking each file displays the details of that file. For example, selecting

Figure 5-43

The Driver File Details dialog box

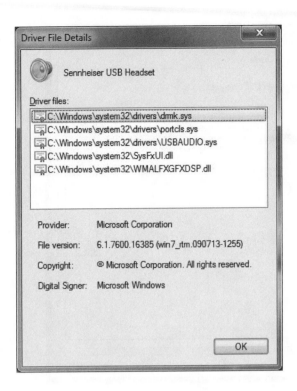

C:\Windows\system32\drivers\dmk.sys shows a file version of 6.1.7600.16385 (win7_rtm.090713-1255). This information is helpful during troubleshooting. Not only can a user tell someone who is helping to troubleshoot a device driver issue the version of the driver, but the user can also state the exact version of the files inside the driver.

- **Update Driver:** Opens the Update Driver Software dialog box where you can search automatically for updated driver software or browse the computer for driver software. You can update a driver from a CD or DVD, or locate a driver you downloaded from a manufacturer's Web site.

- **Roll Back Driver:** Allows you to roll back to a previous version of a driver. If this is the first driver you have installed for a device, this button will be grayed out and unselectable because there are no previous drivers to roll back to.

- **Disable:** Disables the device.

- **Uninstall:** Uninstalls the device driver.

- **Details:** Shown in Figure 5-44, this tab displays many properties of a device. Open the Device description drop-down list to display a long list of property details. Whichever property you choose displays its value in the Value text box. Figure 5-45 shows some of the many properties you can choose.

For example, choosing the property hardware IDs lists two values that identify this hardware. You usually have multiple hardware IDs to try to match between the physical device and a driver. The hardware ID begins with the most specific and moves to the most generic. For example, Figure 5-46 displays USB\VID_1395&PID_0002&REV_0004&MI_00, which may indicate that this is a Sennheiser USB headset driver for Windows 7. The USB\VID_1395&PID_0002&MI_00 hardware ID is a Sennheiser USB headset for any operating system.

Figure 5-44

The Details tab

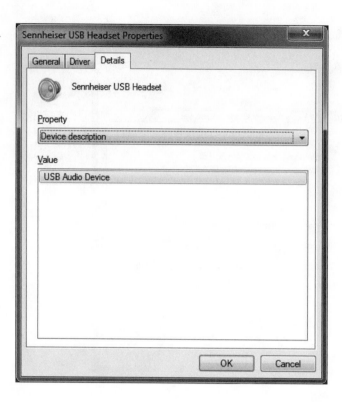

Figure 5-45

A list of properties

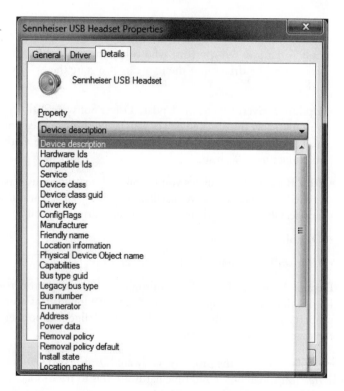

CERTIFICATION READY
How is third-party
software installed for
devices?
5.1

The hardware IDs and the compatible IDs are pieces of information in a driver that help the PnP device driver process identify the closest match between a physical device and the device driver. Regardless of which type of device you are installing or using—audio, video, printer, and so on—driver management is always the same.

Figure 5-46

Hardware IDs

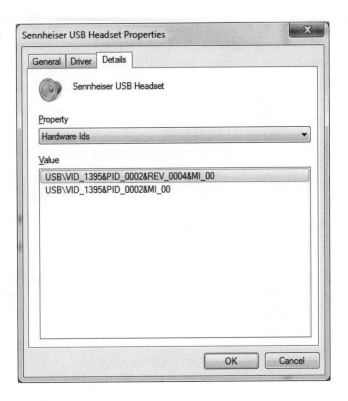

 INSTALL THIRD-PARTY SOFTWARE FOR A DEVICE

GET READY. To install third-party software for a device, perform the following steps:

1. Read the device manufacturer's instructions for installing device software. Connect the device before or after installation, as instructed.

2. Start the application's installation program.

   • If installing from a CD/DVD, insert the application's installation media into your computer's CD/DVD drive. The installer program should run automatically.

   • If installing an application you downloaded from the Web, or if the installer program doesn't start automatically when inserting a CD/DVD, open Windows Explorer, browse to the location of the application's installer program (such as **setup.exe**), and then double-click it.

3. Follow the prompts to install the application.

4. Restart Windows.

5. Test the device's functionality.

These steps are similar to installing any software application, as addressed in Lesson 4. During the installation, you might be prompted to accept a license agreement, select a location on your computer in which to install the software files, and perhaps enter a product ID or key.

 UPDATE A THIRD-PARTY DEVICE DRIVER IN DEVICE MANAGER

GET READY. To update a third-party device driver in Device Manager, perform the following steps:

1. Download the device's latest driver from the manufacturer's Web site and save it to your Downloads folder. For this exercise, you do not need to download the installation program, just the driver file.

2. Log on to the computer as the Administrator or with an account with administrative privileges.

3. Open Device Manager. (Click **Start**, type **device man** in the **Search programs and files** search box, and then select **Device Manager** from the resulting list.)

4. Expand the device type node of the device whose driver you want to update.

5. Right-click the device and select **Update Driver Software**.

6. In the Update Driver Software page that displays (see Figure 5-47), click **Browse my computer for driver software**.

Figure 5-47

The Update Driver Software page

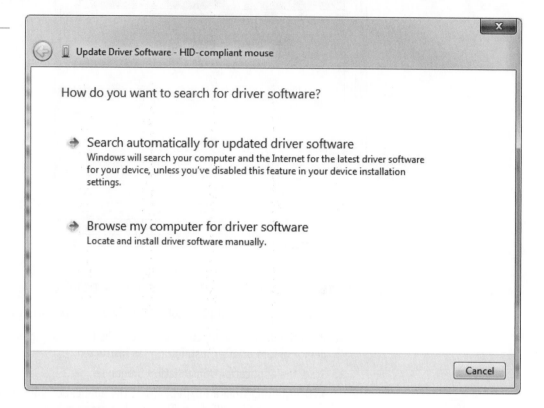

7. On the next screen, click **Let me pick from a list of device drivers on my computer**.

8. On the resulting page, click **Have Disk**.

9. In the **Copy manufacturer's files from** drop-down list, select the drive where the software is located (or click **Browse** to navigate to the location).

10. Click any INF file that displays in the file list and then click **Open**. (INF files are the only files that Device Manager accepts for setting up drivers.)

11. In the Install From Disk dialog box, click **OK**.

12. Select the newly added hardware in the text box and then click **Next**.

13. If a warning message displays regarding compatibility with your hardware, click **Yes** to continue. The Windows 7 Update Driver Software Wizard installs the updated drivers for your hardware.

14. Follow any additional instructions to complete the driver installation.

15. You may be prompted to restart your computer after driver installation is complete.

Much like when you install printers, when you're trying to decide which driver to install (Microsoft versus device manufacturer), it's usually best to choose the manufacturer's driver because it often contains software in addition to the drivers and some graphical user interface (GUI) tools that can help you manage devices at a more granular level. However, third-party manufacturers are increasingly providing their drivers to Microsoft to be part of Windows Update. This way, whenever a device driver is needed, it can be installed from Windows Update.

There are some pesky drivers out there that don't install easily. Some tips for troublesome drivers are:

1. When you first connect the device, if the driver does not install automatically, disconnect the device and reconnect it. If the device requires power, ensure the power is turned on.

2. If you connect a new device but it doesn't appear in Device Manager, click the *Scan for hardware changes* icon on the toolbar in Device Manager.

3. If you allowed the Microsoft driver to be installed for a device and you are not getting the full functionality of the device, such as a duplex printer with no option for duplexing, install the driver from the manufacturer.

➕ **MORE INFORMATION**

To learn more about Device Manager, visit http://windows.microsoft.com/en-US/windows7/products/features/device-management

SKILL SUMMARY

IN THIS LESSON, YOU LEARNED TO:

- The two primary types of disks are basic and dynamic.
- The tool that allows you to manage drives, disks, and partitions is Disk Management, found in the Computer Management snap-in.
- The two types of partitions styles are master boot record (MBR) and GUID partition table.
- The four main types of volumes are simple, spanned, striped, and mirrored, and you can easily distinguish them in Disk Management based on color coding.
- Windows 7 supports several types of storage: USB, IEEE 1394, network storage, and iSCSI.
- Windows Live SkyDrive, OneNote to SkyDrive, and Windows Live Mesh are cloud storage and services available to Windows users.
- Printing devices can be local or networked, or even available over the Internet. You can perform most printer support from the Devices and Printers applet. A print queue is a "holding area" in memory that holds prints jobs until the printer is finished printing the entire document.
- Device Manager helps you manage system devices such as audio, video, processors, and many more. Using Device Manager, you can add new devices, manage the drivers, determine when to use a Microsoft driver versus the manufacturer's driver, and get details on every file the driver installs.
- When you connect a Plug-and-Play (PnP) device to a computer, Windows detects the device and automatically installs the drivers.
- The main tool for managing non-printing devices in Windows 7 is Device Manager.

■ Knowledge Assessment

Fill in the Blank

Complete the following sentences by writing the correct word or words in the blanks provided.

1. There are two types of disks that are recognized by Windows 7: _____ and _____.

2. When creating spanned, striped, or mirrored volumes, you must allow for a _____ disk.

3. Spanned volumes are also referred to as _____ because the space on the first disk must be filled before data will be stored on the second and subsequent disks.

4. Spanned and _____ volumes must contain at least 2 disks and may contain up to 32.

5. _____ volume may only contain two disks.

6. When viewing your disks in the _____ snap-in you can easily tell the different types of volumes based on the color of the stripe over the volume.

7. The _____ storage device type is used to transfer data over local area networks (LANs), wide area networks (WANs), and even the Internet.

8. From within a Windows _____ you can pause printing, cancel all documents, and resume, or restart a document.

9. You can determine the version of files that a device driver installs and their complete paths by using _____.

10. _____ is a part of the Windows Live Essentials suite and enables you to keep data synchronized between computers and some mobile devices.

Multiple Choice

Circle the letter that corresponds to the best answer.

1. Which of the following can you create on a dynamic drive? (Choose all that apply.)
   a. Striped partition
   b. Striped volume
   c. Simple volume
   d. Spanned volume
   e. Mirrored partitions
   f. Striped partitions

2. Which Microsoft cloud storage solution requires software to be installed on the client computer?
   a. Windows Live SkyDrive
   b. Windows Live Mesh
   c. OneNote to SkyDrive
   d. Hotmail

3. After creating a document on Windows Live SkyDrive, which of the following is the easiest way to let someone know a new document is available?
   a. Call them on the phone and tell them, leave a message if not there
   b. Send them a document with the link embedded
   c. Share the document or folder
   d. Sync your computer with their computer

4. Which of the following is a feature that Windows Live Mesh offers that Windows SkyDrive does not?
   a. The ability to sign in using your Live Windows Logon ID
   b. 200 GB of free space
   c. Remote control of another machine
   d. The ability to share folders and documents with others

5. Which of the following is *not* a quick-start icon in Windows Live SkyDrive?
   a. Word
   b. Excel
   c. Outloook
   d. OneNote

6. Which of the following is used to quickly determine if a device had a bad device driver?
   a. Disk Manager
   b. Device Manager
   c. Driver Manager
   d. Control Panel

7. Which of the following can you synchronize using Windows Live Mesh? (Choose all that apply.)
   a. Folders on different computers
   b. Files on cell phones
   c. Internet Explorer favorites
   d. Microsoft Office settings

8. Which of the following requires its own power connector?
   a. eSATA
   b. USB
   c. FireWire
   d. USB 2.0

9. Which of the following stores an exact copy of data from the first member of the volume to the second member?
   a. Simple
   b. Spanned
   c. Striped
   d. Mirrored

10. Which of the following tasks can be completed with Device Manager?
    a. Update a driver's software
    b. Disable a driver
    c. Uninstall a driver
    d. Change a device's hardware ID
    e. Scan for hardware changes

True / False

Circle T if the statement is true or F if the statement is false.

T | F 1. Windows Live Mesh allows you to remote control machines that do not have the Windows Live Mesh software installed.

T | F 2. After you have created volumes and users have stored data on those volumes, you can easily change your partition style from MBR to GPT and back again with no difficulties.

T | F 3. When you add a new disk to a computer and open the Disk Management utility, you are automatically prompted to initialize the disk.

T | F 4. A GPT partition style is used for larger hard drives of up to 9.4 zeta bytes.

T | F 5. When creating mirrored volumes, you can use more disk space from one disk than the other.

■ Competency Assessment

Scenario 5-1: Ensuring Availability

Sheila, a programmer in your company, is developing an application for an important client. Her computer runs Windows 7, and she has a second disk installed that is currently not being used. What are some things you can do to ensure that her system is highly available?

Scenario 5-2: Troubleshooting a Printer Driver

Axel runs the warehouse for Mighty Bubbles Beer Distributor. He called you to report that the new wireless laser jet printer he recently purchased does not work. He connected it to the USB port on his computer running Windows 7 Professional and turned on the printer, but the printer does not appear in the Devices and Printers window. How should you advise Axel to help troubleshoot the problem?

■ Proficiency Assessment

Scenario 5-3: Providing Redundancy on a Client Computer

You provide support for a commercial bioengineering lab. Mizuki is a chemist at the lab, and she recently inherited a computer from the IT department that has two large hard disks and runs Windows 7 Ultimate. One hard disk provides ample disk space for her programs and data files, but she would like to use the other disk for redundancy to better protect her system and files. What should you do to provide the redundancy on her client computer?

Scenario 5-4: Using Cloud Services

The sales and marketing department at Fat Tire Bikes consists of two salespeople, a graphic designer, a copywriter, and a layout person.

Tonya and Aaron are the salespeople. Tonya is responsible for the western United States and Aaron covers the eastern United States. They tend to use the same files for all sales presentations, client follow-ups, and so on. When one modifies a template, it's important that the other gets the updated file as soon as possible.

The marketing employees share several Word documents and PowerPoint presentations, in addition to a large folder of graphical images. It's important for them to have shared access to a Marketing folder that contains the shared files.

What should you do to help the sales and marketing employees work more efficiently?

Understanding File and Print Sharing

EXAM OBJECTIVE MATRIX

SKILLS/CONCEPTS	EXAM OBJECTIVE DESCRIPTION	EXAM OBJECTIVE NUMBER
Understanding File and Printer Sharing Basics		
Understanding HomeGroup	Understand file and print sharing.	4.2
Creating Public, Basic, and Advanced Shares	Understand file and print sharing.	4.2
Mapping Drives	Understand file and print sharing.	4.2
Understanding Permissions	Understand file and print sharing.	4.2
Setting Up Printer Sharing	Understand file and print sharing.	4.2
Troubleshooting Printers		

KEY TERMS

advanced sharing

basic sharing

effective permissions

HomeGroup

inherit

mapping a drive

network discovery

network location

NTFS permissions

permissions

printer driver

printer sharing

Public folder

share permissions

troubleshooter

workgroup

As the IT technician at Interstate Snacks, Inc., you've been asked to set up file and printer sharing for all of the computers at a remote warehouse. The employees there do not need constant access to the network at the main Interstate facility. All of the computers at the remote location are running Windows 7 Professional. There are two printers in the warehouse; one is attached to the supervisor's computer, the other is attached to a computer in the middle of the warehouse that all employees use to print pallet labels for outgoing shipments. Some folders on the supervisor's computer contain confidential files that need to be protected from access by other employees.

■ Understanding File and Printer Sharing Basics

 THE BOTTOM LINE Windows 7 provides many ways to share files or printers on a network. The first step is to ensure that file and print sharing is turned on in the advanced sharing settings in Network and Sharing Center. Some networking methods, such as HomeGroup, also require that your network location be set to Home network.

Microsoft offers several ways for Windows 7 users to share resources such as files and printers, either on the same computer (between accounts) or on a network, without the need for a server. For example, you can share files from any folder on your computer by setting up basic or advanced sharing, or by moving files to the Public folder. Another method is by using HomeGroup, the networking feature that's built into Windows 7.

To share files and printers with users on other computers, you need to have a wired or wireless network set up. In a typical wired environment, each computer has a network adapter that is connected to other computers and a hub, switch, or router with Ethernet cables. Wireless networks are easier to set up and maintain. Each computer's wireless network adapter connects "over the air" to a router or wireless access point within range.

Windows 7 offers three broad categories of network locations: Home, Work, and Public (see Figure 6-1). A *network location* is a collection of security settings that's appropriate for the type of network you want to connect to.

Figure 6-1

Network locations in Windows 7

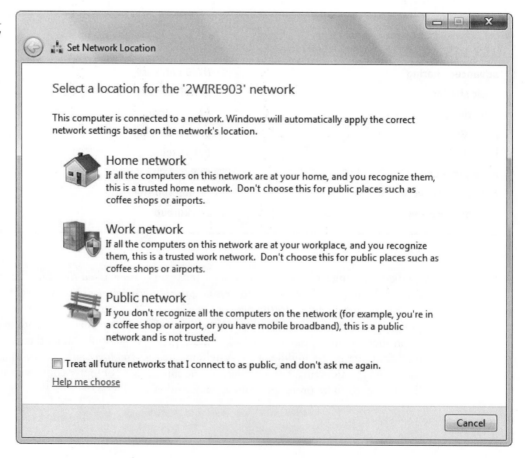

For example, the Home network location is the most trusting and is conducive to file and printer sharing—network discovery is turned on by default. The Work network location also has network discovery turned on but provides stricter security than Home. For example, you can't join a homegroup using the Work network location. The Public network location is used when you connect to public networks, like those offered at airports and libraries. Network discovery is turned off by default so other users can't see your computer. Public networks may be convenient but they are notoriously unsafe, so the Public network location is designed to help protect your computer against unauthorized access and malicious software.

TAKE NOTE *Network discovery* is a Windows feature that enables your computer to find other computers and devices (such as printers on a connected network). It also lets you control whether other computers can see your computer on the same network.

Whether wired or wireless, you must turn on file and printer sharing on each computer that will share files and/or printers. To do so, click the network icon in the notification area of the task bar and then click Open Network and Sharing Center. In the task pane on the left, click the *Change advanced sharing settings* link. Click the down arrow to the right of Home or Work. The advanced sharing settings are shown in Figure 6-2.

Figure 6-2

Advanced sharing settings in Windows 7

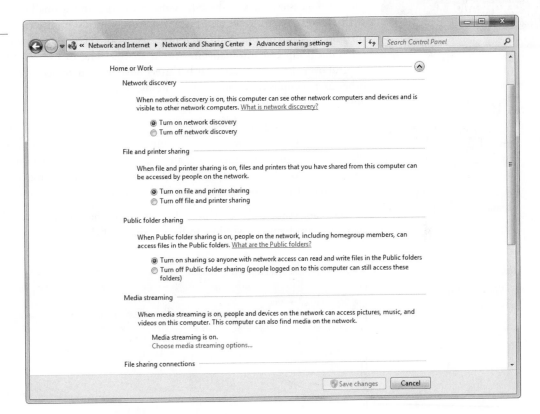

Notice that network discovery, file and printer sharing, and Public folder sharing are all turned on. These settings allow you the maximum flexibility for sharing files in a small office/home office environment.

Finally, if your network includes a mix of computers running Windows 7 and Windows Vista or Windows XP, and you want to share files between the computers, you should use a workgroup. A *workgroup* is a logical grouping of networked computers that can "see" each other on a network. You're prompted to set up a workgroup when installing Windows, and many computers are set up to be a part of a workgroup named WORKGROUP by default. To see if your computer is part of a workgroup, click Start, right-click Computer, and then click Properties. Scroll down to the Computer name, domain, and workgroup settings section. The workgroup name is displayed there.

The following sections walk you through your file and printer sharing options in Windows 7.

➕ MORE INFORMATION

To learn how to set up a small office/home office network, visit http://windows.microsoft.com/en-US/windows7/What-you-need-to-set-up-a-home-network. For more information on workgroups, see http://windows.microsoft.com/en-US/windows7/Networking-home-computers-running-different-versions-of-Windows

■ Understanding HomeGroup

⬇ THE BOTTOM LINE

HomeGroup is a new feature in Windows 7 that greatly simplifies file and printer sharing on small office/home office networks. Using HomeGroup, you can share libraries and printers, but you don't have a lot of control over which users may share the items.

CERTIFICATION READY
What is a HomeGroup?
4.2

One of the easiest ways to share files and printers across a small office/home office network is with *HomeGroup*, the file and printer sharing solution built into Windows 7. Once you set up a homegroup on one computer, other networked computers running Windows 7 can join the homegroup and automatically see the shared libraries and printers. You also have some control over the level of access other users have to your shared items. You can choose to let other users simply view and use your items, or configure settings for modifying, deleting, and adding items to your shared libraries.

TAKE NOTE ✱

"HomeGroup" is the name of the Windows 7 feature. You set up a "homegroup" that other computers connect to for sharing files and printers.

Computers that are members of a homegroup display in the navigation pane in the Homegroup section of Windows Explorer. Just click the name of the computer whose files you want to access, then navigate to the folder or file as you normally do in Windows Explorer. If you don't see a computer that's a member of a homegroup in the navigation pane, the computer might be powered off, in sleep mode, or hibernating.

You can also see at a glance which libraries you're sharing. The Details pane at the bottom of the Windows Explorer window indicates Shared if the library is shared (see Figure 6-3).

Figure 6-3

The Windows Explorer Details pane indicates shared libraries

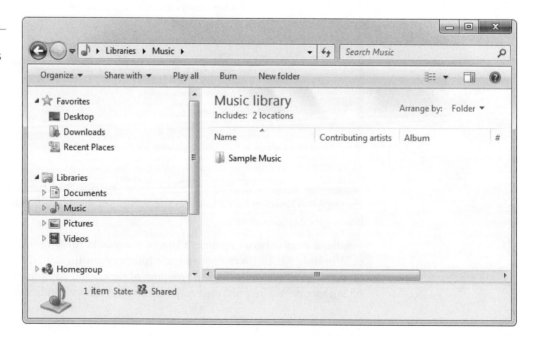

Although HomeGroup is easy to set up and use, there are a few caveats:

- In Windows 7 Home Basic and Starter editions, you can only join a homegroup—you cannot create one.
- You can join only one homegroup at a time. If your computer is already joined to a homegroup, you must leave that homegroup to join another.
- You can't limit access to shared items to individual users. Anyone using a computer that's a member of the homegroup can access the shared content.
- Non-Windows 7 computers (such as those running Windows Vista, Windows XP, Mac OS, or Linux) require additional setup steps in order to access shared items in the homegroup.
- You must already have a network set up (either wired or wireless).
- To create or join a homegroup, your computer's network location must be set to "Home network" (in the Network and Sharing Center).
- Do you use your laptop computer at work? If the computer connects as part of a domain at work, you can still join it to a homegroup at home. You'll be able to use folders and printers shared by other computers in the homegroup, but you won't be able to share any of your computer's folders with the group for security purposes.

HomeGroup makes networking a snap for even new computer users. However, as with most technology, things can go wrong. If you run into any problems using HomeGroup, Microsoft provides a HomeGroup troubleshooter that steps you through the troubleshooting process.

CREATE A HOMEGROUP

GET READY. To create a homegroup, perform the following steps:

1. Ensure that your network setting is set to Home.
2. Click the network icon in the notification area of the taskbar, and then click **Open Network and Sharing Center.** The Network and Sharing Center window indicates the current network location (see Figure 6-4). If network location is set to Work network,

Figure 6-4

The Network and Sharing Center

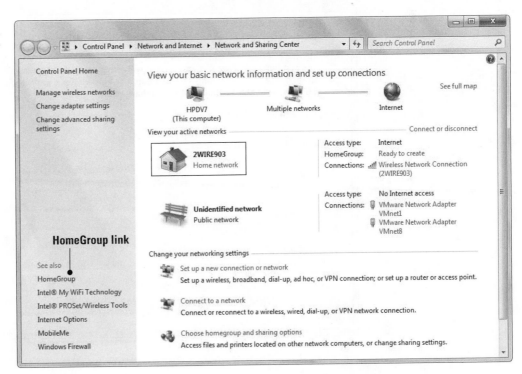

click the link. In the Network Locations window that displays, click **Home network**
and then click **Close**.

3. From the Network and Sharing Center window, click **HomeGroup** in the task pane
(left pane).

4. In the next window, click **Create a homegroup** (see Figure 6-5). The Create a
Homegroup Wizard starts.

Figure 6-5

Starting the Create a
Homegroup Wizard

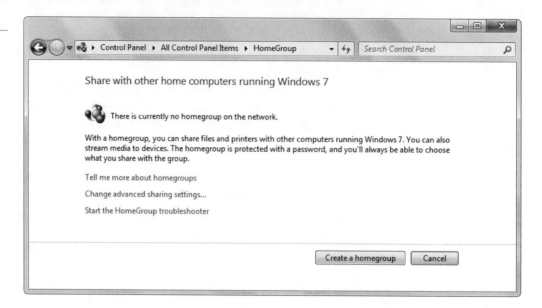

5. Select what you want to share with other members of the homegroup (see Figure 6-6).
You can change your selections later if you decide to discontinue sharing one or more
items. Click **Next**.

Figure 6-6

Selecting items to share

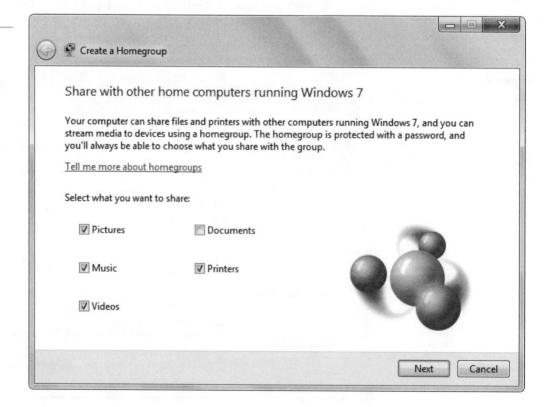

6. Windows 7 creates the homegroup settings and then displays a password (see Figure 6-7). Write down the number or click the **Print password and instructions** link to print it; you'll need the password when joining other computers to the homegroup.

Figure 6-7

The homegroup password displays

Create a Homegroup

Use this password to add other computers to your homegroup

Before you can access files and printers located on other computers, add those computers to your homegroup. You'll need the following password.

Write down this password:

5WV49PA1M7

Print password and instructions

If you ever forget your homegroup password, you can view or change it by opening HomeGroup in Control Panel.

How can other computers join my homegroup?

Finish

TAKE NOTE *

Uppercase and lowercase matter in the homegroup password. Be sure to enter the exact password as shown when joining computers to the homegroup.

7. Click **Finish** to complete the process.

The HomeGroup window now shows that your computer belongs to a homegroup and displays the items that are shared (see Figure 6-8). This window also includes links to additional

Figure 6-8

The HomeGroup window confirms that a homegroup was created

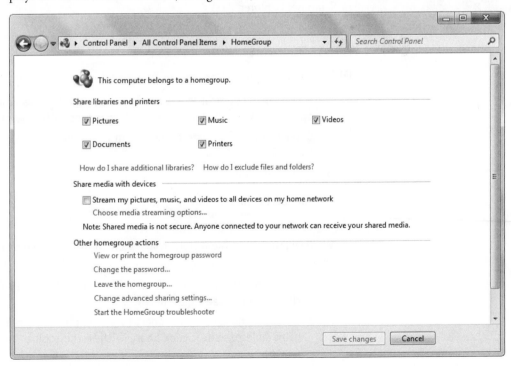

Control Panel ▸ All Control Panel Items ▸ HomeGroup   Search Control Panel

This computer belongs to a homegroup.

Share libraries and printers

☑ Pictures   ☑ Music   ☑ Videos

☑ Documents   ☑ Printers

How do I share additional libraries?   How do I exclude files and folders?

Share media with devices

☐ Stream my pictures, music, and videos to all devices on my home network
   Choose media streaming options...
   Note: Shared media is not secure. Anyone connected to your network can receive your shared media.

Other homegroup actions

   View or print the homegroup password
   Change the password...
   Leave the homegroup...
   Change advanced sharing settings...
   Start the HomeGroup troubleshooter

Save changes   Cancel

actions you can take with HomeGroup, such as viewing or changing the homegroup's password, leaving the homegroup, and troubleshooting the homegroup's connectivity.

You can close the HomeGroup window if you like. Now that you've set up a homegroup, you will learn how to go to another Windows 7 computer to join it to the homegroup.

 JOIN A HOMEGROUP

GET READY. To join a computer to a homegroup, perform the following steps:

1. Log on to another Windows 7 computer on the network and ensure that the network location is set to Home in the Network and Sharing Center. (Refer to Step 1 in the "Create a Homegroup" section of this lesson if you need help.)

2. Click **Start > Control Panel.** In the Network and Internet section, click the **Choose homegroup and sharing options** link and then click **Join now.**

3. Select the types of files that this computer user wants to share with the rest of the homegroup. Click **Next.**

4. Type the homegroup password and click **Next.**

 TAKE NOTE * If you don't know the homegroup password, go to a computer that's already a member of the homegroup and then click Start > Control Panel > Choose homegroup and sharing options > View or print the homegroup password.

X REF

Recall from Lesson 3 that you can stream media files across a network using HomeGroup.

5. Click **Finish.**

Repeat these steps on all other Windows 7 computers that you want to join to the homegroup. Each user can decide which item, if any, she wants to share with the homegroup. If a user doesn't share items, her user name will not display in the Homegroup listing (left pane) in Windows Explorer.

 CONTROL HOMEGROUP ACCESS

GET READY. To control homegroup access, perform the following steps:

1. Click **Start > Control Panel** and then click the **Choose homegroup and sharing options** link in the Network and Internet section to open the HomeGroup window.

2. Deselect the appropriate check box in the Share libraries and printers section (see Figure 6-9).

3. Click **Save changes.**

To exclude specific files or folders within a library:

1. Open Windows Explorer.

2. Navigate to the file or folder you want to exclude from sharing and select it.

3. Do one of the following:

   • To prevent access to the file or folder, click **Share with** in the toolbar and then click **Nobody** (see Figure 6-10).

   • To restrict homegroup members to viewing a shared file or folder (rather than being able to write), click **Share with** in the toolbar and then click **HomeGroup (Read).**

Figure 6-9

Uncheck a library check box to prevent sharing

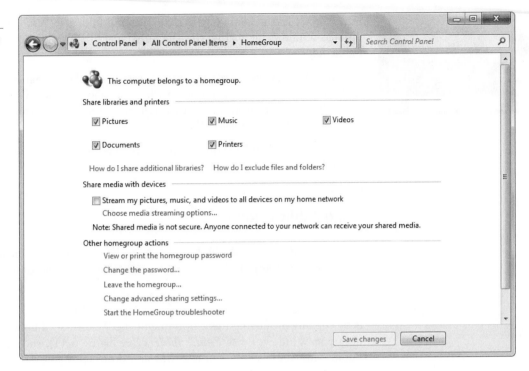

Figure 6-10

The Share with menu

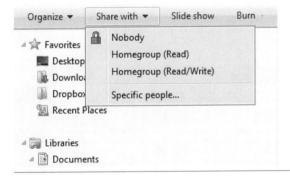

➕ **MORE INFORMATION**

For more information about Windows 7 HomeGroup, visit http://windows.microsoft.com/en-US/windows7/products/features/homegroup, http://windows.microsoft.com/en-US/windows7/help/home-sweet-homegroup-networking-the-easy-way, and http://technet.microsoft.com/en-us/library/ee449408(WS.10).aspx. You can learn more about file sharing in Windows at http://windows.microsoft.com/en-US/windows7/File-sharing-essentials. If you need help connecting non-Windows 7 computers to a homegroup, visit http://windows.microsoft.com/en-us/windows7/help/sharing-files-and-printers-with-different-versions-of-windows

■ Creating Public, Basic, and Advanced Shares

THE BOTTOM LINE

Windows 7 provides Public folders and traditional file sharing capabilities to meet your networking needs. Public folders are a quick-and-easy way to share files with network users and with other users on your computer. Basic and advanced sharing allow you to control who may access specific files and folders located in your libraries. Advanced sharing offers the most options and is therefore the best choice for protecting confidential information.

HomeGroup isn't the only way to share files and folders in Windows 7. You can also use traditional Windows file sharing to share individual files or folders, or move files or folders to a Public folder.

Traditional Windows file sharing offers greater control over sharing with Public folders. In traditional file sharing, depending on who you choose to share files or folder with, you can generally apply permissions to restrict users to simply viewing (reading) files as well as allow them to modify and/or delete files.

Let's look at Public folders first, since this method is the most convenient of the two methods.

Using Public Folders

If you need to share files with other users who have accounts on your computer or with users on a network, Public folders is a convenient drag-and-drop method.

Perhaps the easiest way to quickly share files and folders with other users on a network is by copying or moving them into one of the Windows 7 Public folders. Each default library in Windows 7 has *Public folders* (see Figure 6-11), such as Public Documents, Public Music, and so on. You just drag and drop items you want to share into the appropriate Public folder. Other users on your computer or on your network can use Windows Explorer to navigate to the files, and then open the files just as if the files were on their own computers.

Figure 6-11

Libraries expanded to show Public folders in Navigation pane

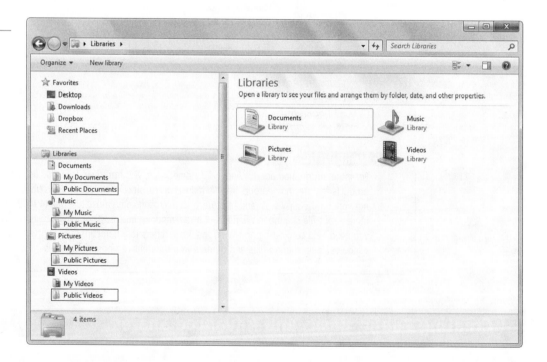

One consideration is that if you simply copy a file to a Public folder to share with someone, you have two instances of that file on your computer. If you want to change the file, you must change it in one place and copy it to the other to keep both versions current. For example, you're working on a spreadsheet named Projects.xlsx in your My Documents folder. You copy it to the Public Documents folder so a co-worker can also view it. When you update Projects.xlsx in My Documents, you also need to save it again or copy the new version to Public Documents. For this reason, if you want to share the most current version of a file at all times using Public folders, you should move the file to the Public folder rather than try to maintain two versions.

Public folders are all about convenience, but they don't offer a lot of control. For example, you can't limit which files or folders are shared in a Public folder—everything is shared. Plus, anyone with network access can read and write files in the Public folders.

Public folder sharing in Windows 7 is turned off by default (except on a homegroup). When Public folder sharing is turned on, anyone on your computer or network can access these folders. When Public folder sharing is turned off, only people with a user account and password on your computer have access. In addition, Windows offers a password-protected sharing feature that you can use to limit Public folder access to people with a user account and password on your computer.

 TURN PUBLIC FOLDER SHARING ON OR OFF

GET READY. To turn Public folder sharing on or off, perform the following steps:

1. Click any Public folder, click the **Share with** menu on the toolbar, and then click **Advanced sharing settings** (see Figure 6-12).

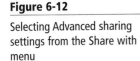

Figure 6-12

Selecting Advanced sharing settings from the Share with menu

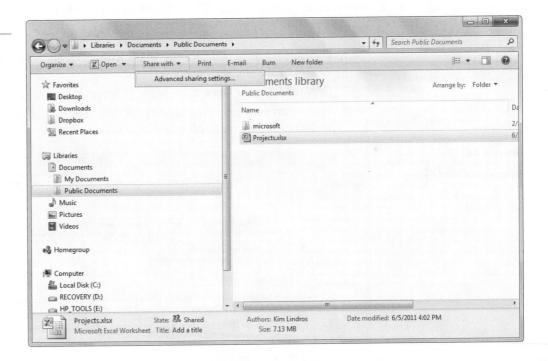

2. Click the **Home or Work** down arrow to access the profile settings.
3. In the **Public folder sharing** section, select an option to turn sharing on or off. Figure 6-13 shows the option selected to turn sharing on.
4. Click **Save changes** at the bottom of the Advanced sharing settings window. If you're prompted for an administrator password or confirmation, type the password or provide confirmation.

Figure 6-13

Public folder sharing options

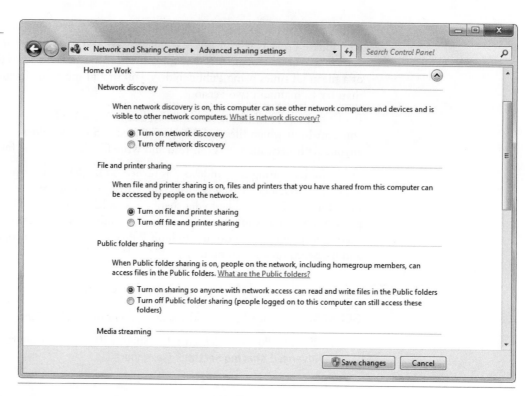

TURN PASSWORD-PROTECTED SHARING ON OR OFF

GET READY. To turn password-protected sharing on or off, perform the following steps:

1. Click any Public folder, click the **Share with** menu on the toolbar, and then click **Advanced sharing settings**.

2. Click the **Home or Work** down arrow to access the profile settings.

3. In the **Password protected sharing** section, select an option to turn password-protected sharing on or off (see Figure 6-14).

Figure 6-14

Password protected sharing options

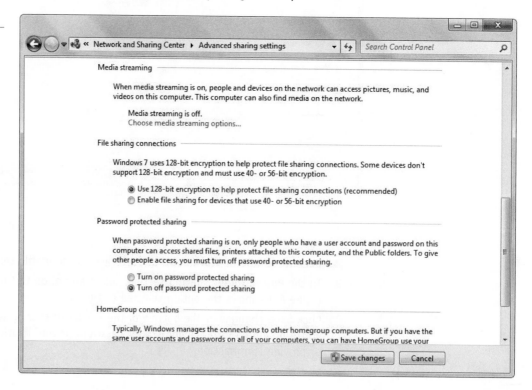

4. At the bottom of the Advanced sharing settings window, click **Save changes**. If you're prompted for an administrator password or confirmation, type the password or provide confirmation.

Remember, by turning on password-protected sharing in Control Panel, you can limit Public folder access to people with a user account and password on your computer.

➕ MORE INFORMATION

You can learn more about file sharing in Windows 7 at http://windows.microsoft.com/en-US/windows7/File-sharing-essentials and http://windows.microsoft.com/en-US/windows7/Share-files-with-someone. For specific information about sharing files with the Public folder, go to http://windows.microsoft.com/en-US/windows-vista/Sharing-files-with-the-Public-folder

---

Using Basic and Advanced Shares

If you need more control over who has access to your shared files and folders, use Windows basic or advanced sharing.

HomeGroup and Public folders are easy, convenient methods of sharing files with other users. However, we often store confidential information on our computer drives that must remain protected from some or all other users. HomeGroup allows you to share entire libraries, which includes those confidential files if they're stored in your My Documents folder. Public folders give you more control over what is shared—you copy or move files to a Public folder to make them available to other users. However, what if you want to leave a document or folder in place (that is, not transfer it to a Public folder) and still share it with others but without sharing other files and folders in the same library?

Traditional Windows file sharing allows you to restrict access to shared specific files and folders, and choose which users have access. **Basic sharing** allows you to share a file or folder with a specific user and restrict the user to Read or Read/Write actions. **Advanced sharing** offers the greatest amount of control; you can:

- Share files, folders, or an entire drive
- Choose users or groups with which to share files and folders
- Limit the number of users who may use a file or folder at the same time, mainly for security purposes
- Set permissions on shared files and folders, such as allowing users Read, Change, or Full Control
- Choose which files are available to users offline

TAKE NOTE*

You'll learn about permissions later in this lesson.

To set up basic or advanced shares, you must make sure file sharing and network discovery are turned on. A best practice is to also turn on password-protected sharing for security purposes.

➡ SET UP A BASIC SHARE

GET READY. To set up a basic share for a specific user, perform the following steps:

1. In Windows Explorer, navigate to the file or folder you want to share. This exercise assumes you are not working with Public folders.

2. Right-click the file or folder, select **Properties**, click the **Sharing** tab in the Properties dialog box (see Figure 6-15), and then click the **Share** button. Alternately, right-click the file or folder, click **Share with**, and then click **Specific people**.

Figure 6-15

The Sharing tab in the
Properties dialog box

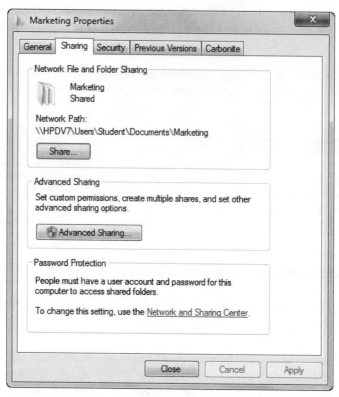

3. The File Sharing Wizard starts. Click the arrow next to the text box, click a name from the list, and then click **Add** (see Figure 6-16). Alternately, if you know the user name of the person you want to add, type it in the text box and click **Add**.

Figure 6-16

The File Sharing Wizard

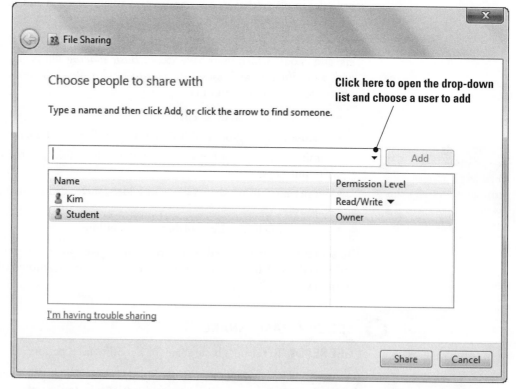

4. In the **Permission Level** column, click the down arrow for the new user and select **Read** or **Read/Write** (see Figure 6-17). Read allows the user to open and view items but not make changes or delete them. Read/Write allows users to open, modify, and delete items. You can also remove the user by clicking **Remove**.

5. When you're finished, click **Share**. If you're prompted for an administrator password or confirmation, type the password or provide confirmation.

Figure 6-17

Selecting permissions

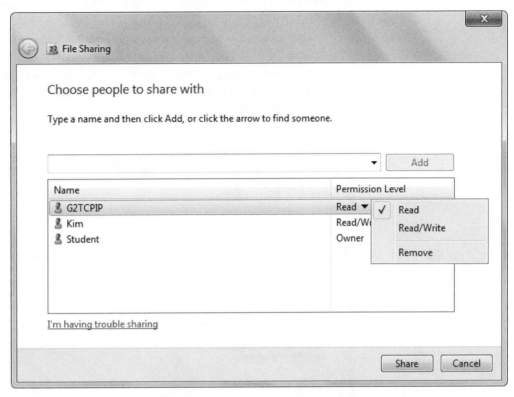

6. After you set up a basic share for a user, Windows lets you send a confirmation to that user via e-mail, or you can copy and paste a link to the shared item and send it to the user via e-mail or instant messaging, for example. (See Figure 6-18.)

7. When you're finished, click **Done**.

Figure 6-18

Notification options after setting up a basic share

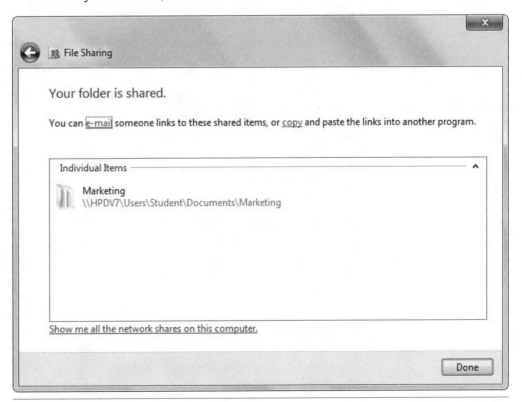

SET UP AN ADVANCED SHARE

GET READY. To set up an advanced share, perform the following steps:

1. In Windows Explorer, navigate to the file, folder, or drive you want to share. This exercise assumes you are not working with Public folders.

2. Right-click the item to be shared, select **Properties**, click the **Sharing** tab in the Properties dialog box (see Figure 6-19), and then click the **Advanced Sharing** button. If you're prompted for an administrator password or confirmation, type the password or provide confirmation.

Figure 6-19

The Sharing tab in the Properties dialog box

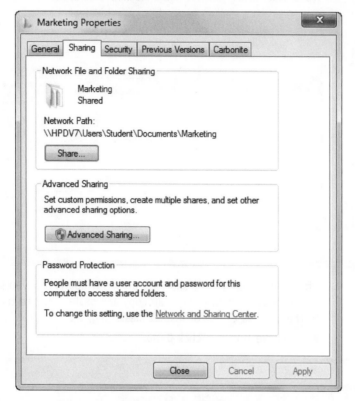

3. In the Advanced Sharing dialog box, select the **Share this folder** check box (see Figure 6-20).

Figure 6-20

The Advanced Sharing dialog box

4. Use the **Limit the number of simultaneous users to** spin box to select the number of users who may access the item simultaneously.

5. In the **Comments** text box, type a description of the shared item (if desired). See Figure 6-21.

Figure 6-21

The Advanced Sharing dialog box with information added

6. To specify users or groups, or change permissions, click the **Permissions** button. The Permissions dialog box displays (see Figure 6-22).

Figure 6-22

The Permissions dialog box

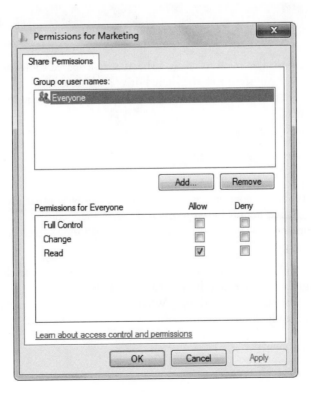

7. Click **Add** to add a user or group. (You can also click **Remove** to remove a user or group from the share.) The Select Users or Groups dialog box displays (see Figure 6-23).

Figure 6-23

The Select Users or Groups dialog box

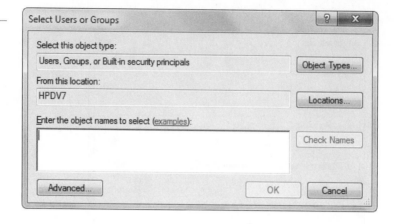

8. Type a user or group name in the text box or click **Locations** to find a user or group to add. When you're finished, click **OK**.

9. In the Permissions dialog box, select a user or group, select the check boxes for the permissions you want to assign, and then click **OK**.

10. When you're finished, click **OK** to close the Advanced Sharing dialog box.

Now your selected user or group can share your file, folder, or drive. You'll learn more about permissions later in this lesson.

Mapping Drives

THE BOTTOM LINE

Drive mapping allows you to create a shortcut to a shared folder across a network. Instead of finding and connecting to the shared drive each time you log on, you can create a mapped drive that is available at all times. Just double-click the mapped drive to access the shared folder.

CERTIFICATION READY
What is a mapped drive?
4.2

Once you share a folder or drive on your computer with other users, an easy way for them to get to the shared item is by *mapping a drive*. A mapped drive is a shortcut to a shared folder or drive on another computer across a network. Windows Explorer makes this process easy and straightforward.

By default in Windows 7, network drive letters start from the back of the alphabet (Z: is the first default drive letter that displays) and work down, so as not to interfere with local drives (which start with A: and work up). When mapping a drive, you can select any drive letter that's not already in use.

A mapped network drive is displayed in Windows Explorer under Computer in the navigation pane.

 MAP A DRIVE

GET READY. To assign a drive letter to a shared folder on the network, perform the following steps:

1. Open Windows Explorer.
2. Press the **Alt** key to display the Explorer menu bar (see Figure 6-24).

Figure 6-24

The Explorer menu bar displays near the top of the Windows Explorer window after pressing the Alt key

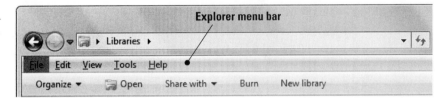

3. Click the **Tools** menu (see Figure 6-25) and then choose **Map network drive**.

Figure 6-25

Selecting the Map network drive command

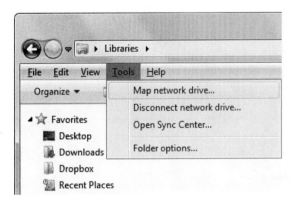

4. The Map Network Drive Wizard starts. In the drop-down menu, select a drive letter of your choice (see Figure 6-26).
5. Click **Browse** and then navigate to the shared folder you want to map to (see Figure 6-27). Alternately, type the Universal Naming Convention (UNC) path of the folder. A UNC is a naming format that specifies the location of a resource on a local area network. The UNC format is *computername**sharename**filepath*. The *computername* and *sharename* variables refer to the computer or server on which the folder resides. The *filepath* variable is the name of the folder you're mapping.
6. Select the shared folder and then click **OK**.

Figure 6-26

Selecting a drive letter from
the drop-down list

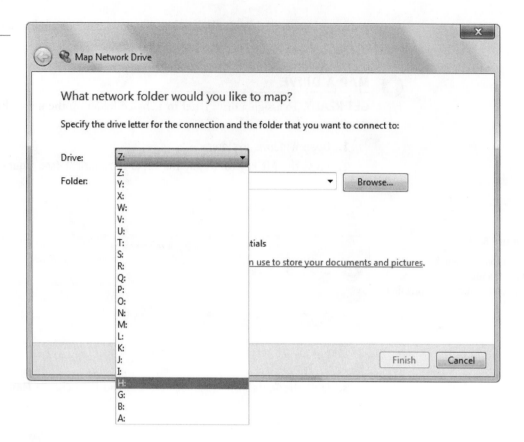

Figure 6-27

Browsing for a drive or folder
to map to

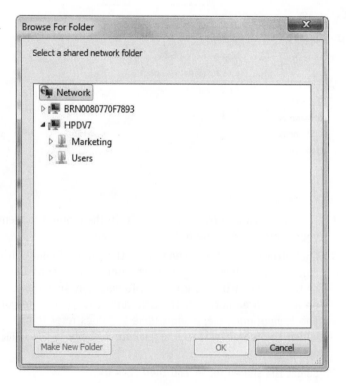

7. By default the **Reconnect at logon** check box is selected. This means the drive mapping will persist until you manually disconnect it (using the Disconnect network drive entry in the Tools menu in Windows Explorer). When you're done, click **Finish**.

The mapped drive displays in the Windows Explorer navigation pane (see Figure 6-28). Click it to access the shared folder.

Figure 6-28

A shared folder with a drive mapping

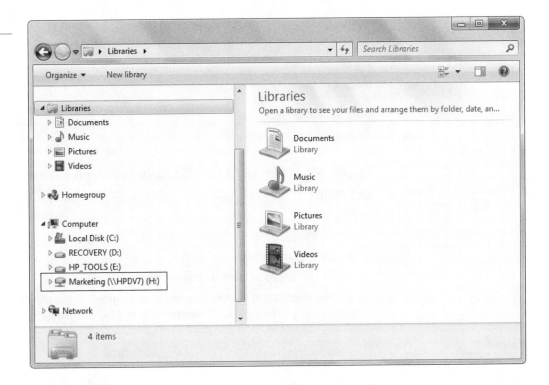

✚ MORE INFORMATION

For more information about mapping drives in Windows 7, visit http://windows.microsoft.com/en-US/windows7/Create-a-shortcut-to-map-a-network-drive

■ Understanding Permissions

↓ THE BOTTOM LINE

Permissions allow you to restrict the actions other users may take on shared items, such as files, folders, drives, and so on.

You've seen permissions when sharing files and folders. *Permissions* are rules you apply to users and groups to limit actions they can take on shared resources, such as files, folders, drives, network shares, and even printers. For example, you can restrict some users to only view (read) files, but allow other users to modify and/or delete files in the same folder.

TAKE NOTE*

Permissions can be granted or revoked by the owner of a resource, system administrators, and users with administrative accounts.

Basic permissions on files and folders in Windows 7 are described in Table 6-1.

Table 6-1

Basic File and Folder
Permissions in Windows 7

PERMISSION LEVEL	DESCRIPTION
Full control	Allows users to view and change files and folders, to create new files and folders, and to run programs in a folder.
Modify	Allows users to change files and folders but they cannot create new ones.
Read & execute	Allows users to view the contents of files and folders and to run programs in a folder.
Read	Allows users to view the contents of a folder and to open files and folders.
Write	Allows users to create new files and folders and to change files and folders.

CHECK AND MANAGE PERMISSIONS FOR A FILE OR FOLDER

GET READY. To check the permissions of a file or folder in Windows 7, perform the following steps:

1. In Windows Explorer, right-click a file or folder and then click **Properties**.
2. Click the **Security** tab.
3. In the **Group or user names** section, click a user name or group.
4. The permissions for the selected user or group display in the Permissions section (lower portion) of the Properties dialog box. See Figure 6-29.

Figure 6-29

Viewing permissions for a file
or folder

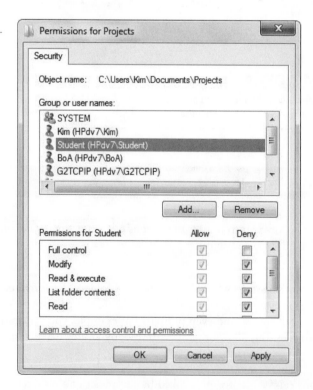

To change a permission for a user, perform the following steps:

1. With the user selected in the Properties dialog box, click **Edit**. The Permissions dialog box displays.

2. In the Group or user names section, click a user name.

3. Select and deselect the boxes in the Permissions section to allow or deny access. (See Figure 6-30.)

Figure 6-30

Changing permissions

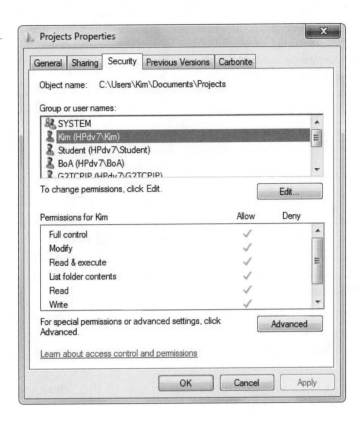

4. Click **OK** to apply the permissions and close the dialog box.

Clicking the Advanced button on the Security tab in the Properties dialog box lets you fine-tune permissions.

+ MORE INFORMATION

To learn more about permissions, visit http://windows.microsoft.com/en-US/windows7/What-are-permissions

Understanding NTFS, Share, and Effective Permissions

Windows 7 includes share and NTFS permissions. Share permissions apply to users who connect to a shared folder over a network; NTFS permissions apply to users who log on locally or from across a network. Effective permissions for an object, such as a folder, are permissions granted to a user or group based on the permissions granted through group membership and any permissions inherited from the parent object.

CERTIFICATION READY
To whom does an NTFS permission apply?
4.2

Share permissions apply to users who connect to a shared folder over a network; *NTFS permissions* apply to users who log on locally or from across a network. You set share permissions in a folder's Properties dialog box on the Sharing tab, and you set NTFS file permissions using the options on the Security tab. If you set share permissions and NTFS permissions on a shared folder, the more restrictive permissions apply to users who access the shared folder.

TAKE NOTE *

NTFS permissions are far more granular (detailed) than share permissions and apply only to NTFS-formatted volumes.

For example, let's say you grant a user named Stacie the Read permission on a network share. However, her account has the Full Control NTFS permission on the same folder. Because the Read permission is more restrictive, Stacie has only Read access when connecting over the network.

Another important permissions concept is inheritance. In a file system, a folder with subfolders is considered the parent folder. The subfolders are considered child folders. After you set permissions on a parent folder, new files and subfolders that are created in the folder *inherit* these permissions, as shown in Figure 6-31.

Figure 6-31

Parent and child folder permission inheritance

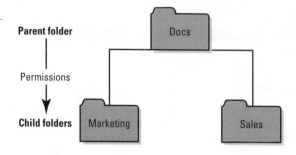

TAKE NOTE *

To set NTFS permissions, open a command prompt window and use the iCacls.exe tool.

The concept of inheritance is important to keep in mind when setting NTFS permissions. When users:

- Copy files and folders, the files and folders inherit permissions of the destination folder (see Figure 6-32).
- Move files and folders within the same volume, they retain their permissions (see Figure 6-33).
- Move files and folders to a different volume, they inherit the permissions of the destination folder (see Figure 6-34).

Figure 6-32

Copying files or folders

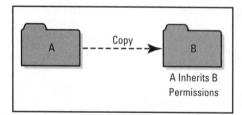

Figure 6-33

Moving files or folders within an NTFS volume

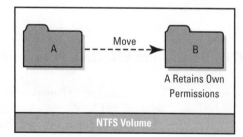

Figure 6-34

Moving files or folders from one NTFS volume to another

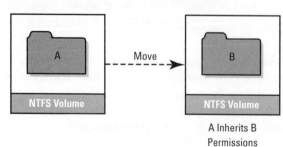

Effective permissions for an object, such as a folder, are permissions granted to a user or group based on the permissions granted through group membership and any permissions inherited from the parent object. Windows does not include share permissions as part of the effective permissions.

To view effective permissions for a folder, for example, right-click the folder, click Properties, click the Security tab, select a user or group, click the Advanced button, and then click the Effective Permissions tab in Advanced Security Settings dialog box (see Figure 6-35).

Figure 6-35

The Effective Permissions tab

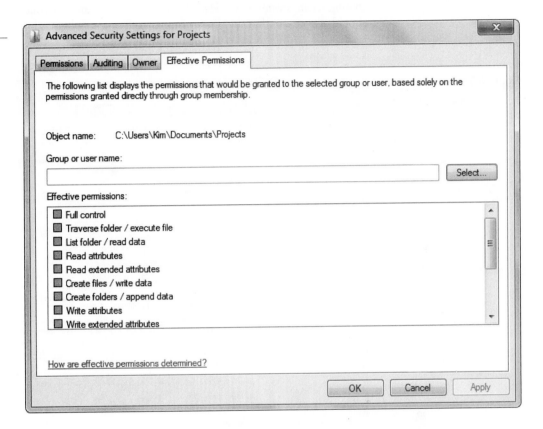

Understanding the different levels of permissions can be a challenge for a newbie. You should research Windows permissions thoroughly before making major changes to permissions.

✚ MORE INFORMATION

For more information about NTFS and share permissions, visit http://technet.microsoft.com/en-us/library/cc754178.aspx and http://technet.microsoft.com/en-us/library/cc726004.aspx. To learn more about effective permissions, visit http://technet.microsoft.com/en-us/library/cc772184.aspx

■ Setting Up Printer Sharing

THE BOTTOM LINE

Printer sharing allows a computer user to share his or her attached printer with other users on a network. Use the Devices and Printers applet to manage and share printers.

As you learned about file sharing earlier in this lesson, you probably noticed that printer sharing was included in some of the file-sharing methods. Windows 7 ties file and printer sharing together in many instances. For example, the HomeGroup window lets you select libraries to share and includes a Printers check box. The Advanced sharing settings window in Control Panel also includes a File and printer sharing section.

Sharing printers is, in some ways, even easier than sharing files. You can share a printer that's connected to your computer with a cable, such as a universal serial bus (USB) cable, share a networked printer connected directly to a router, or share a wireless network printer. This section focuses on directly attached printers using a cable.

To share any printer, you must ensure that file and printer sharing is turned on in the Advanced sharing settings window (accessed from the Network and Sharing Center). See Figure 6-36. You should also ensure that the printer is operating properly by sending a test page to the printer.

Figure 6-36

The Advanced sharing settings window

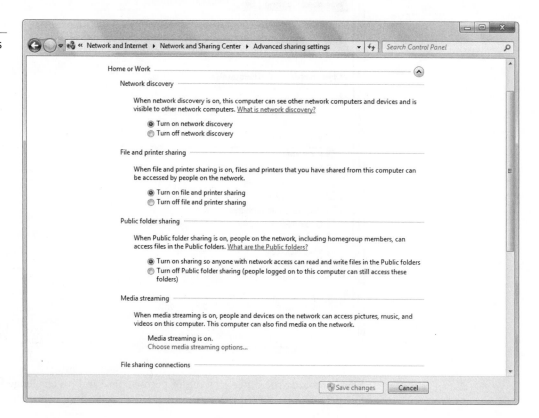

Windows 7 provides the Devices and Printers applet to let you manage one or more printers from a single interface. From here you can add a printer, see what's printing, and remove a printer. As shown in Figure 6-37, Devices and Printers handles more than just printers.

You have two primary ways to work with a printer: Device Stage and the Properties dialog box. Device Stage is a window that's unique to each device in Devices and Printers. Just double-click a printer's icon to open its Device Stage window (see Figure 6-38). You can see jobs that are printing, whether a printer error has occurred, select the default page orientation, click links to go directly to manufacturer information on the Web, and access the printer's properties by clicking the *Customize your printer* link.

You can also access a printer's properties by right-clicking a printer's icon and then selecting *Printer properties*. Using the tabs in the printer's Properties dialog box (see Figure 6-39), you can configure printer properties, install a new printer driver, share a printer, select a different printer port, limit the time of day the printer is available, enforce security, and much more.

Figure 6-37

The Devices and Printers
window

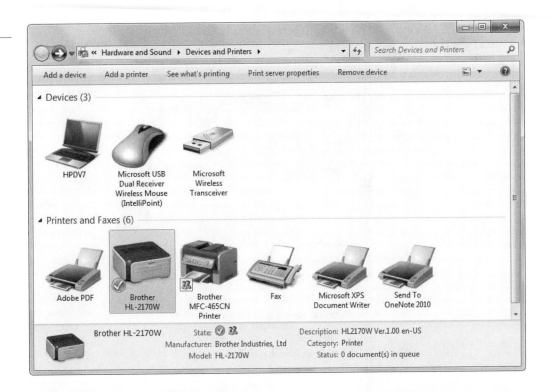

Figure 6-38

A printer's Device Stage
window

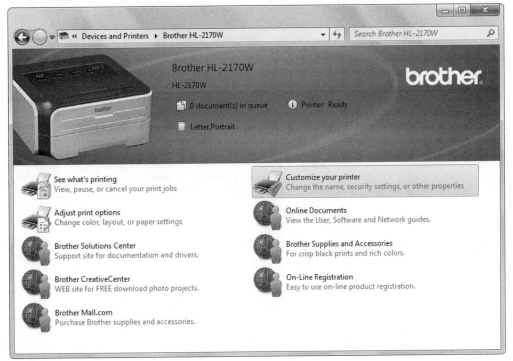

SHARE AN ATTACHED PRINTER

GET READY. To share a printer that's attached to your computer, perform the following steps:

1. Open Devices and Printers by clicking **Start** > **Devices and Printers**.
2. Right-click the printer you want to share and choose **Printer properties**.
3. Click the **Sharing** tab (see Figure 6-40).
4. Select the **Share this printer** check box and then click **OK**.

Figure 6-39

A printer's Properties
dialog box

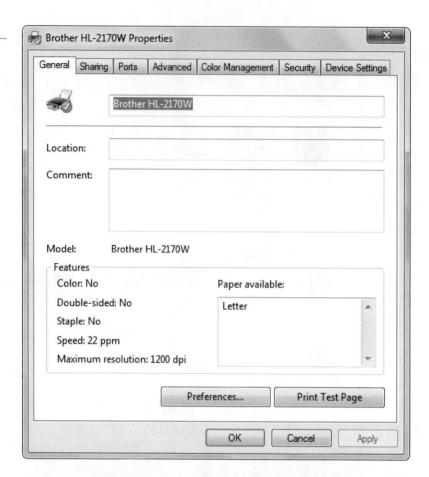

Figure 6-40

The Sharing tab

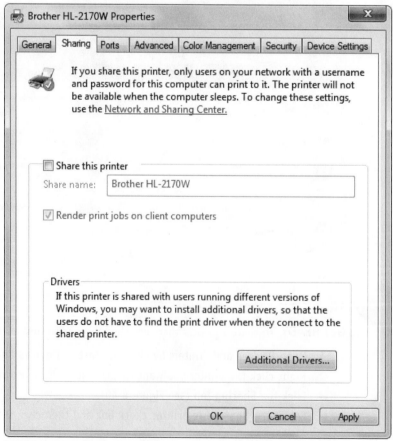

Other users on your network need to add a network printer to their computers (using Devices and Printers, in Windows 7) and then connect to the shared printer.

MORE INFORMATION

For more information about printer sharing, visit http://windows.microsoft.com/en-US/windows-vista/Share-a-printer

Understanding Print Drivers

> Hardware and peripherals, including printers, require a driver in order to run in Windows. The Devices and Printers applet gives you access to utilities for viewing print driver information and updating drivers.

CERTIFICATION READY
What is a print driver?
4.2

As you learned in Lesson 5, each piece of hardware and peripherals require a driver in order to run in Windows. Printers are no exception. A *printer driver* is a small software program that prepares application data to print to a specific printer.

One way to view a printer's driver information is by using the Printer server properties menu in Devices and Printers. The Drivers tab in the Printer Server Properties dialog box lists all printers installed on the computer. Just double-click the printer of interest to view driver information in the Driver Properties dialog box (see Figure 6-41).

Figure 6-41

The Driver Properties dialog box

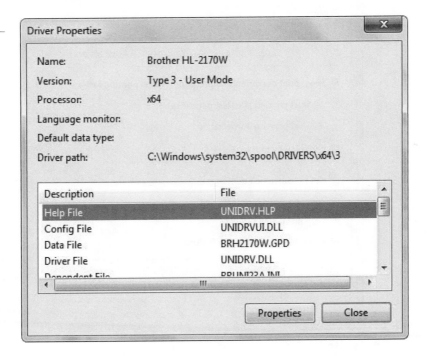

Printer manufacturers, like all device manufacturers, update drivers occasionally to fix bugs or to add capabilities for newly released operating systems. For example, if your printer had been working well for some time, but after you installed new software or upgraded your operating system the printer stopped working, you might need to update its driver.

Windows Update checks for new drivers for many devices and installs them during regular updates. However, sometimes you must manually update a driver. (Windows Update might not have a driver for a specific printer due to compatibility issues, for example, or because the manufacturer recently released a driver that's not yet part of Windows Update.) One method is to use the Add Printer Driver Wizard described in the following exercise. In some cases, it's best to visit the manufacturer's Web site, locate the latest driver for your printer, and download it. In most cases, the driver comes with an installer program, allowing you to double-click the EXE file and install the driver.

 UPDATE A PRINTER'S DRIVER

GET READY. To update a printer's driver, perform the following steps:

1. Open Devices and Printers by clicking **Start > Devices and Printers**.
2. Right-click a printer and choose **Printer properties**.
3. On the Advanced tab (see Figure 6-42), select the printer in the **Driver** drop-down list and then click **New Driver**.

Figure 6-42

The Advanced tab

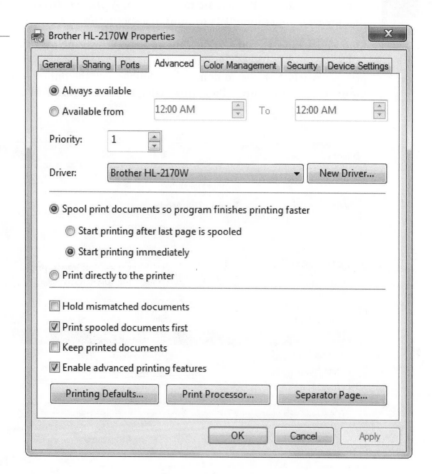

4. The Add Printer Driver Wizard starts. Click **Next**.
5. On the Printer Driver Selection screen (see Figure 6-43), scroll through the Manufacturer list and select your printer's manufacturer.
6. In the **Printers** list, find and select your printer model and then click **Next**.
7. Click **Finish**.

Figure 6-43

The Printer Driver Selection screen

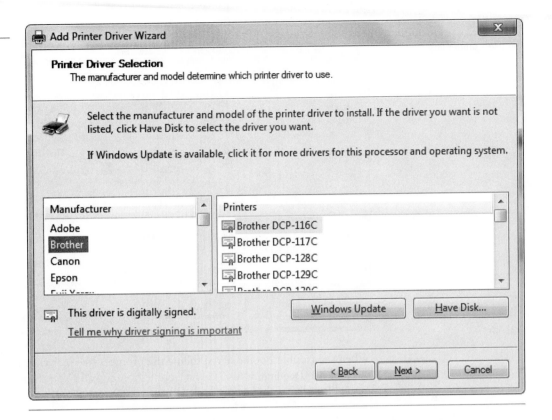

If the wizard was unable to update your driver, go to Devices and Printers, double-click the printer, and follow a link to the manufacturer's Web site to download the latest driver. Then return to Step 6 in this exercise and click Have Disk to install the driver manually. If the driver isn't preselected, you might have to browse to the location of the driver.

■ Troubleshooting Printers

THE BOTTOM LINE

Technicians and users alike occasionally have to troubleshoot printer problems. Device Stage, accessed through Devices and Printers, is a good first place to check for clues to the source of printer problems. You can also use a Windows troubleshooter to help resolve issues quickly.

Troubleshooting some printer problems is pretty simple. Make sure the power is on, ensure that the cable is securely connected to the printer and PC, ensure the printer's tray has paper, and check the printer's level of toner or ink, replacing the cartridge if necessary.

Other problems are more complicated and require investigation on your part. The first place to check is Device Stage for the printer that's not working. Device Stage displays the status of the printer along with any error messages that may indicate the problem. If Device Stage doesn't offer enough information, try a Windows 7 *troubleshooter*. Windows troubleshooters are wizard-driven tools that walk you through a software or hardware issue to help you resolve it.

To use a troubleshooter, click Start and in the *Search programs and files* search box, type *trouble* and then click Troubleshooting in the resulting list. In the Troubleshooting window, in the Hardware and Sound section, click the *Use a printer* link (see Figure 6-44).

Figure 6-44

The Use a printer link

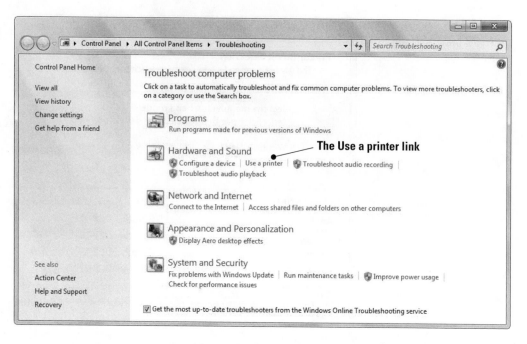

When the troubleshooter starts, follow the prompts to select your printer and narrow down the problem (see Figure 6-45). The troubleshooter walks you through a series of questions, much like a live technician would, to help you resolve the issue.

Figure 6-45

Using the printer troubleshooter

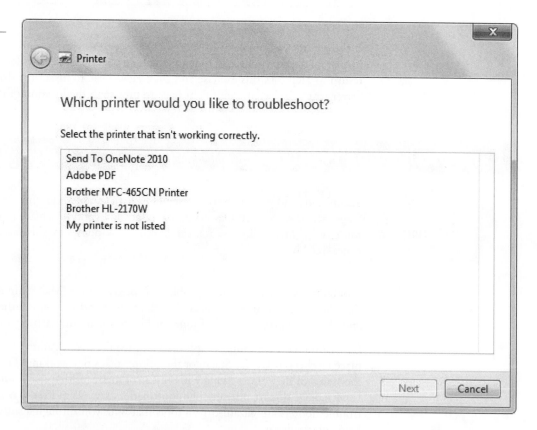

Much like with any device, simply powering it off, waiting a minute, and powering it back on clears memory problems. When troubleshooting shared printers, remember to check that the network is making connections between computers. The problem may be network related rather than printer related.

Sometimes the Print Spooler service has stopped communicating with the printer. The example in Lesson 4 described a printer with several duplicate print jobs and an unresponsive print queue. Restarting the printer didn't resolve the problem, so the next likely step was to restart the Print Spooler service in the Services console to clear the print queues.

➕ MORE INFORMATION

For more information about troubleshooting directly connected printers, visit http://windows.microsoft.com/en-US/windows-vista/Troubleshoot-printer-problems. To learn more about network printing issues, go to http://windows.microsoft.com/en-US/windows-vista/Troubleshoot-network-printer-problems

SKILL SUMMARY

IN THIS LESSON YOU LEARNED:

- Windows 7 provides many ways to share files or printers on a network. The first step is to ensure that file and print sharing is turned on in the advanced sharing settings in Network and Sharing Center. Some networking methods, such as HomeGroup, also require that your network location be set to Home network.

- HomeGroup is a new feature in Windows 7 that greatly simplifies file and printer sharing on small office/home office networks. Using HomeGroup, you may share libraries and printers, but you don't have a lot of control over which users may share the items.

- Public folders are a quick-and-easy way to share files with network users and with other users on your computer. Basic sharing and advanced sharing allow you to control who may access specific files and folders located in your libraries. Advanced sharing offers the most options and is therefore the best choice for protecting confidential information.

- Drive mapping allows you to create a shortcut to a shared folder across a network. Rather than having to find and connect to the shared drive each time you log on, you create a mapped drive that is available at all times. Just double-click the mapped drive to access the shared folder.

- Permissions allow you to restrict the actions other users may take on shared items, such as files, folders, drives, and so on.

- Windows 7 includes share and NTFS permissions. Share permissions apply to users who connect to a shared folder over a network; NTFS permissions apply to users who log on locally or from across a network. Effective permissions for an object, such as a folder, are permissions granted to a user or group based on the permissions granted through group membership and any permissions inherited from the parent object.

- Printer sharing allows a computer user to share his or her attached printer with other users on a network. Use the Devices and Printers applet to manage and share printers.

- Hardware and peripherals, including printers, require a driver in order to run in Windows. The Devices and Printers applet gives you access to utilities for viewing print driver information and updating drivers.

- Technicians and users alike occasionally have to troubleshoot printer problems. Device Stage, accessed through Devices and Printers, is a good first place to check for clues to the source of printer problems. You can also use a Windows troubleshooter to help resolve issues quickly.

■ Knowledge Assessment

Fill in the Blank

Complete the following sentences by writing the correct word or words in the blanks provided.

1. A _____ is a collection of security settings that's appropriate for the type of network you want to connect to.

2. Each default library in Windows 7 has _____, created to easily share documents, music, and so on with network users.

3. _____ allows you to share a file or folder with a specific user and restrict the user to Read or Read/Write actions.

4. After you set permissions on a parent folder, new files and subfolders that are created in the folder _____ these permissions.

5. _____ permissions apply to users who log on locally or by using Remote Desktop.

6. A Windows 7 _____ walks you through a series of questions, much like a live technician would, to help you resolve printer and other issues.

7. _____ allows you to share files, folders, or an entire drive, set permissions on shared files and folders (Read, Change, or Full Control), and more.

8. _____ is the built-in file and printer sharing feature in Windows 7 that's designed for small office/home office networks.

9. A _____ is a small software program that prepares application data to print to a specific printer.

10. _____ permissions for an object, such as a folder, are permissions granted to a user or group based on the permissions granted through group membership and any permissions inherited from the parent object.

Multiple Choice

Circle the letter that corresponds to the best answer.

1. Which of the following is *not* a network location in Windows 7?
   a. Home
   b. Office
   c. Work
   d. Public

2. When your peer-to-peer network has a mix of Windows 7, Windows Vista, and Windows XP computers, which of the following should be used for file sharing?
   a. Public folders
   b. HomeGroup
   c. A workgroup
   d. A domain

3. What can be done with a homegroup? (Choose all that apply.)
   a. Share libraries
   b. Share attached printers
   c. Allow users to view but not modify or copy shared files
   d. Choose which folders users may access

4. Once you share a folder on your Windows 7 computer with other users, which of the following can be done to make it easy for those users to get to the shared folder?
   a. Create a workgroup
   b. Create effective permissions
   c. Create NTFS permissions
   d. Map a drive

5. Regarding NTFS permissions, which of the following is *not* true?
   a. Copied files and folders inherit permissions of the destination folder
   b. Copied files and folders retain permissions of the source folder
   c. Files and folders moved within the same partition retain their permissions
   d. Files and folders moved to a different partition inherit the permissions of the destination folder

6. Which of the following Windows 7 permissions allows users to view and change files and folders, create new files and folders, and run programs in a folder?
   a. Write
   b. Modify
   c. Read and execute
   d. Full control

7. Which of the following Public folders is *not* created by default?
   a. Public Documents
   b. Public Music
   c. Public Pictures
   d. Public Projects

8. Which Windows 7 feature is used to turn Public folders on or off?
   a. Advanced sharing settings
   b. The Computer window
   c. Network and Sharing window
   d. Devices and Printers window

9. Which Windows 7 feature is used to add a printer?
   a. Devices and Printers
   b. Device Manager
   c. Printer troubleshooter
   d. Programs and Features

10. What is used to view a printer's driver information?
    a. Printer troubleshooter
    b. Printer server properties menu in Devices and Printers
    c. Printer's Properties dialog box, Sharing tab
    d. Printer's Properties dialog box, Drivers tab

True / False

Circle T if the statement is true or F if the statement is false.

T F 1. You can join two or more homegroups at a time.

T F 2. When creating a homegroup, you can share libraries but not printers.

T F 3. Public folder sharing in Windows 7 is turned off by default (except on a homegroup).

T F 4. Share permissions apply to users who connect to a shared folder over a network.

T F 5. Windows Update checks for new drivers for many devices and installs them during regular updates.

Competency Assessment

Scenario 6-1: Picking an Appropriate File-Sharing Method

Arnie, a supervisor in a small content translation company, wants to share a status spreadsheet with seven co-workers on a regular basis. His computer runs Windows 7. The peer computers all run Windows 7 and are connected through a wireless network. What method of file sharing should you set up for the supervisor?

Scenario 6-2: Creating and Configuring a Homegroup

Meredith's Pet Shop has three computers in the back office, all running Windows 7. Meredith wants them to share all files in their Documents and Pictures libraries and share a printer attached to one of the computers. How should she set this up?

Proficiency Assessment

Scenario 6-3: Restricting Permissions

You are setting permissions on a network share named Marketing. Currently, Bob and Aileen's accounts have Full Control over the Marketing folder. However, you want to restrict both users so that they can revise files within the Marketing folder and create new ones, but cannot revise executing programs. What permissions should you apply?

Scenario 6-4: Mapping a Network Drive

Samuel needs to be able to access the \Projects\Documents\98-349\ folder on the network often and quickly. He doesn't want to click through several folders to get to the one he needs. What can you do to help Samuel?

Maintaining, Updating, and Protecting Windows 7

EXAM OBJECTIVE MATRIX

SKILLS/CONCEPTS	EXAM OBJECTIVE DESCRIPTION	EXAM OBJECTIVE NUMBER
Exploring Built-in Maintenance Tools	Understand maintenance tools.	6.2
Maintaining the Windows Registry	Remove malicious software.	3.3
Updating the System	Understand updates.	6.3
Defending Your System from Malicious Software	Remove malicious software.	3.3

KEY TERMS

Action Center

Disk Cleanup

Disk Defragmenter

endpoint

firewall

fragmented

hotfix

malicious software (malware)

Microsoft Forefront Endpoint Protection

Microsoft Security Essentials

Microsoft Update

Microsoft Windows Malicious Software Removal Tool

service pack

signature

spyware

Task Scheduler

trigger

Windows Defender

Windows Firewall

Windows registry

Windows Update

A primary part of your IT technician position at Interstate Snacks involves maintaining company computers. To keep support costs down, you use free tools that are built into Windows or downloadable from the Microsoft Web site. The tools include Disk Defragmenter, Disk Cleanup, Windows Update, Windows Defender, and Microsoft Security Essentials. With the exception of Disk Cleanup, these tools have built-in scheduling features. You plan to use Task Scheduler to automate Disk Cleanup to run once a week and to start the accounting software every day at 8:30 a.m. for all accounting employees.

■ Exploring Built-in Maintenance Tools

THE BOTTOM LINE

Windows 7 comes with many built-in maintenance tools that help to keep computers running at top performance. These tools include Disk Defragmenter, Disk Cleanup, Task Scheduler, and the Action Center Maintenance feature.

Microsoft began bundling computer maintenance utilities in its early versions of Windows and has improved and expanded on them ever since. The latest utilities provide nearly any type of maintenance you might need, such as defragmenting disks, removing unnecessary files, scheduling tasks, troubleshooting problems, backing up files, and more.

In the following sections, you learn about some of the most popular Windows built-in utilities: Disk Defragmenter, Disk Cleanup, Task Scheduler, and the Maintenance section of Action Center. You can find many of the maintenance tools in the System Tools folder (click **Start > All Programs > Accessories > System Tools**).

Understanding Disk Defragmenter

Disk Defragmenter can speed up your computer's performance by defragmenting data on your hard disk. In Windows 7, the utility is set to automatically run once a week.

CERTIFICATION READY
What is Disk Defragmenter?
6.2

A hard disk is divided into many sectors, each of which can hold a small amount of data for a file. The hard disk's arm moves across a disk to "read" each sector in order to display a file or run a program. As more and more files are added to the disk the information becomes *fragmented*, which means it is spread across sectors on different parts of the disk.

Disk Defragmenter is a utility that helps improve your computer's performance by moving sectors of data on the hard disk, so that files are stored sequentially. This minimizes the movement a hard disk's arm must make to read all of the sectors that make up a file or program.

TAKE NOTE*

Solid state drives (SSDs) differ from hard disks. An SSD uses solid state memory to store data rather than writing data to sectors. Therefore, an SSD does not need to be defragmented.

Disk Defragmenter first analyzes your hard disk to determine the level of fragmentation, and then it defragments the disk if necessary.

In Windows 7, Disk Defragmenter is scheduled to run once a week by default. Although you may continue to use your computer while your hard disk is being defragmented, you might notice a performance hit if you're working on large files or running several programs at once, for example. If you're often working on your computer when the hard disk is being analyzed and defragmented, you can change the schedule when Disk Defragmenter runs automatically.

 RUN DISK DEFRAGMENTER

GET READY. To run Disk Defragmenter, perform the following steps:

1. Click **Start > All Programs > Accessories > System Tools > Disk Defragmenter**. (Alternately, click **Start** and in the **Search programs and files** search box, type **defrag** and then click **Disk Defragmenter** from the resulting list.) If prompted for administrative privileges, type the password or provide confirmation.

Figure 7-1

The Disk Defragmenter window

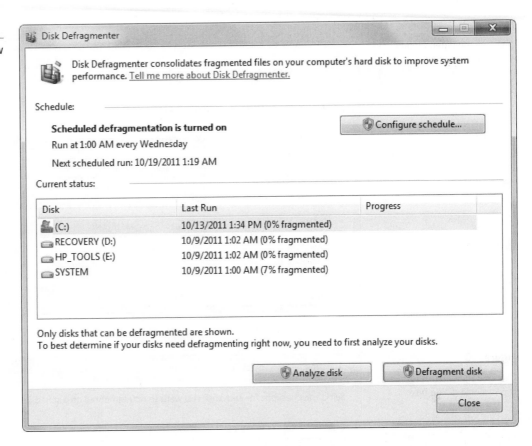

2. Click **Defragment disk**.

The defragmentation process can take several minutes to well over an hour to complete, depending on the size and level of fragmentation of the hard disk.

IT technicians and other advanced users may want to use the command-line version of Disk Defragmenter, in order to run reports and use advanced commands. To use the utility at a command-line, click Start, type **cmd** in the *Search programs and files* search box, select cmd.exe from the resulting list, and then in the command window, type **defrag/?** and press Enter. Re-issue the command using any of the command-line parameters that display.

 CHANGE THE DISK DEFRAGMENTER SCHEDULE

GET READY. To change the Disk Defragmenter schedule, perform the following steps:

1. In Disk Defragmenter (refer to Figure 7-1 if necessary), click **Configure schedule.** The Disk Defragmenter: Modify Schedule dialog box displays (see Figure 7-2).

2. To change how often Disk Defragmenter runs, click the Frequency drop-down arrow and select **Daily**, **Weekly**, or **Monthly**. If you choose Weekly or Monthly, click the Day drop-down arrow, and select a day of the week or a day of the month.

3. To change the time of day when Disk Defragmenter runs, click the **Time** drop-down arrow and select a time.

4. To change the volumes that are scheduled to be defragmented, click the **Select disks** button (see Figure 7-3). Deselect any volumes you don't want scanned, and then click **OK**.

5. Click **OK**, and then click **Close**.

Figure 7-2

Disk Defragmenter: Modify
Schedule dialog box

Figure 7-3

Disk Defragmenter: Select Disks
For Schedule dialog box

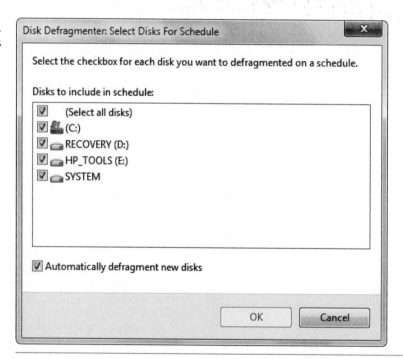

➕ MORE INFORMATION

To learn more about improving disk performance with Disk Defragmenter, visit http://windows.microsoft.com/en-US/windows7/Improve-performance-by-defragmenting-your-hard-disk

Understanding Disk Cleanup

Disk Cleanup helps you remove unnecessary files from your computer, such as downloaded program files, temporary Internet files, those that are left after running software, and much more.

CERTIFICATION READY
How does Disk Cleanup
help you maintain a
Windows 7 computer?
6.2

Another handy maintenance tool in Windows 7, and many previous versions of Windows, is *Disk Cleanup*. This utility removes many different kinds of unnecessary files from your computer:

- Downloaded program files
- Temporary Internet files
- Offline Web pages
- Files in the Recycle Bin
- Setup log files
- Temporary files left by programs, often in a TEMP folder
- Thumbnails for photos, videos, and documents used by the Windows interface (if you delete them, Windows re-creates them when needed)
- Windows error reporting files

You choose which files are deleted by Disk Cleanup by selecting and deselecting the boxes for each.

 RUN DISK CLEANUP

GET READY. To run Disk Cleanup, perform the following steps:

1. Click **Start > All Programs > Accessories > System Tools > Disk Cleanup**. (Alternately, click **Start** and in the **Search programs and files** search box, type **clean** and then click **Disk Cleanup** from the resulting list.) If prompted for administrative privileges, type the password or provide confirmation.

2. The Disk Cleanup: Drive Selection dialog box displays (see Figure 7-4). In the **Drives** drop-down list, click the arrow to select the drive you want to clean and then click **OK**.

Figure 7-4

Selecting a drive for Disk Cleanup to scan

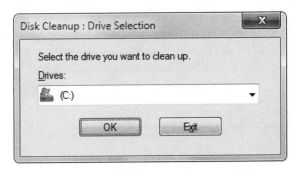

Disk Cleanup scans your disk (see Figure 7-5) to determine how much space it can free up. (You can safely click **Cancel**, if necessary, but you will have to restart Disk Cleanup to clean your disk.)

Figure 7-5

Disk Cleanup scanning a disk

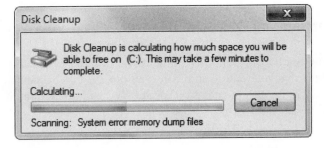

3. The Disk Cleanup dialog box for the selected drive displays (see Figure 7-6). Select the types of files you want the utility to delete; those that are deselected will not be deleted. For many of the file types, you can click **View Files** to see a list of files that will be deleted.

Figure 7-6

The Disk Cleanup dialog box

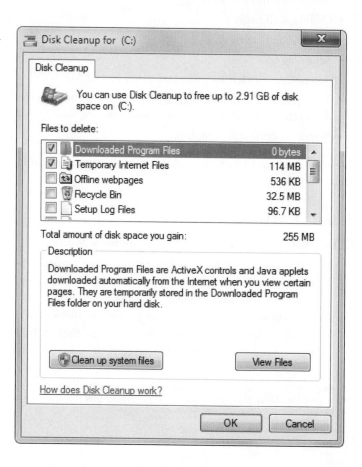

4. When you're ready, click **Clean up system files.**

 **MORE INFORMATION**

To learn more about using Disk Cleanup and the types of files it deletes, visit http://windows.microsoft.com/en-US/windows-vista/Delete-files-using-Disk-Cleanup

Understanding Task Scheduler

Many, but not all, Windows utilities have their own scheduling feature. For those utilities that you want to automate, you can use Task Scheduler. You can also use Task Scheduler to open programs on specific days and times, or at Windows startup.

Task Scheduler enables you to schedule and automate a variety of actions, such starting programs, displaying messages, and even sending e-mails. You create a scheduled task by specifying a *trigger*, which is an event that causes a task to run, and an *action*, which is the action taken when the task runs.

The main Task Scheduler window is shown in Figure 7-7. The left pane lists the Task Scheduler Library, which contains several built-in tasks by Microsoft and other vendors.

Figure 7-7

The main Task Scheduler window with the built-in task libraries expanded

Libraries

Actions pane

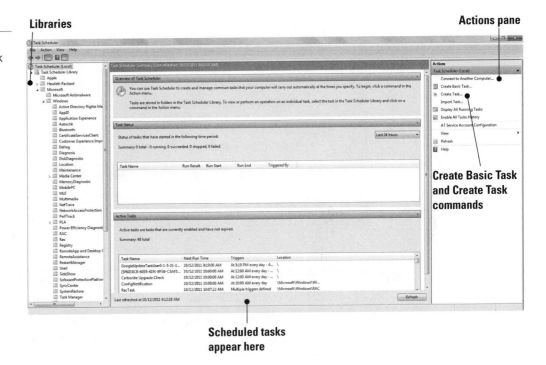

Create Basic Task and Create Task commands

Scheduled tasks appear here

The middle pane has three panes. The Overview pane gives you an overview of Task Scheduler, the Task Status pane displays a summary of tasks that started in a certain time period (for example, within the last 24 hours), and the Active Tasks pane displays scheduled tasks. The information displayed in the middle pane can vary greatly from computer to computer.

On the right of the screen, the Actions pane provides commands for connecting to another computer and scheduling tasks for that computer, creating basic and more advanced tasks, and commands for viewing tasks and their histories. Notice in Figure 7-7 that there are two commands in the Actions pane for creating tasks: Create Basic Task and Create Task. When you use the Create Basic Task command, the Create Basic Task Wizard walks you through the essentials of creating a task. The Create Task command displays the Create Task dialog box (see Figure 7-8), which is the manual way of creating task but gives you more control and options.

To schedule tasks for all users on your computer, you must be logged on as the Administrator. If you're logged on as a Standard user, you can schedule tasks only for your user account.

Figure 7-8

The General tab

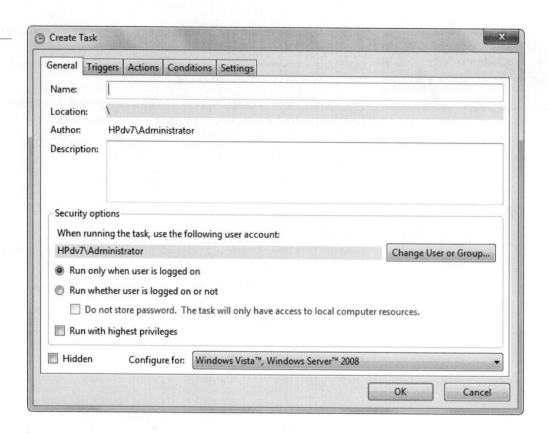

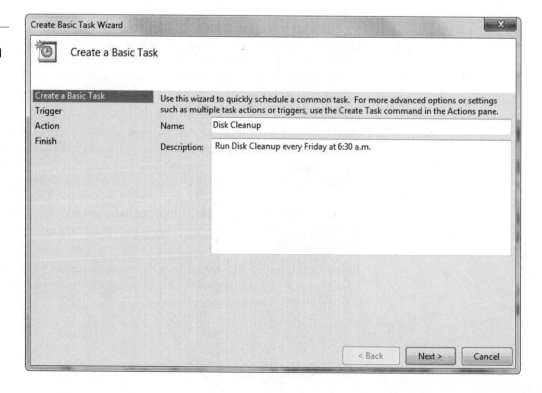

CREATE A TASK USING THE CREATE BASIC TASK WIZARD

GET READY. To create a task using the Create Basic Task Wizard, perform the following steps:

1. Click **Start** > **All Programs** > **Accessories** > **System Tools** > **Task Scheduler**. (Alternately, click **Start** and in the **Search programs and files** search box, type **task**, and then click **Task Scheduler** from the resulting list.)

Figure 7-9

Entering information for a basic task in the initial wizard screen

2. In the Actions pane on the right, click **Create Basic Task**. The Create Basic Task Wizard starts.

3. In the initial screen, type a name for the task and its description (optional). In the example shown in Figure 7-9, the Task Scheduler will run Disk Cleanup every Friday at 6:30 a.m. Click **Next**.

4. The Task Trigger screen enables you to select the frequency the task should occur or an event that triggers the task (see Figure 7-10). The default selection is Daily. For our example, because this task will run weekly, click the **Weekly** radio button and then click **Next**.

Figure 7-10

You can create a task to run daily, weekly, monthly, one time, and more

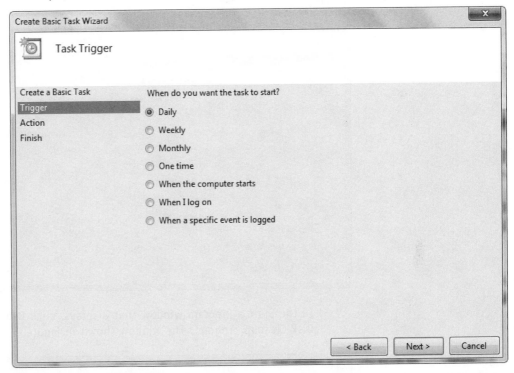

5. In the Weekly screen, select a starting date as well as the time and day of the week the task should run (see Figure 7-11). Click **Next**.

Figure 7-11

Selecting frequency and recurrence of the task

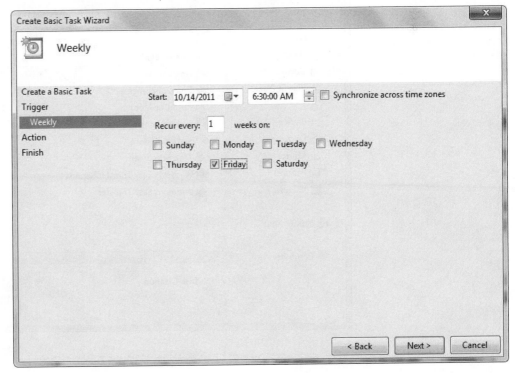

6. On the Action screen (see Figure 7-12), select the action that will be performed when the task runs. Because in this example we want to start a program, leave the default selected and then click **Next**.

Figure 7-12

Selecting the action to be performed

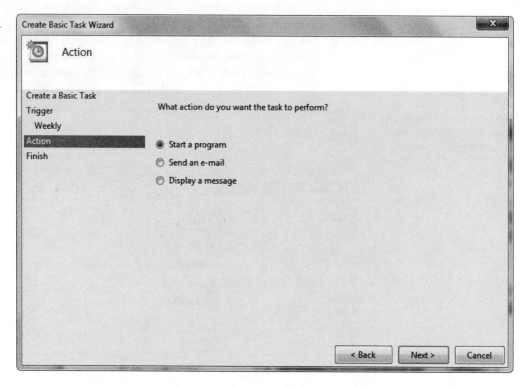

In the Start a Program window that displays, click **Browse** to find the Disk Cleanup program. The window shown in Figure 7-13 displays.

Figure 7-13

Selecting the program to run

Click **Disk Cleanup** and then click **Open**. (If the window in Figure 7-13 does not display, navigate to the Disk Cleanup executable file in C:\Windows\system32\ cleanmgr.exe, click **cleanmgr.exe,** and then click **Open**.) When the Start a Program screen displays again, which now indicates the path to the Disk Cleanup program executable, click **Next**.

7. The Summary screen summarizes the task, indicating when it will run (see Figure 7-14). If everything is correct, click **Finish**. If you need to make any changes, click the **Back** button, make the appropriate changes, and then click **Finish**.

Figure 7-14

Finishing the task creation

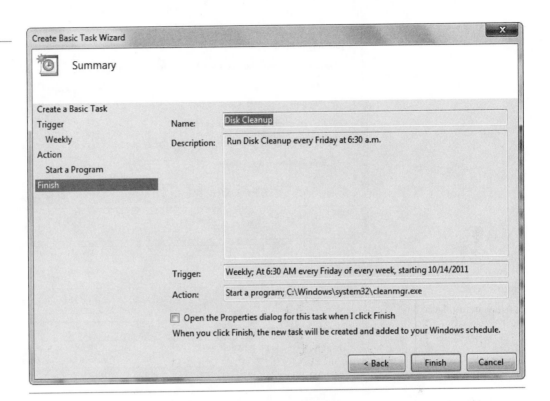

The task is added to Task Scheduler and will run on the trigger date.

 CREATE A TASK MANUALLY

GET READY. To create a task manually, such as scheduling a program to start when Windows starts, perform the following steps:

1. In Task Scheduler, in the Actions pane, click **Create Task**.

2. In the Create Task dialog box, on the General tab, type a **Name** for the task and a **Description** (optional). In the Security Options section, you can click **Change User or Group** to change the account or group the task runs under, and select whether the task should run when the user is logged on or not. Be sure to select the appropriate operating system in the **Configure for** drop-down list. The completed tab is shown in Figure 7-15.

3. Click the **Triggers** tab, and then click **New**. In the New Trigger dialog box, click the **Begin the task** drop-down arrow (see Figure 7-16) and select one of the options, such as **At startup**.

Figure 7-15

Adding information to the
General tab

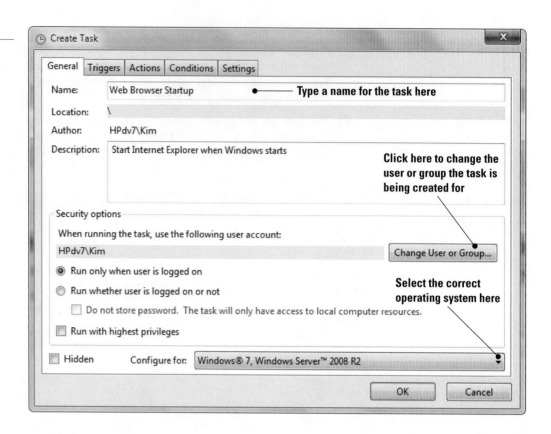

Figure 7-16

The New Trigger dialog box

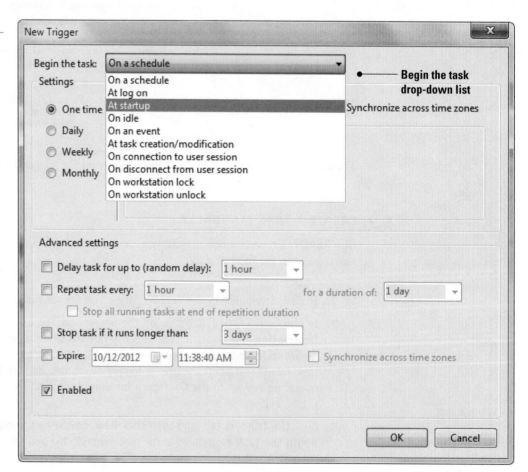

With this option selected, the New Trigger dialog box changes (see Figure 7-17). Configure advanced settings, if needed, and then click **OK**.

Figure 7-17

The New Trigger dialog box after selecting the At startup option

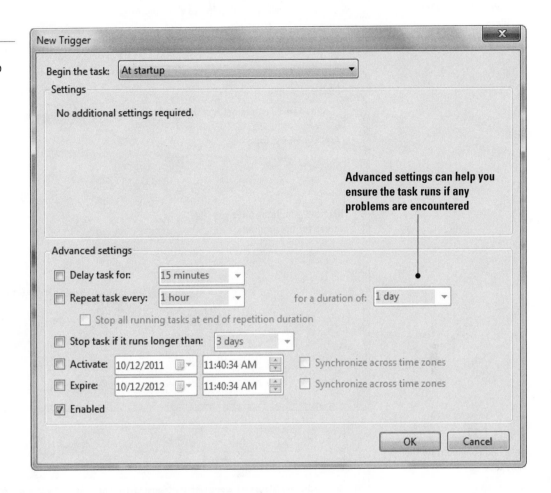

4. In the Create Task dialog box, click the **Actions** tab, and then click **New**. In the New Action dialog box, click **Browse**, navigate to the program's executable file (in this example, navigate to C:\Program Files\Internet Explorer\ and locate the Internet Explorer 9 executable named iexplore.exe), select it, and then click **Open**. The New Action dialog box should look similar to Figure 7-18.

5. Click **OK**.

6. In the Create Task dialog box, click the **Conditions** tab. In addition to the trigger, you can specify conditions under which the task should run (see Figure 7-19). For example, the power conditions are selected in an effort to avoid running a laptop's battery down unnecessarily. Make selections as appropriate.

7. Click the **Settings** tab. Here you can control task behavior (such as whether the user should be able to run the task on demand), how often the task should attempt to restart if it fails, and so on. Make selections as appropriate.

8. When you're finished configuring settings, click **OK**.

TAKE NOTE* To delete a task from Task Scheduler, double-click it in the Active Tasks pane and click Delete in the Action pane.

Figure 7-18

The New Action dialog box after selecting the program to run

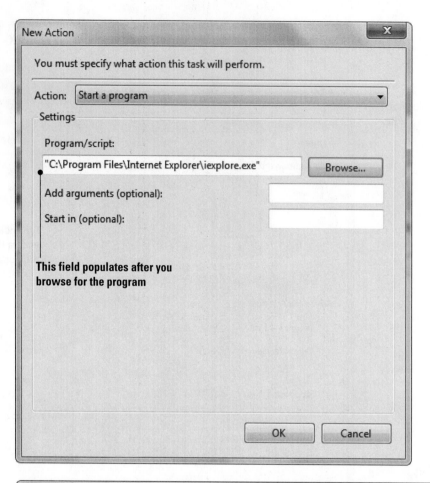

Figure 7-19

Selecting conditions for the new task

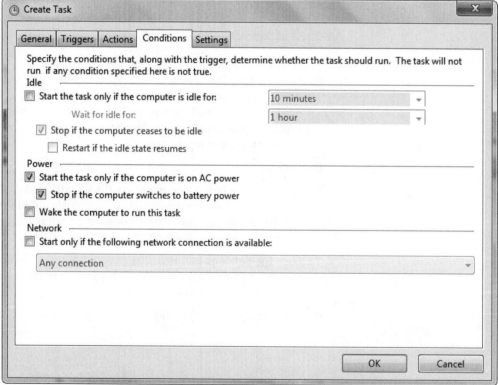

The task is added to Task Scheduler. You can see the task listed in the Active Tasks pane at the bottom of the main Task Scheduler window.

> ### ➕ MORE INFORMATION
>
> To learn more about scheduling tasks in Windows 7, visit http://windows.microsoft.com/en-US/windows7/schedule-a-task

Understanding Action Center

> Windows 7 Action Center is an improvement upon Security Center in previous versions of Windows. Within Action Center, you can view the status of security features (firewall, antivirus software, etc.) and maintenance (backups, updates, etc.).

Action Center provides a single interface in which you can view the status of security and maintenance features (see Figure 7-20) and it alerts you to problems you need to correct and usually provides a way to fix it. (You'll learn about the security features of Action Center later in this lesson.)

Figure 7-20

Action Center

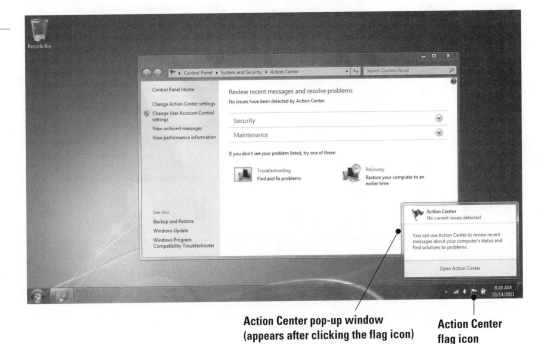

Action Center pop-up window
(appears after clicking the flag icon)

Action Center flag icon

The quickest way to open Action Center is from the desktop. Click the flag icon in the notification area of the taskbar icon, and then click Open Action Center in the pop-up window. If no issues are pending, both the Security section and the Maintenance section are collapsed. When an issue needs your attention, one or both sections are expanded and the problem is described. Items can be displayed with yellow or red bars. A yellow bar indicates a suggested change; a red bar indicates a change that should be taken care of immediately.

In the expanded Maintenance section (see Figure 7-21), Action Center tracks four features:

- **Check for solutions to problem reports:** From here you can check for solutions, view the Windows 7 privacy policy, change settings to choose how often to check for solutions to problems reports, and view a graph of the system's reliability history.
- **Backup:** This section provides information about the status of Windows Backup on your computer. You'll learn about Windows Backup in Lesson 8.
- **Check for updates:** This section refers to Windows Update, which provides updates to the operating system and many installed programs. You'll learn about Windows Update later in this lesson.
- **Troubleshooting: System Maintenance:** This section displays messages related to the automatic troubleshooting feature in Windows 7, which actively monitors your system for any maintenance issues.

Figure 7-21

Action Center Maintenance section

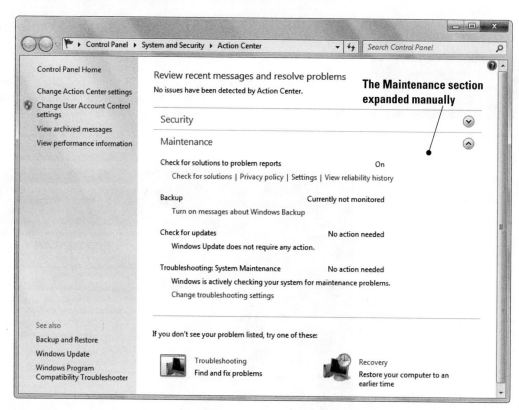

You might not need to visit Action Center very often; you might need to visit only when an issue occurs. Windows 7 notifies you of any pending issues by displaying a red X under the flag in the notification area.

➕ **MORE INFORMATION**

For details about Action Center in Windows 7, visit http://windows.microsoft.com/en-US/windows7/What-is-Action-Center

Understanding System Information

System Information displays a wealth of information about your computer's hardware, drivers, and system software. If you're having any type of system-related issues, you should check System Information for possible clues as to the source of the problem.

System Information is a utility that displays details about your computer's hardware components, software, and drivers. You can use System Information to simply gather information about your computer or to diagnose issues. To open System Information, click Start, type **system info** in the *Search programs and files* search box, and then select System Information in the resulting list. The main System Information window is shown in Figure 7-22.

Figure 7-22

The System Information window

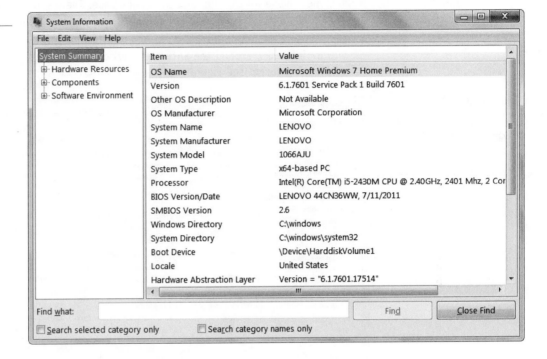

The left pane includes the following categories:

- **System Summary:** This category displays general information about your computer. You can view the name of the operating system, the name of the computer (system), the type of processor, and much more.

- **Hardware Resources:** This category displays details about your computer's hardware, such as whether any conflicts exist and the status of input/output (I/O) devices.

- **Components:** This category displays information about hardware devices and their drivers, such as disk drives, network adapters, and computer ports.

- **Software Environment:** This category displays details about system drivers, current print jobs and network connections, services, startup programs, and other system-related items.

System Information provides a search feature that enables you to quickly find specific information about your system. Just type the information you're looking for in the Find what box at the bottom of the window. For example, to see which programs launch at startup, type **startup** in the Find what box and then click Find. You can narrow your search by selecting either the *Search selected category only* or *Search category names only* check boxes at the bottom of the System Information window.

When attempting to diagnose a system problem, it can be useful to export information in System Information to a text file to send to a fellow support technician or post on a troubleshooting forum on a Web site. System Information enables you to save information to an .nfo file format, which you can open from System Information, or export information to a standard text file with a .txt file extension.

SAVE SYSTEM INFORMATION TO A TEXT FILE

GET READY. To save System Information to a text file, perform the following steps:

1. Click **Start**, type **system info** in the **Search programs and files** search box, and then select **System Information** in the resulting list.
2. In the System Information Windows, click **File > Export**.
3. Type a name for the file, and then click **Save**. The resulting file is very long and contains all of the information collected by System Information.
4. To export specific information from System Information, such as the list of currently running tasks, expand the **Software Environment** category in the left pane and select **Running Tasks** (see Figure 7-23).

Figure 7-23

Selecting specific information to export to a text file

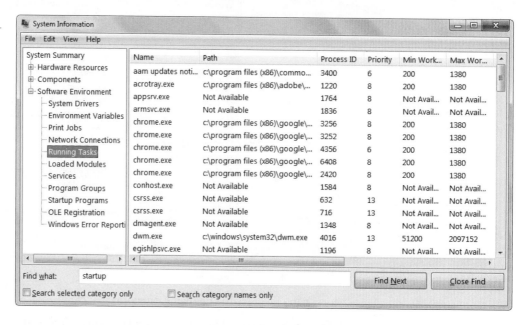

5. Click **File > Export**, type a name for the file, and then click **Save**.

You can open the text files in Notepad, WordPad, or any word processing program.

 **MORE INFORMATION**

For details about the System Information utility in Windows 7, visit http://windows.microsoft.com/en-US/windows7/What-is-System-Information

■ Maintaining the Windows Registry

THE BOTTOM LINE

The Windows registry is a database of configuration settings for your computer. It's often referred to as the "brains" of a Windows operating system. The registry is self-sufficient and rarely requires maintenance, but you can use a reputable registry cleaner occasionally to remove settings that are no longer used.

The *Windows registry* is a database in Windows that stores user preferences, file locations, program configuration settings, startup information, hardware settings, and more. In addition, the registry stores the associations between file types and the applications that use them. For example, the registry holds the information that tells Windows to open the default media player program (usually Windows Media Player) when you double-click a music or movie file.

The registry is made up of keys, subkeys, and values, as shown in Figure 7-24. Registry keys are similar to folders in Windows Explorer in that the keys can have subkeys (like subfolders). Subkeys have values that make up the preferences, configuration settings, and so on of the operating system. Whenever you change a preference, install software or hardware, or essentially make any changes to the system, the changes are reflected in the Windows registry.

Figure 7-24

A portion of the Windows registry

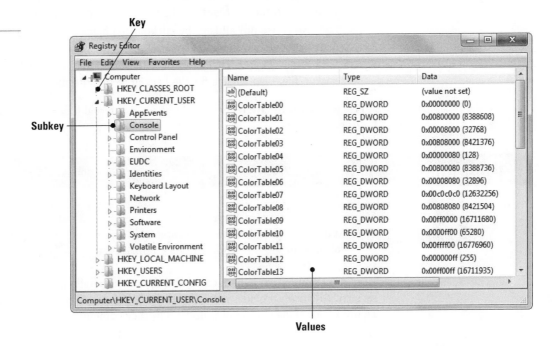

Over time, some settings in the registry are no longer needed. Registry settings take up a relatively small amount of disk space, and the settings can remain in the registry without affecting the performance of the computer. However, a registry setting can also become corrupt. Microsoft doesn't provide tools to repair the registry directly, but registry cleaners are available that remove unnecessary settings (for programs that are no longer installed, for example) and can repair many problems.

TAKE NOTE * Some registry cleaners can actually harm your computer. Be sure to get a reputable program to avoid contaminating your PC with spyware and viruses.

You should back up your registry before running any maintenance program on it. Microsoft provides the Registry Editor utility to make changes to the registry and back it up. To open Registry Editor, click **Start** and in the *Search programs and files* search box, type **regedit**, and then select regedit.exe from the resulting list. The Registry Editor window displays, which should look similar to Figure 7-24 shown previously.

Only users with advanced computer skills and IT professionals should edit the registry. Changing or deleting a critical setting can prevent your computer from operating upon reboot. However, nearly anyone can safely back up the registry.

BROWSE AND BACK UP THE WINDOWS REGISTRY

GET READY. To browse and then back up the Windows registry, perform the following steps:

1. Open Registry Editor by clicking **Start**, typing **regedit** in the **Search programs and files** search box, and selecting **regedit.exe** from the resulting list.

2. Expand keys in the left pane to view the associated subkeys. To view Microsoft-related subkeys, for example, click the clear triangle to the left of **HKEY_CURRENT_USER** key, click the **Software** subkey, and then click the **Microsoft** subkey. Browse the list of Microsoft subkeys.

3. Similarly, expand the **HKEY_LOCAL_MACHINE** key, expand the **SOFTWARE** subkey, and then expand the **Microsoft** subkey. Another set of Microsoft-related subkeys displays.

4. Collapse (close up) all keys by clicking the black triangles to the left of each expanded entry in the left pane.

5. Click **File > Export**, navigate to the location where you want to save the registry backup file, type a name for the backup in the **File name** text box, and then click **Save**.

A best practice is to save registry backups to an external location, such as a USB flash drive, a CD/DVD, or a network drive.

■ Updating the System

THE BOTTOM LINE

Microsoft provides several ways to help you keep your Windows system patched and updated using hotfixes, service packs, updated drivers, and more. Windows Update and Microsoft Update are the primary update tools.

Keeping a Windows system patched and updated is vitally important to maintaining proper security. Microsoft provides regularly scheduled updates via the *Windows Update* feature (see Figure 7-25), along with critical updates as they come up.

Figure 7-25

The Windows Update window

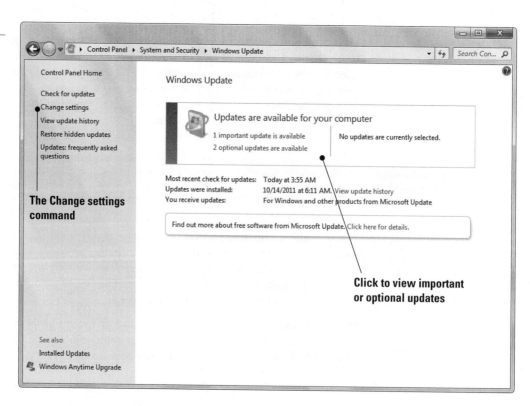

Microsoft releases regular, critical updates usually on the second Tuesday of the month (referred to as Patch Tuesday), although the company might release them more often to fix serious security vulnerabilities. These updates install automatically if you have automatic updating turned on.

To check your Windows Update settings, click the *Change settings* command in the task pane of the Windows Update page. The Change settings page (see Figure 7-26) allows you to choose whether you want to receive updates automatically (recommended) or per your own schedule. If you want Windows Update to download updates but let you choose which ones to install, or have Windows Update check for updates and let you choose which ones to download and install, click the *Important updates* drop-down arrow and select your preferred option.

Figure 7-26

The Change settings page

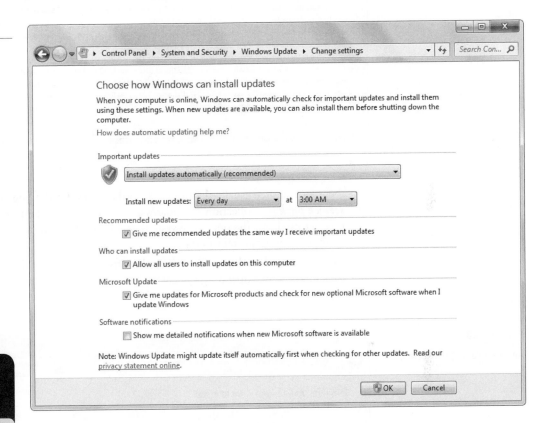

CERTIFICATION READY
What are the three main types of updates installed by Windows Updates?
6.3

CERTIFICATION READY
How do Windows Update and Microsoft Update deliver updates to Windows computers?
6.3

CERTIFICATION READY
What is a hotfix?
6.3

On the Change settings page, notice the ***Microsoft Update*** option. When this option is selected, Microsoft delivers updates for additional Microsoft software, not just the Windows operating system.

You view all of the updates that have been applied to your computer by returning to the main Windows Update page and clicking the *View update history* command in the task pane. The View update history window (see Figure 7-27) shows the name of each update, whether it installed successfully or not, the type of update (Important, Recommended, or Optional), and the date installed. Double-click any update to get more information.

Even with automatic updates enabled, some updates are not installed automatically; Microsoft gives you the option to install them. To view these updates, click one of the links in the Updates are available for your computer section of the Windows Update window. Windows Update pushes three types of updates to your computer:

- **Important updates:** These include security and critical updates, hotfixes, service packs, and reliability improvements. A ***hotfix*** is a patch that typically fixes a bug in software. If the bug creates a security issue or results in a part of the software malfunctioning,

Figure 7-27

Viewing the Windows Update history

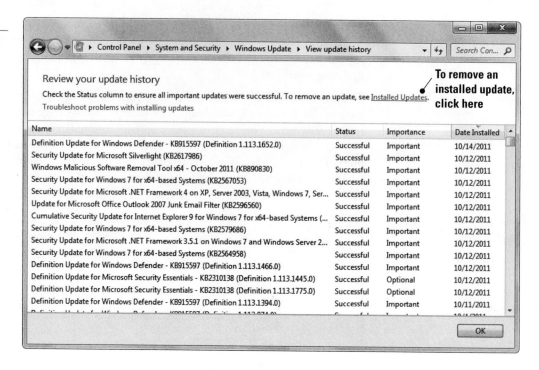

the manufacturer usually distributes a hotfix soon after the bug is detected. A Windows *service pack* is a collection of updates and hotfixes since the product was released. The product might be the operating system or Microsoft software. Figure 7-28 shows an example of an important update.

• **Recommended updates:** These include software updates and new or improved features to help keep your operating system and software running optimally.

Figure 7-28

An example of an important update

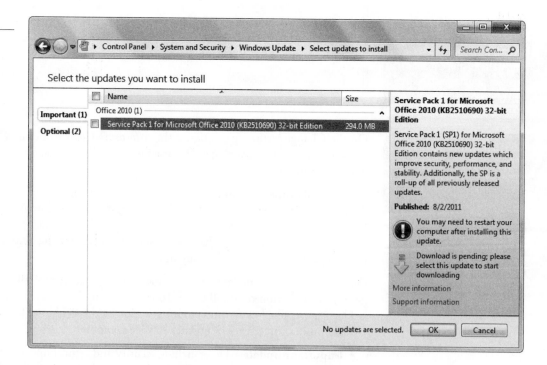

- **Optional updates:** These include items such as optional device drivers for components on your computer, or new or trial Microsoft software. Figure 7-29 shows an example of optional updates (in this case, device drivers).

Figure 7-29

An example of optional updates

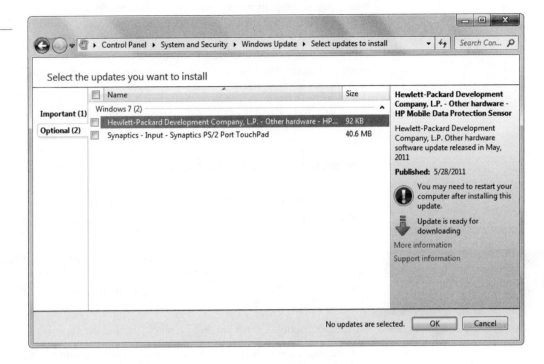

To install any of these updates, select the box next to the name of the update and then click OK. Many updates require you to restart your computer for the update to take effect. You can usually continue working and then restart when it's convenient. However, it's best to restart immediately if one or more critical updates have been installed.

Administrators in all but very small environments often use Windows Server Update Services (WSUS) to gather Windows updates and hotfixes and then distribute them to client computers. WSUS runs on a Windows server. The service downloads updates and hotfixes to the server, allowing the administrator to install them on test computers that are configured similar to actual user computers. If the tests do not result in any problems, the administrator approves the updates or hotfixes, and WSUS then installs them on client computers over the network.

➕ **MORE INFORMATION**

For more information about Windows Update, visit http://windows.microsoft.com/en-US/windows7/products/features/windows-update. To learn about the Microsoft update management process, go to http://technet.microsoft.com/en-us/library/cc700845.aspx

■ Defending Your System from Malicious Software

THE BOTTOM LINE

One of the most challenging problems for computer users and administrators is to prevent viruses, worms, and other types of malware from infecting your computer. The Windows 7 Action Center: Security section helps you manage your computer's security. Microsoft Windows Defender and Microsoft Security Essentials help to prevent spyware and malware infections, respectively.

With thousands of different viruses, worms, and other forms of *malicious software (malware)* ready to attack any computer connected to the Internet, it's vitally important to use antivirus and antispyware software in addition to a firewall.

Many protection companies sell stand-alone antivirus, antispyware, and firewall programs that are bundled into Internet security products that usually provide additional features (such as antispam and anti-phishing filters, parental controls, and password vaults). At a minimum, every computer should have antivirus and antispyware software installed along with a firewall; every computer should also use the security settings found in the latest Web browsers.

The following sections review tools available in Windows 7 and downloadable from the Microsoft Web site that enable you to protect your computer from malware.

Understanding Action Center

The Security section of Action Center lets you view the status of many different security features and fix security vulnerabilities if any are present.

CERTIFICATION READY
How does the Action Center help to protect a computer?
3.3

You learned the essentials of Action Center earlier in this lesson. Although Action Center provides some information regarding maintenance, it really shines on security issues. And it should—Action Center is the new and improved version of the Windows Security Center that was featured in Windows XP SP2 and Windows Vista.

By default, Action Center tracks seven security features (see Figure 7-30):

- **Network firewall:** This feature monitors your computer's firewall, through which network and Internet traffic flows. Windows 7 comes with Windows Firewall, which should be turned on if no other firewalls are present.

Figure 7-30

Action Center's Security section

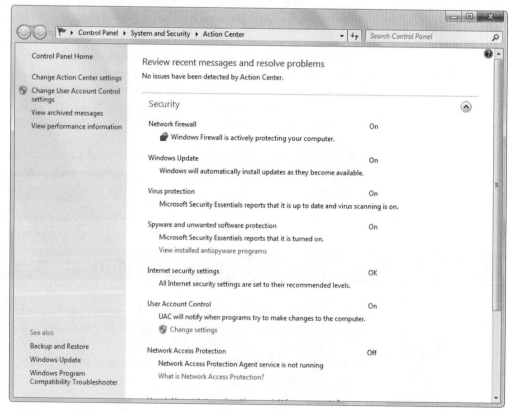

- **Windows Update:** This feature indicates whether Windows Update is enabled.
- **Virus protection:** Virus protection software installed on your computer is monitored with this feature. If no software is present or if it's out of date, you'll be notified here.
- **Spyware and unwanted software protection:** Action Center monitors Windows Defender (which comes bundled with Windows 7, and which you'll learn about shortly) and other third-party antispyware solutions.
- **Internet security settings:** These settings are configured through the Security tab in Internet Explorer 9's Internet Options dialog box. You learned about Internet Explorer security zones in Lesson 3. If any zone is configured so that it poses a threat to your computer, you'll be notified here.
- **User Account Control:** In this section, you can see whether User Account Control (UAC) is enabled and you can click the Change settings link to configure it.
- **Network Access Protection (NAP):** This feature applies mainly to enterprise environments. With NAP enabled, the network can detect whether the computer meets baseline security standards for the organization. If not, the computer is not allowed access to the full network and must be updated or reconfigured before access is granted.

If any of these features require your attention, the Action Center flag in the notification area displays a red X. Click the flag to open Action Center and address important security issues. Important items that need your attention are designated with red bars.

Understanding Windows Firewall

> Windows Firewall comes with Windows 7 and other Windows versions to protect your computer from traffic entering through communications ports.

A *firewall* is a software program or device that monitors traffic entering and leaving a computer. This term comes from the building trades where it refers to a special barrier designed to delay the advance of fire from one area to another. In the computer world, threats and attacks are the "fire" advancing on computers connected to the Internet and from malicious insiders.

TAKE NOTE *

Networks have firewalls, too—similar to computers but usually much more robust.

Microsoft provides ***Windows Firewall*** with Windows 7, Windows Vista, and Windows XP operating systems. The firewall is turned on automatically in new installations of the operating systems. To access Windows Firewall, click Start and in the *Search programs and files* search box, type **firewall**, and then select Windows Firewall from the resulting list. The Windows Firewall page displays whether the program is enabled (see Figure 7-31) and what it's protecting.

Sometimes a firewall works too well, blocking communications that you want to allow! For example, a newly installed program that needs to communicate with the Internet might not work because it's blocked by the firewall. In this case, click the *Allow a program or feature through Windows Firewall* command in the task pane of the Windows Firewall page. The Allowed Programs page displays (see Figure 7-32). To change settings, click the *Change settings* button. Click the *Allow another program* button. Scroll the list to locate the program, select it, click Add, and then click OK.

It's best to have only one firewall running on a computer. If you install an Internet security product, the new software should automatically turn off Windows Firewall. If you check Action Center and see that two firewalls are running, open the Windows Firewall page, click *Turn Windows Firewall on or off* in the task pane, select the *Turn off Windows Firewall* option, and then click OK. Reboot your computer, and then immediately check Action Center again to verify that only one firewall is enabled.

Figure 7-31

The Windows Firewall page

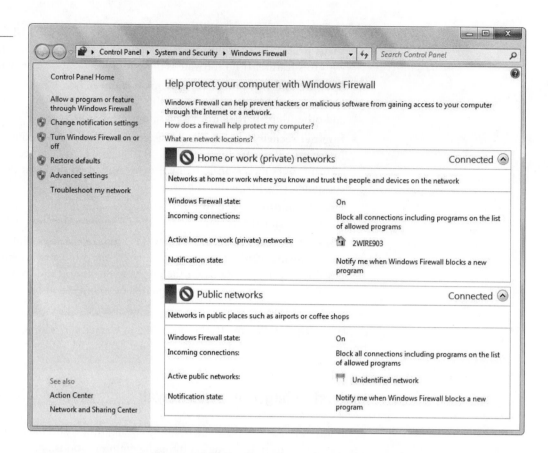

Figure 7-32

The Windows Firewall Allowed Programs page

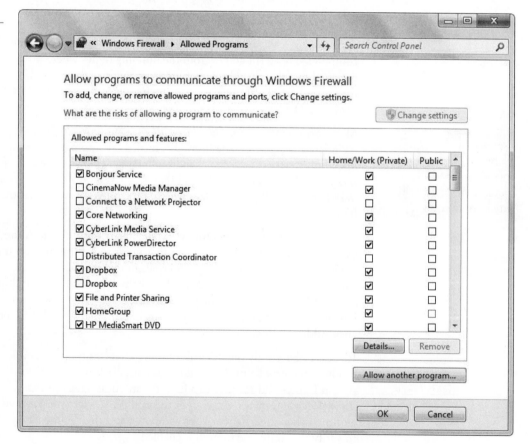

Understanding Windows Defender

> Windows Defender is a free software program that provides antispyware protection for a Windows computer.

Spyware is a type of program that installs on your computer without your permission, monitors your computing activities, and reports the activity back to the spyware writer or a third party. Some legitimate companies use spyware to gather profile information about their customers for direct marketing and product development efforts; however, most spyware is malicious in nature.

A free antispyware program provided by Microsoft is ***Windows Defender***, which comes bundled with Windows 7. The Windows Defender window is shown in Figure 7-33. You can set Windows Defender to run in the background, constantly monitoring your computer for spyware. When it detects spyware, the program quarantines it (so the spyware can't run on your computer) or deletes it. Quarantining is handy in case Windows Defender mistakenly deems a "good" program as spyware; by only quarantining it, you're provided with an opportunity to restore the program.

Figure 7-33

The Windows Defender main page

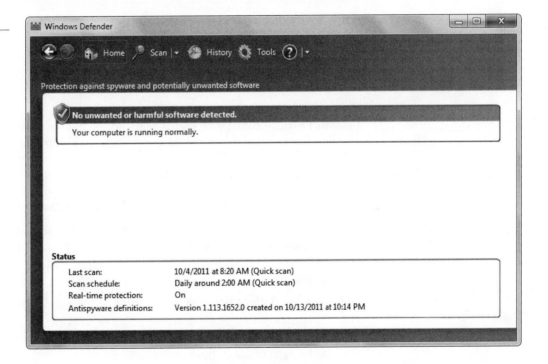

To open Windows Defender, click Start, type **defender** in the *Search programs and files* search box, and then select Windows Defender from the resulting list. If Windows Defender is not already running, click the link in the pop-up box that displays to enable Windows Defender. You might have to start the service manually in the Services MMC snap-in, or you might have to restart your computer. If you have other anti-malware software running on your computer, such as the latest version of Microsoft Security Essentials (covered in the next section), Windows won't allow you to start Windows Defender.

To run a scan of your computer, click the down arrow next to the Scan icon at the top of the window (see Figure 7-34) and then select Quick scan, Full scan, or Custom scan.

Figure 7-34

Windows Defender's scanning options

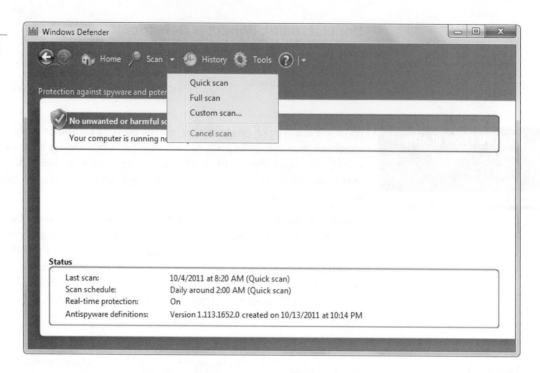

A quick scan checks critical files and those most often affected by spyware. A full scan checks all files on your hard disk and can take several hours to complete, depending on the number of files on your computer. A custom scan lets you choose which files or folders to scan.

Windows Defender comes with several configurable options, such as scheduling, default behavior when a threat is detected, an exception list, and much more.

 CONFIGURE WINDOWS DEFENDER

GET READY. To configure Windows Defender, perform the following steps:

1. Click **Start** > **All Programs** > **Windows Defender**. Alternately, click **Start**, type **defender** in the **Search programs and files** search box, and then click **Windows Defender** in the resulting list.

2. In Windows Defender, click the **Tools** icon at the top of the window.

3. Click the **Options** link. The Options page displays (see Figure 7-35).

4. To change the automatic scanning schedule, click the drop-down lists and select a new frequency (either **Daily** or a particular day of the week), an **Approximate time**, and a **Type** of scan (**Quick** or **Full**).

5. In the left pane, click **Default actions**. You can set default behaviors when Windows Defender detects a severe, high, medium, or low alert item (see Figure 7-36). All options in the drop-down lists include the choice to **Quarantine** or to **Remove**. The medium and low alert levels also include the **Allow** option.

6. To exclude specific files or folders from the scans, click **Excluded files or folders** in the left pane, click the **Add** button, navigate to the file or folder you want to exclude, select it, and then click **OK**.

7. To exclude certain file types, click **Excluded file types** in the left pane. Type a file extension in the text box next to the Add button for the type of file that does not need to be scanned (such as *.jpg, *.tif, or *.pdf) and then click **Add**.

Figure 7-35

The Windows Defender Options page

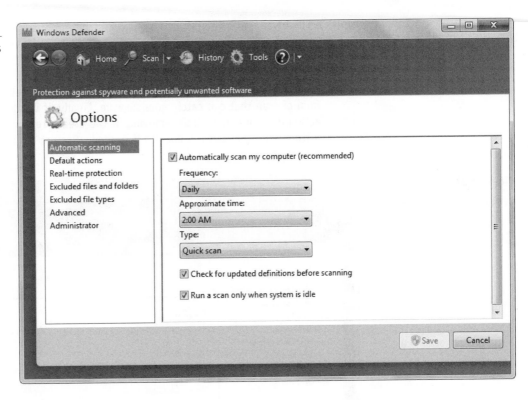

Figure 7-36

Setting default behaviors for alert levels

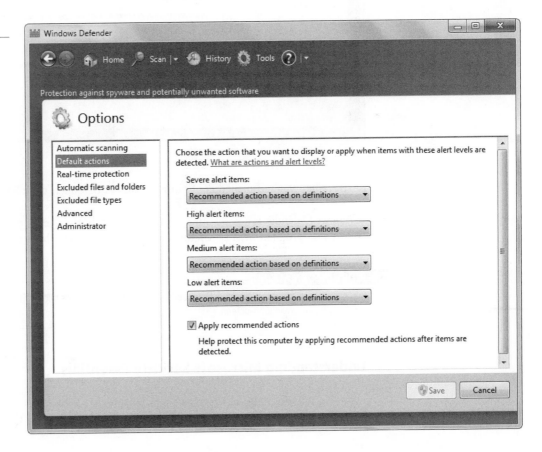

8. Click **Advanced** in the left pane. The advanced options (see Figure 7-37) include scanning archive files, scanning e-mail (including attachments), and scanning removable drives (such as a connected USB flash drive). You can also tell Windows Defender to use heuristics when scanning files; heuristics is a process or method that looks for partial matches to spyware rather than a complete match. This is a deeper form of scan that can catch more spyware. Finally, if Windows Defender must take action on a threat, such as removing it, the **Create restore point** option creates a restore point you can roll back to if needed. (Restore points are covered in Lesson 8.)

Figure 7-37

Setting advanced options

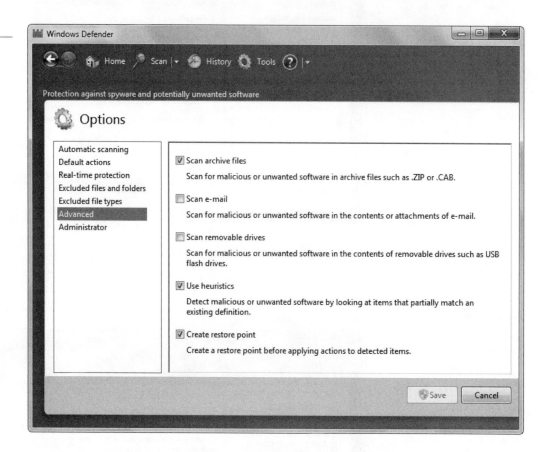

9. When you're finished configuring Windows Defender, click **Save**.

Windows Defender is a good antispyware program, but it doesn't protect you as well as a more feature-rich program such as Microsoft Security Essentials, which is covered in the next section.

➕ **MORE INFORMATION**

You can learn more about Windows Defender by visiting http://windows.microsoft.com/en-US/windows7/products/features/windows-defender

Understanding Microsoft Security Essentials

Microsoft Security Essentials is a program that helps protect your computer from viruses and other malware. You can run Microsoft Security Essentials for free on up to 10 computers.

Windows 7 doesn't include antivirus software, but every computer that interacts with other computers or the Internet should have antivirus software installed. As previously mentioned in this section, you can buy and install third-party antivirus software or an Internet security suite. You can also use the free antivirus software provided by Microsoft: Microsoft Security Essentials.

To download Microsoft Security Essentials, go to the Microsoft Security Essentials Web site or the Microsoft Download Center.

Microsoft Security Essentials (see Figure 7-38) protects your computer from viruses and many other forms of malware. The program is updated regularly by the Microsoft Update service to ensure the signatures, the anti-malware engine, and the application itself are kept up to date. A *signature* is a sequence of text or code that's programmed into a virus and uniquely identifies it. Antivirus software uses an anti-malware engine to find viruses and other malware on a computer. Because new threats appear every day, Security Essentials downloads new signatures daily and uses the Dynamic Signature Service to push the updates to your computer almost immediately.

Figure 7-38

The Microsoft Security Essentials main window

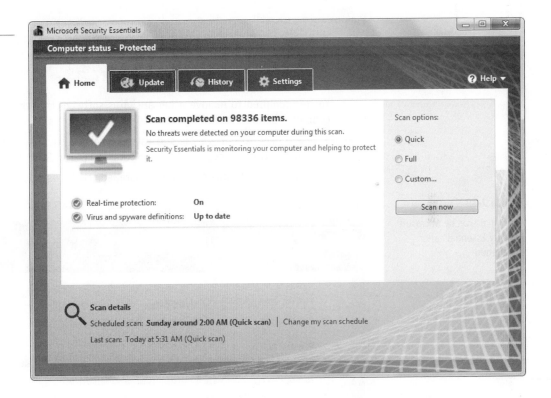

Like Windows Defender, Security Essentials offers three types of scans: quick, full, and custom. A quick scan checks critical files and those most often affected by spyware. A full scan checks all files on your hard disk and can take several hours to complete, depending on the number of files on your computer. A custom scan lets you choose which files or folders to scan. Just select the type of scan you want to run on the Home tab and then click *Scan now*.

INSTALL MICROSOFT SECURITY ESSENTIALS

GET READY. To install Microsoft Security Essentials, perform the following steps:

1. Download the Microsoft Security Essentials installation program to your hard disk, such as to your Downloads folder. The installation file is named mseinstall.exe. Don't disconnect from the Internet after downloading the file; you must be connected to the Internet to complete the installation of Microsoft Security Essentials.

 **TAKE NOTE*** You must be running a genuine version of Windows in order to install Microsoft Security Essentials. A genuine version of Windows is one that is published and licensed by Microsoft.

2. In Windows Explorer, locate and double-click **mseinstall.exe**. If prompted for administrative privileges, type the password or provide confirmation.
3. In the installation wizard, click **Next**.
4. Accept the license agreement and then click **Next**.
5. Choose or decline participation in the Customer Experience Improvement Program and then click **Next**.
6. Leave the **If no firewall is turned on, turn on Windows Firewall (Recommended)** option selected and then click **Next**.

TAKE NOTE* Making sure a firewall is enabled is highly important. You must have your computer connected to the Internet when installing Microsoft Security Essentials or the installation will fail. So, the firewall helps protect the computer for the short time that the computer is vulnerable to online attacks.

7. You're prompted to remove other antivirus software that might be installed on your computer before continuing.
   - If you need to remove the software, cancel the wizard, go to Control Panel, uninstall the program, and reboot your computer. Start from Step 2 in this exercise.
   - If no other antivirus software is installed, click **Install**.

Figure 7-39

The initial scan by Microsoft Security Essentials after installation

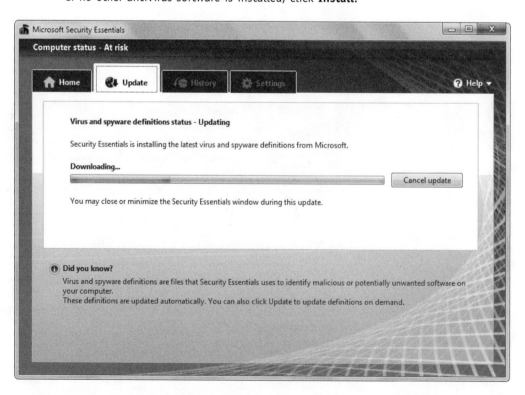

8. After the software installs, the final screen of the wizard provides the option to perform a system scan. Click **Finish**. The software immediately checks for updates for its definitions and signatures, and scans your system (see Figure 7-39). The red bar displayed at the top of the window indicates that the computer is at risk. Once the updates are installed, the status bar will change to green and indicate "protected."

Your computer is now constantly monitored by Security Essentials, and offers real-time protection against malware.

 CONFIGURE MICROSOFT SECURITY ESSENTIALS

GET READY. To configure Microsoft Security Essentials, perform the following steps:

1. In Microsoft Security Essentials, click the **Settings** tab.
2. To change the schedule for quick scans, click the drop-down lists to select options (see Figure 7-40). Change the Scan type to **Full scan** and then set the **When** option and the **Around** option, too. It's best to schedule a full scan, which can take hours, to run overnight or on a weekend—whenever you're least likely to use the computer.

Figure 7-40

The Settings tab in Microsoft Security Essentials

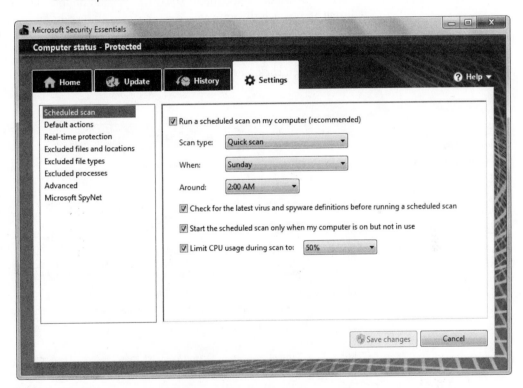

3. Change any other settings as you wish. The settings are very similar to those in Windows Defender, which was covered previously.

When you're finished configuring Security Essentials, click the *Save changes* button.

+ MORE INFORMATION

To download Microsoft Security Essentials, go to http://www.microsoft.com/en-us/security_essentials/default.aspx or visit the Microsoft Download Center at http://www.microsoft.com/download/en/default.aspx. For details about how Microsoft Security Essentials works, go to http://www.microsoft.com/en-us/security_essentials/ProductInformation.aspx

Using the Malicious Software Removal Tool

> If your anti-malware software cannot remove a virus or worm from a computer, try the Microsoft Malicious Software Removal Tool.

CERTIFICATION READY
How is the Microsoft Windows Malicious Software Removal Tool used to remove malware from a computer?
3.3

Computers can become infected even with the best protection software running in the background. If you know your computer is infected with malware, such as Blaster, Mydoom, EyeStyle, or Poison, download and run the *Microsoft Windows Malicious Software Removal Tool.* This utility scans your computer for dangerous malware and attempts to remove it immediately.

You can download the Malicious Software Removal Tool from the Microsoft Safety & Security Center or the Microsoft Download Center. The tools work with computers running Windows 7, Windows Vista, Windows XP, Windows 2000, and Windows Server 2003. If you're running an x64 version of Windows 7, go to http://www.microsoft.com/download/en/details.aspx?displaylang=en&id=9905.

Download the software to your Downloads folder (or another folder that's easy to access). In Windows Explorer, navigate to the installation file (which may be windows-kb890830-v4.1.exe or windows-kb890830-x64-v4.1.exe) and double-click it. Follow the prompts to install and launch the software.

When the Microsoft Windows Malicious Software Removal Tool window displays, click Next. You have the option of performing a quick, full, or customized scan (see Figure 7-41). Select one and then click Next.

Figure 7-41

Malicious Software Removal Tool scanning options

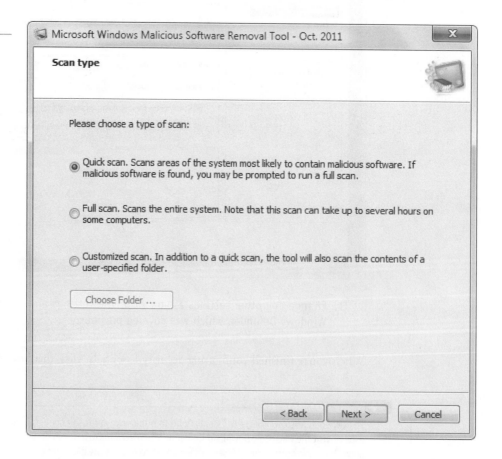

When the detection and removal process is complete, the tool displays a report that indicates which, if any, malware was detected and whether it was removed. Click Finish.

Microsoft releases an updated version of the Malicious Software Removal Tool on Patch Tuesday each month, or more often if security threats are detected before the next Patch Tuesday updates. Microsoft recommends that you run the tool regularly, such as every week or two, as a supplement to your real-time antivirus software.

A complementary (and free) product is the Microsoft Safety Scanner. This utility also scans your hard disk on demand for viruses and other malware, but is not meant to be a replacement for a full-featured antivirus program such as Microsoft Security Essentials.

➕ MORE INFORMATION

To learn more about the Malicious Software Removal Tool and Microsoft Security Scanner, visit http://www.microsoft.com/security/pc-security/malware-removal.aspx

Understanding Windows Forefront Endpoint Protection

> Microsoft Forefront Endpoint Protection works with System Center Configuration Manager 2007 to provide security for network-connected computers in the enterprise.

CERTIFICATION READY
How is Microsoft Forefront Endpoint Protection used to protect client computers in the enterprise?
3.3

Microsoft Forefront Endpoint Protection is a combination of antivirus/anti-malware and management software for desktops, laptops, and other client *endpoints* in a business environment. If you have more than 10 client computers to protect in your organization, Microsoft recommends that you use Forefront Endpoint Protection rather than Microsoft Security Essentials. The client interface for Forefront Endpoint Protection 2010 is shown in Figure 7-42.

Figure 7-42

The Forefront Endpoint Protection 2010 client interface

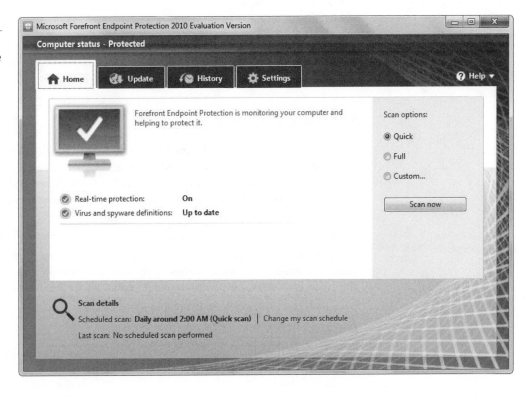

Forefront Endpoint Protection 2010 is built on System Center Configuration Manager. Configuration Manager provides centralized management of client computers along with the ability to secure them, and it supports WSUS for distributing Windows updates and hotfixes. In busy organizations with 10, 20, 30, or more client computers to manage, administrators have a hard time staying on top of management and threat-detection tasks if they must visit each computer physically. Forefront Endpoint Protection allows most management and security updates and tasks to be performed over the network, using automated tasks and policies that apply to many computers at once.

System Requirements

Forefront Endpoint Protection 2010 requires a Microsoft System Center Configuration Manager 2007 site that has Forefront Endpoint Protection Server installed. The following systems are fully supported:

- Windows 7 (x86 or x64)
- Windows 7 XP mode
- Windows Vista (x86 or x64) or later versions
- Windows XP Service Pack 2 (x86 or x64) or later versions
- Windows Server 2008 R2 (x64) or later versions
- Windows Server 2008 R2 Server Core (x64)
- Windows Server 2008 (x86 or x64) or later versions
- Windows Server 2003 Service Pack 2 (x86 or x64) or later versions
- Windows Server 2003 R2 (x86 or x64) or later versions

You can also install Forefront Endpoint Protection 2010 on the following operating systems, with some limitations. You have to install the software manually, you cannot manage the clients centrally, and you cannot apply policies to them:

- Windows 7 Starter
- Windows 7 Home Premium
- Windows Vista Basic
- Windows Vista Home Premium
- Windows XP Home Edition

Deploying to Clients

You can install Forefront Endpoint Protection directly (manually) on client computers that are not running the Configuration Manager agent, or you can run the installation software from a server in a domain environment with Forefront Endpoint Protection Server installed. Remember, if you install the software directly on client computers, you will not be able to manage the clients centrally nor apply policies to them.

To deploy Forefront Endpoint Protection to client computers in a domain, you must verify prerequisites, uninstall any existing antivirus software, create Forefront Endpoint Protection policies, configure Forefront Endpoint Protection definition updates, deploy the Forefront Endpoint Protection client software, and verify that the deployment was successful.

Microsoft recommends the following general steps for deploying Forefront Endpoint Protection to clients in a domain environment:

1. Create Forefront Endpoint Protection policies according to your organization's requirements, set policy precedence, and then assign policies to one or more deployment collections.

2. Configure Forefront Endpoint Protection definition update methods based on the settings defined in the Forefront Endpoint Protection policies created in Step 1.

3. Deploy the Forefront Endpoint Protection installation package to client computers.

With Forefront Endpoint Protection deployed, you can perform a quick or full scan on one or more computers simultaneously from the Configuration Manager console.

✚ MORE INFORMATION

For more information about Microsoft Forefront Endpoint Protection, visit http://www.microsoft.com/en-us/server-cloud/forefront/endpoint-protection.aspx

---

SKILL SUMMARY

IN THIS LESSON YOU LEARNED:

- Windows 7 comes with many built-in maintenance tools that help to keep computers running at top performance. These tools include Disk Defragmenter, Disk Cleanup, Task Scheduler, and the Action Center Maintenance feature.

- Disk Defragmenter can speed up your computer's performance by defragmenting data on your hard disk. In Windows 7, the utility is set to automatically run once a week.

- Disk Cleanup helps you remove unnecessary files from your computer, such as downloaded program files, temporary Internet files, those that are left after running software, and much more.

- Task Scheduler enables you to automate tasks that don't have scheduling features built in. You can also use Task Scheduler to open programs on specific days and times, or at Windows startup.

- Windows 7 Action Center is an improvement upon Security Center in previous versions of Windows. Within Action Center, you can view the status of security features (firewall, antivirus software, etc.) and maintenance (backups, updates, etc.).

- System Information displays a wealth of information about your computer's hardware, drivers, and system software. If you're having any type of system-related issues, you should check System Information for possible clues as to the source of the problem.

- The Windows registry is a database of configuration settings for your computer. The registry is self-sufficient and rarely requires maintenance, but you can use a reputable registry cleaner occasionally to remove settings that are no longer used.

- Microsoft provides several ways to help you keep your Windows system patched and updated, using hotfixes, service packs, updated drivers, and more. Windows Update and Microsoft Update are the primary update tools.

- Windows Firewall is the native firewall in Windows 7 and many other versions of Windows. It monitors inbound and outbound traffic to allow safe traffic to flow and to prevent unsafe traffic from reaching your computer.

- Windows Defender is a free program from Microsoft that monitors your computer for spyware and quarantines or removes it upon detection.

- Microsoft Security Essentials is another free program from Microsoft that provides constant, real-time protection from viruses and other malware.

- If your anti-malware software cannot remove a virus or worm from a computer, try the Microsoft Windows Malicious Software Removal Tool.

- Microsoft Forefront Endpoint Protection works with System Center Configuration Manager 2007 to provide security for network-connected computers in the enterprise.

■ Knowledge Assessment

Fill in the Blank

Complete the following sentences by writing the correct word or words in the blanks provided.

1. A disk that is _____ has file data spread across many different sectors.

2. _____ is a utility that removes many different kinds of unnecessary files from your computer.

3. In Task Scheduler, a _____ is an event that causes a task to run.

4. The _____ is a database in Windows that stores user preferences, file locations, program configuration settings, startup information, hardware settings, and more.

5. Microsoft provides regularly scheduled updates to the Windows operating system via the _____ feature.

6. _____ delivers updates for Microsoft software in addition to the Windows operating system.

7. _____ describes a wide variety of malicious software, such as viruses and worms, that attack computers.

8. A _____ is a collection of updates from Microsoft since the last version of Windows or another Microsoft product was released.

9. _____ is Microsoft's free antispyware program.

10. _____ enables you to centrally manage the security of client computers and devices in an enterprise.

Multiple Choice

Circle the letter that corresponds to the best answer.

1. Which Windows built-in utility helps you delete unnecessary files from your computer?
   a. Disk Defragmenter
   b. Disk Cleanup
   c. Task Scheduler
   d. Registry Editor

2. Which Windows built-in utility helps improve your computer's performance by moving sectors of data on the hard disk?
   a. Disk Defragmenter
   b. Disk Cleanup
   c. Task Scheduler
   d. Registry Editor

3. In Task Scheduler, which command creates a task using a wizard?
   a. Create Task
   b. Create Scheduled Task
   c. Create Task Automatically
   d. Create Basic Task

4. In Windows Defender and Microsoft Security Essentials, which of the following scans is *not* available?
   a. Quick
   b. Full

    c. Partial

    d. Custom

5. Which of the following is *not* part of the Maintenance section in Action Center?

    a. Check for solutions to problem reports

    b. Virus protection

    c. Backup

    d. Check for updates

6. If Action Center detects a maintenance or security issue that needs your attention, an X is displayed under the flag in the notification area. What color is the flag?

    a. Red

    b. White

    c. Yellow

    d. Orange

7. How often does Disk Defragmenter run by default?

    a. Every day

    b. Once a week

    c. Biweekly

    d. Once a month

8. Which program is always updated on Patch Tuesday?

    a. Windows Defender

    b. Microsoft Security Essentials

    c. Malicious Software Removal Tool

    d. Windows Firewall

9. If, for example, your computer is infected with MyDoom, which tool should be used to remove it?

    a. Malicious Software Removal Tool

    b. Windows Firewall

    c. Windows Defender

    d. Task Scheduler

10. Which system does Microsoft Forefront Endpoint Protection require?

    a. Windows Server 2008 R2

    b. Windows Server 2008 R2 or later versions

    c. System Center Configuration Manager 2007

    d. Windows 7

True / False

Circle T if the statement is true or F if the statement is false.

T F 1. Microsoft includes Windows built-in maintenance tools in the Maintenance Tools folder in Accessories.

T F 2. Disk Cleanup can be run on demand but the utility does not have its own scheduling feature.

T F 3. Windows Update provides hotfixes and service packs for Windows computers.

T F 4. Windows Defender can run simultaneously with Microsoft Security Essentials, as a complementary program.

T F 5. Windows Firewall is enabled automatically in new installations of Windows 7.

■ Competency Assessment

Scenario 7-1: Automating Computer Maintenance and Program Launching

Maria is a busy freelance writer who uses her computer many hours a day to research and write articles for several national magazines and newspapers. Her computer, which runs Windows 7 Professional, must be running at peak performance with little downtime. Maria has little time to devote to computer maintenance tasks. She also uses Internet Explorer 9 and Microsoft Word 2010 every day and would like them to start automatically when Windows starts. Maria asks you for advice how to maintain her computer with relatively little effort, and how to configure her computer to start programs automatically. What do you tell her?

Scenario 7-2: Removing Viruses Safely

You are a support person for a computer consulting company. Rajeem is an independent tax consultant who calls you to report that he believes he infected his computer with a virus after downloading and installing a tax-related utility from the Web. How do you advise him to check his computer and resolve the problem, if necessary?

■ Proficiency Assessment

Scenario 7-3: Gathering System Information

In an effort to troubleshoot an issue on a client computer, you posted a message on an online PC support forum. The forum moderator posts a message asking you to list all of the programs that launch at startup on the affected computer. What is the easiest way to provide this information?

Scenario 7-4: Distributing Windows Updates Across a Network

You support Richman Investments, a brokerage firm that employs 20 brokers. Each broker has his own client computer, and the firm has a server running Windows Server. All of the client computers are configured identically.

Over the past six months, some Windows updates have caused the computers to hang, leaving the brokers without computers to conduct business. How can you ensure that the Windows updates that install on client computers will not cause usability issues?

Understanding Backup and Recovery Methods

EXAM OBJECTIVE MATRIX

SKILLS/CONCEPTS	EXAM OBJECTIVE DESCRIPTION	EXAM OBJECTIVE NUMBER
Understanding Local, Network, and Automated Backup Methods	Understand backup and recovery methods.	6.1
Creating a System Image		
Creating a Repair Disc		
Understanding System Restore	Understand backup and recovery methods.	6.1
Using System Restore		
Understanding Recovery Boot Options	Understand backup and recovery methods.	6.1

KEY TERMS

backup

recovery boot options

restore

restore point

system image

system repair disc

System Restore

Volume Shadow Copy service

Windows Backup

At Interstate Snacks, Inc., management wants to ensure that their users' data is backed up. The IT group has requested that you prepare user training materials to teach employees how to back up and restore their data. You need to learn as much as possible about these technologies to provide accurate materials and in-depth training.

■ Understanding Local, Network, and Automated Backup Methods

↓
THE BOTTOM LINE With Windows 7, backups are better than ever. In this section, you'll learn about local, manual, and network backups and how to automate them.

CERTIFICATION READY
How are local, online, and automated backups created?
6.1

A *backup* is a properly secured copy of files and folders—and sometimes settings—usually saved in a compressed format. A backup is created so you can *restore* the files and settings in the event of data loss from a hard disk failure, accidental erasure or disk formatting, or natural events. Most users hope they never need backups. When they do need backups, however, they need them *now!* And if they don't have backups, it's often too late—their files might be gone forever.

Windows Backup uses the Backup and Restore utility that comes with many Windows versions and enables you to back up and recover files. Windows Backup has been around in one form or another for quite a while. In the past, due to performance issues, many companies and individuals employed third-party backup and restore solutions. With Windows 7, the backup utility is greatly improved over previous Windows editions.

The initial Windows Backup page is shown in Figure 8-1. To begin the first backup on this computer, you would click the *Set up backup* link. Before you learn about backups in depth, there are other system protection features you should know about. The *Create a system image* option located on the upper-left of the page creates a complete backup of your computer. You can use a system image to fully restore a crashed computer. The *Create a system repair disc* option creates a CD or DVD disc you can use to restore your computer if it crashes and no longer boots. You'll learn about system images and creating a system repair disc later in this lesson.

As detailed in Lesson 7, the Action Center link allows you to manage pop-up messages from the system tray and change your User Account Control (UAC) and Windows Update settings

Figure 8-1

The main Windows Backup page

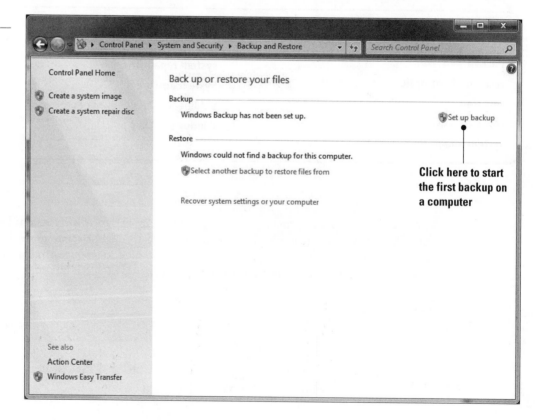

(among other system settings). Windows Easy Transfer (covered in Lesson 1) helps you migrate data and user settings from an old computer.

Windows Backup is designed to back up application data and settings. It does not back up the following:

- Program files, unless part of a system image
- Files stored on a FAT formatted volume
- Files in the Recycle Bin
- Temporary files on drives smaller than 1 gigabyte (GB)
- Files located on other computers across your network (mapped network drives), on the Internet, or on the same drive you are storing the backup; only local files are included in the backup

You can store backups on CD/DVD, to another internal disk, to an external drive, or to a network drive. (Only Windows 7 Professional, Ultimate, and Enterprise editions enable you to back up your files to a network.) If you're using an external drive that's a universal serial bus (USB) drive, you must have enough storage space to store your backup. Tape drives are no longer supported for storage of your backups.

To ensure that your data is protected, you should first create a full backup of your data files and settings. By default, Windows Backup stores incremental changes and appends them to your existing backup when backing up to either a hard drive or a network location. If you back up to CD or DVD, you will have an option to create a new, full backup each time.

Windows Backup is set to run automatically each week, adding new or modified information to your backup file. You can change the default schedule of Windows Backup to a day and time that works best for you, which means a time you're least likely to be working on the computer.

TAKE NOTE*

Although you can back up to an internal disk on the same computer, what happens if your computer crashes or gets damaged in a fire or flood? The purpose of a backup is to have a working copy of data in the worst-case scenario. A best practice is to save the backup to some type of media that's easy to access and store, separate from the computer that contains the original data. If the backup contains critical files, consider saving the backup media in a fireproof cabinet or safe, or in an offsite location. You could store your backup on an internal drive of a server across the network—that's different than saving it to an internal disk on the same computer as the original files.

To perform a backup, you need to be logged on using an account with local or domain administrative permissions, or as a member of the Backup Operators group. Restoring files is different. Even a standard user is able to restore his own data files. An administrator or a member of the Backup Operators group can restore anyone's files as well as the entire system.

CREATE A BACKUP

GET READY. To create a backup using Windows Backup, perform the following steps:

1. Click **Start,** type **backup** in the **Search programs and files** search box, and then select **Backup and Restore** from the resulting list. Alternately, click **Start > Control Panel** and in the System and Security section, click **Backup your computer.** If prompted for an administrator password or confirmation, type the password or provide confirmation. If you attempt to run the backup utility as a non-administrative account, you can expect to see the error message displayed in Figure 8-2.

Figure 8-2

An error message as a result of attempting to run Windows Backup as a non-administrative user

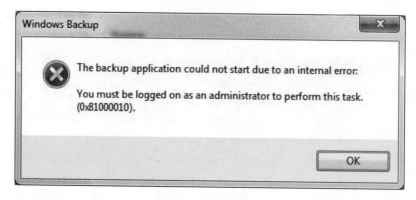

> **TAKE NOTE** *
>
> If Windows Backup is not enabled, you must turn it on to create backups. Enabling Windows Backup also enables the ***Volume Shadow Copy service***, which is what allows you to create restore points and backups of your system.

CERTIFICATION READY
Which options can be selected when creating a backup?
6.1

2. If this is the first time you are creating a backup on your computer, click the **Set up backup** link. The backup wizard starts.

3. Select where you want to save your backup files. The available types of media you can back up to include CDs/DVDs, internal drives, external drives, USB drives, and network locations (if using Windows 7 Professional, Ultimate, or Enterprise).

   • To store your backup on CD/DVD, an internal drive, or an external drive, select one of the available local backup destinations (see Figure 8-3) and then click **Next**.

Figure 8-3

Selecting where to store your backup

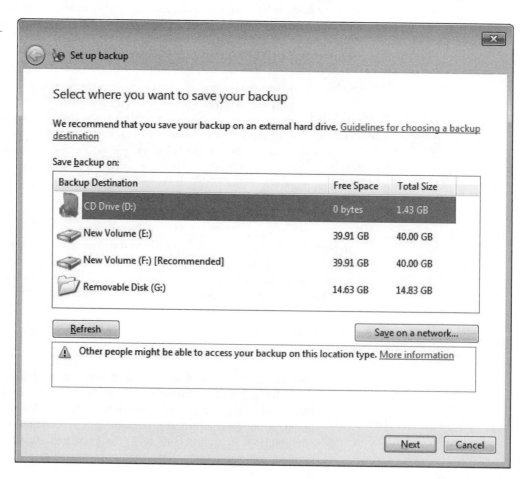

- To store your backup on a network drive, click the **Save on a network** button and then click **Next**. On the Select a network location page shown in Figure 8-4, in the **Network Location** text box, type a Universal Naming Convention (UNC) to a shared folder on your network and a **Username** and **Password** that has read/write access to the shared folder you specified in the UNC path. Click **OK.**

Figure 8-4

Storing your backup on the network

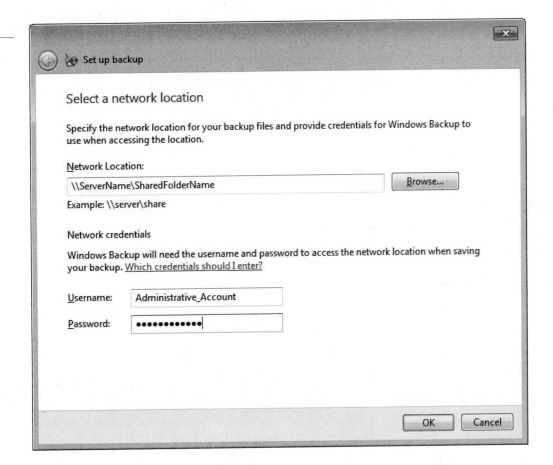

4. On the What do you want to back up? page, you have two options:
   - **Let Windows choose (recommended):** Select this to back up the following:
     ○ All data that is saved in local libraries for all user accounts on the computer.
     ○ Default Windows folders (including Downloads, AppData, Contacts, Desktop, Favorites, Links, Saved Games, and Searches).
     ○ A system image. If you are saving your backup to a NTFS-formatted partition and there is enough available disk space for a full system image, the Windows operating system, drivers, installed programs, and registry settings will be included in the backup.
   - **Let me choose:** If you select this option and then click **Next**, you can expand your libraries, drives, and folders to select only what you want to back up (see Figure 8-5). Notice that you cannot expand the folders to back up individual files.

   Make your selections and click **Next**.
5. The Review your backup settings page displayed in Figure 8-6 gives you the opportunity to review your choices and to set up a schedule for how often you would like backups to occur. If you leave the default schedule, backups will run **Every Sunday at 7:00 PM.**

TAKE NOTE *

You can back up individual folders, libraries, or drives, but you cannot back up individual files.

Figure 8-5

Choosing what to back up

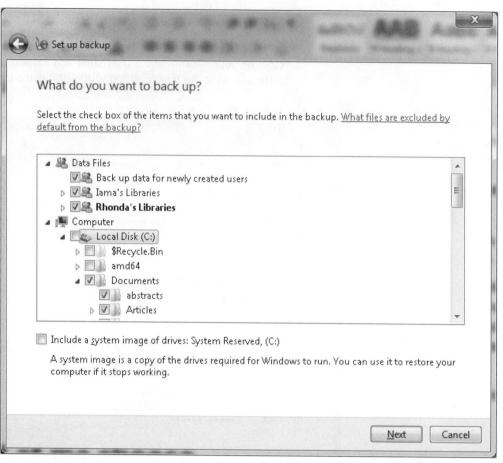

Figure 8-6

Reviewing your backup settings

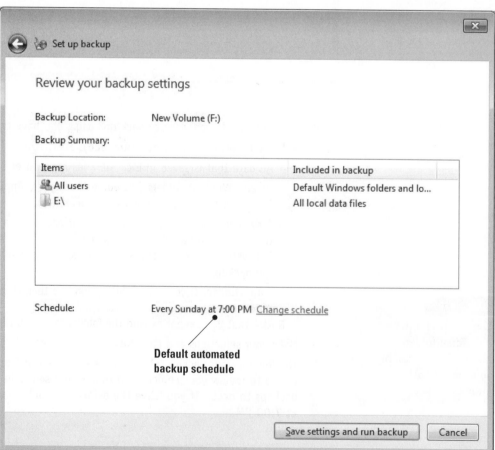

To change the schedule or disable it, click the **Change schedule** link. The How often do you want to back up? page displays (see Figure 8-7):

- To disable scheduled (automatic) backups, deselect the **Run backup on a schedule (recommended)** box.
- To change the schedule, you can change **How often** (**Daily**, **Weekly** or **Monthly**), **What day** (any day of the week), and **What time** (a 24-hour time frame).

After making your selections, click **OK**.

Figure 8-7

Scheduling backups

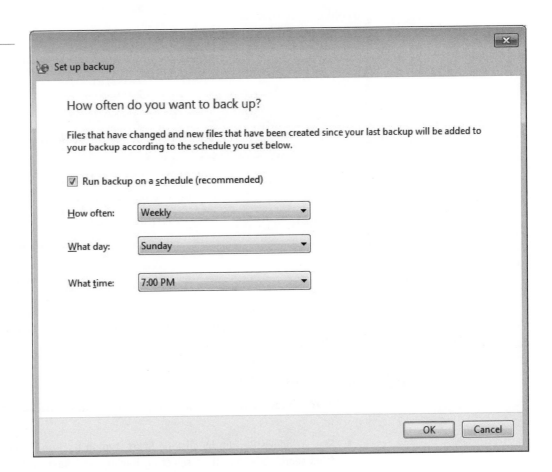

6. On the Review your backup settings page, click **Save settings and run backup.**

After the backup runs, the Back up or restore your files page will look similar to Figure 8-8. Notice that, in this example, the location is set to the E: volume, which currently has 39.83 GB of free space. The backup size is 74.99 MB. And because the schedule was turned on and set to 10:00 PM every Friday night, the next backup is scheduled for the following Friday and every Friday thereafter. The last backup date and time stamp lets you know the last time the backup completed successfully. If you want to change the settings, click *Change settings*. The Set up backup wizard runs again. Using the wizard, you can change your destination to back up to what you want backed up and you can configure the automatic backup schedule.

The *Manage space* link allows you to browse to where your backups are stored. From there you can double-click a backup and then restore it (you will learn more about restores in the next section). You can also view and delete data and system image backups in case you need space for future backups. There are two new options on this page: The *Turn off schedule* link (located in the Control Panel Home section) at the top left of the page and the *Back up now*

Figure 8-8

After backups have run

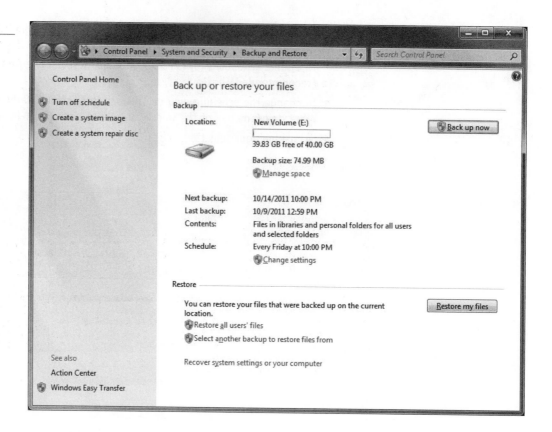

button (located at the top right of the page). You can create a manual backup anytime by clicking the *Back up now* button.

RESTORE FROM A BACKUP

GET READY. To restore data from a backup using Windows Backup, perform the following steps:

1. Start Windows Backup by clicking **Start**, typing **backup** in the **Search programs and files** search box, and then selecting **Backup and Restore** from the resulting list.

2. If you are logged on as a user with administrative permissions and want to restore another user's data, click the **Restore all users' files** link in the Restore section of the Backup and Restore window (refer to Figure 8-8). If you need to restore files or folders for the administrator account you are logged on as, click the **Restore my files** button. The Browse or search your backup for files and folders to restore page displays (see Figure 8-9).

3. By default, files are restored from the latest backup. To choose an older backup, click the **Choose a different date** link and then select the backup you'd like to restore from.

4. On the right, click the **Search** button if you know the name of the folder or document you're looking for (even part of the name will work).

5. Clicking either **Browse for files** or **Browse for folders** displays Figure 8-10, which at first glance might appear to be the same page, but the behavior is not the same. As you probably guessed, **Browse for files** allows you to browse at the file level so you can restore a specific file. **Browse for folders** allows you to go only to the folder level to restore an entire folder.

Notice also that there are three user accounts data that were backed up: Administrator, Lindsey, and Rhonda. If Lindsey logged on to this same computer,

TAKE NOTE*

You can select multiple files using the Shift and Ctrl keys. The Shift key enables you to select files that are listed consecutively. The Ctrl key enables you to select non-consecutive files.

Figure 8-9

Starting the restore process

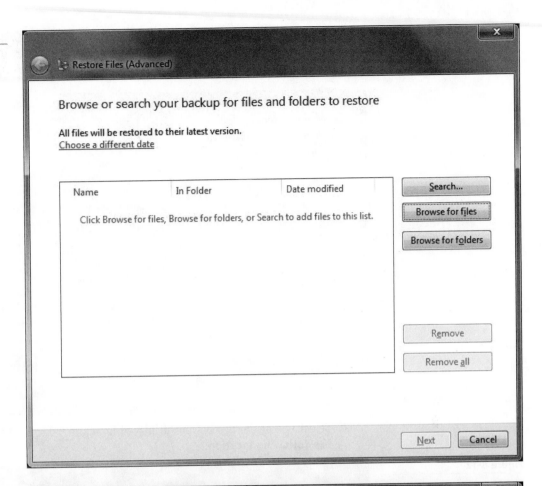

Figure 8-10

Browsing for files and folders

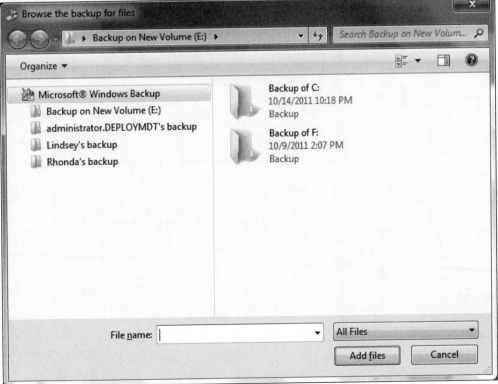

opened the Backup and Restore utility, and clicked **Restore my files**, Figure 8-11 would display (with her Documents folder expanded).

6. Double-click any file (such as Windows 7 IT Training). When you double-click a file, you perform the same function as when you click the file and then click the **Add files** button.

Figure 8-11

Reviewing a folder backup

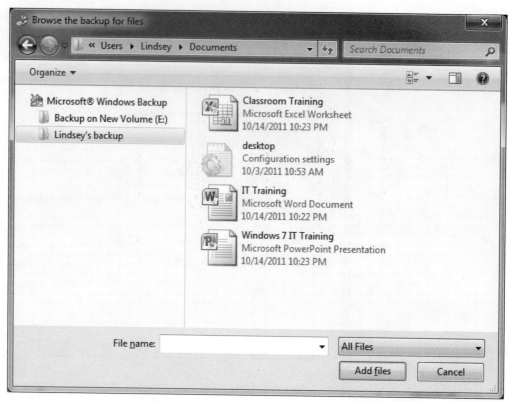

7. Select one of the two options displayed in Figure 8-12: **In the original location** or **In the following location**.

Figure 8-12

Choosing where to restore your files

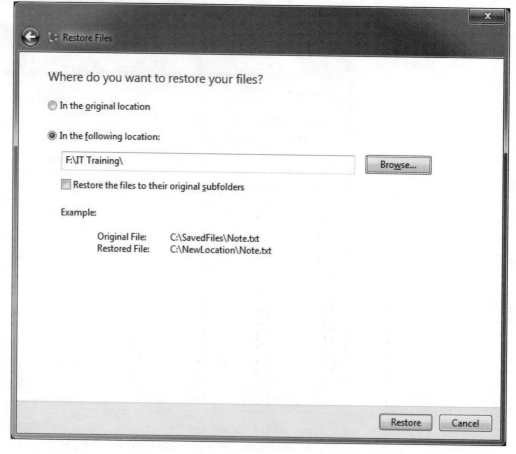

8. Click **Restore.**
9. The Your files have been restored page displays. From this page you can click the **View restored files** link to ensure the correct files were restored to the path you specified.
10. When you have restored your files or folders, click **Finish.**

You can also use the Previous Versions of a file by right-clicking the file and choosing *Restore previous version*. Each time a file is saved with changes, a previous version is created so that you can roll back to an earlier version of a document in case the document becomes corrupted or you just want to view what has changed. If you choose to restore the document, it will be restored to its original location. If you want to restore it to a new location, click the Copy button and browse to the folder where you would like to paste it. The permissions will be inherited from the folder into which you paste the copied file. If you're not sure which version of the file you want to restore, highlight the different versions and click Open to view the contents of each file.

➕ MORE INFORMATION

For more information about Windows 7 Backup and Restore, visit http://windows.microsoft.com/en-US/windows7/products/features/backup-and-restore

■ Creating a System Image

A *system image* is an image of an entire hard drive that includes all files needed to restore your operating system. By default, a system image includes the Windows folder, all system settings, programs, and files. If the drive your operating system resides on fails or the computer fails for any reason, you can use a system image on the same machine (replacing the hardware that caused the failure) or another machine to get your users back up and running as quickly as possible.

A system image restore is an all-or-none process. You cannot pick and choose what gets restored, but you can decide to back up more than just a system image if you like.

There are two methods for creating a system image:

- Creating a system image as part of the automatic Windows Backup process
- Creating a system image manually, which involves running the backup wizard and selecting the drives you want to include in the image

Figure 8-13 shows the backup wizard's What do you want to back up? page (which was previously displayed) with the Include a system image option selected.

You can also click the Create a system image link in the left pane of the Backup and Restore page (refer to Figure 8-8) and then select additional drives or folders for backup on the same page. Just follow the wizard to create your system image.

Figure 8-13

Creating a system image

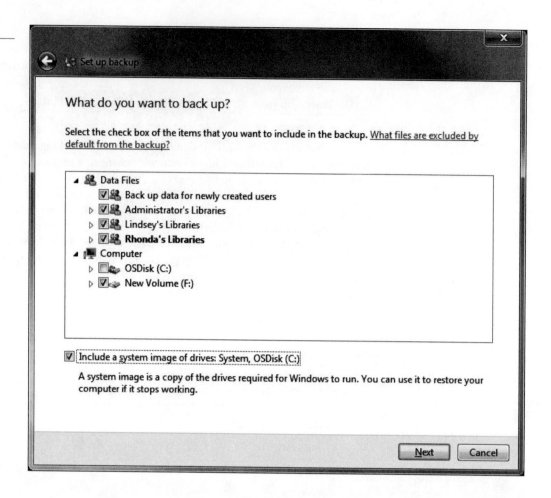

Creating a system image using the backup wizard enables you to store the system image on a CD/DVD, hard drive, USB drive, or a network location. If you are storing your system images on an internal or external hard drive and you begin to run out of space, older system image backups will be deleted to make room for the new backups. If you are storing your system image backups to a network location, only one is saved. This is because the backup utility creates a folder named \WindowsImageBackup\ and within that folder each system image backup is named based on the name of the computer storing the system image backup. So each time a new backup is created the old one is overwritten. If you need to save an older system image backup, copy it to a different location and then create the new system image backup.

 CREATE A SYSTEM IMAGE

GET READY. To create a system image, perform the following steps:

1. Click **Start,** type **backup** in the **Search programs and files** search box, and then select **Backup and Restore** from the resulting list.

2. On the Backup or restore your files page, in the upper-left corner, click the **Create a system image** link.

3. The backup program scans for available storage devices and displays them on the Where do you want to save the backup? page (see Figure 8-14). In this example, the available options are:

- **On a hard disk.** Click the drop-down arrow to select a disk.
- **On one or more DVDs.** Click the drop-down arrow to select the CD or DVD drive.
- **On a network location.** Click **Select** to set your network location UNC path (as you did previously in this lesson).

Make a selection and click **Next**.

Figure 8-14

Storage choices for a system image

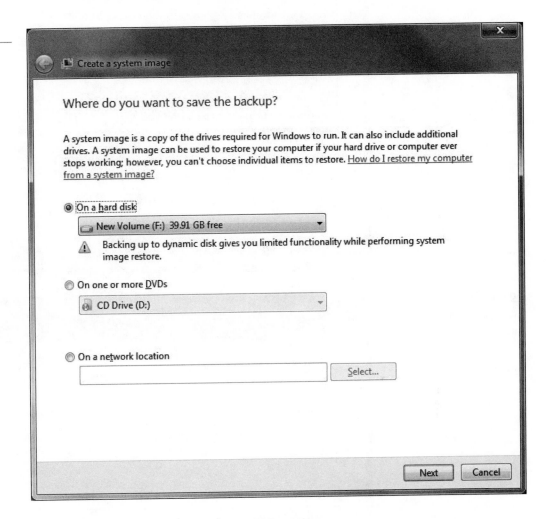

4. The Which drives do you want to include in the backup? page displays (see Figure 8-15). The default selections are the **System** drive and the **OSDisk** disk (the disk on which the operating system is installed). This computer has only two other disks: **E:** (where we are storing the image, so we cannot include it here) and **F:** (which is not currently selected). If you want to include the F: drive, select the check box and then click **Next**.

5. On the Confirm your backup settings page (see Figure 8-16), review where the backup location will be, how much space the backup will need, and a list of drives that will be included in the backup. If everything looks good, click the **Start backup** button.

Figure 8-15

Selecting drives to include in
the system image

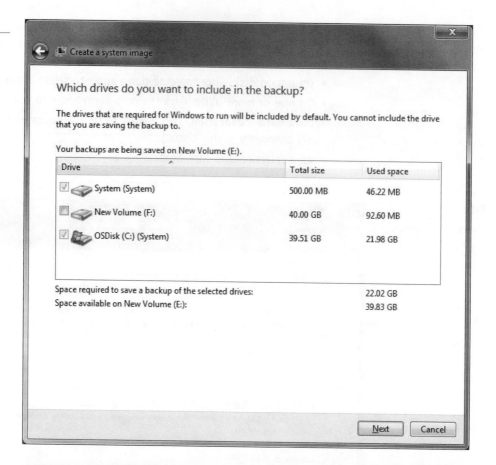

Figure 8-16

Reviewing system image
backup settings

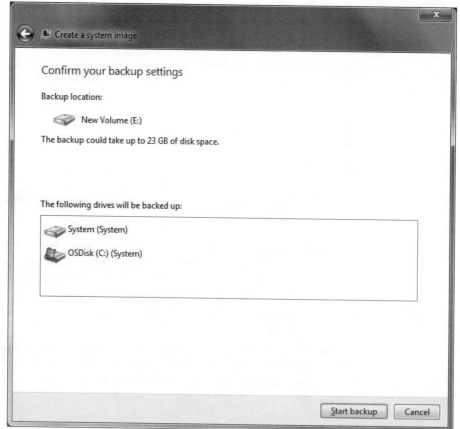

MORE INFORMATION

For details about system images, go to http://windows.microsoft.com/en-US/windows7/Back-up-your-programs-system-settings-and-files

■ Creating a Repair Disc

↓
THE BOTTOM LINE

If your job involves keeping computers up and running, you'll need to be able to repair those systems if the operating system files become corrupted. It's essential for you to have a Windows installation disc or a repair disc on hand. Most organizations today use Microsoft deployment tools to roll out Windows 7, which means that only a few users (if any) will have a Windows installation disc. If that's the case, then creating a repair disc is the next best thing.

When a serious error occurs and you need to restore a system, you'll find the Windows 7 system recovery options to be an invaluable resource. There are two tools that contain the system recovery options:

- The Windows installation disc
- A system repair disc

The Windows installation disc is provided by Microsoft or the computer manufacturer. In some cases, it might be one you created yourself if your organization purchases volume licenses of Windows 7 rather than individual retail copies. A *system repair disc* is a bootable disc you create in Windows 7 that contains Windows system recovery tools. You can use the repair disc to attempt to start a failed computer, or to restore a computer from a system image. In an IT environment, you can create a repair disc for as many technicians as needed.

 CREATE A REPAIR DISC

GET READY. To create your own repair disc, perform the following steps:

1. Open Windows Backup by clicking **Start**, typing **backup** in the **Search programs and files** search box, and then selecting **Backup and Restore** from the resulting list.
2. In the task pane on the left, click **Create a system repair disc** (refer to Figure 8-1 and Figure 8-8). If prompted by UAC, type your administrative credentials or click **Continue**.
3. The Create a system repair disc dialog box displays a drop-down list you can click to select a CD/DVD drive. (If only one CD/DVD drive is available on the system, only one option is available and it's already selected.) Click **Create disc**.

Sometimes it is possible that the files needed to create a system repair disc are not available and you might be prompted to insert a Windows installation disc in order to find those files.

Understanding System Restore

THE BOTTOM LINE

Restoring a system image is usually necessary because of a computer catastrophe or to get a new computer up and running quickly. If a computer has crashed and you have a spare computer (or you can replace the hardware—such as a drive—that caused the crash), restoring the system image can be a quick fix. When a user gets a new computer and she needs to access all the settings and data from her old computer, restoring a system image can take less time than installing Windows and all applications.

CERTIFICATION READY
How does System
Restore help you restore
a system?
6.1

Just as there is more than one method for creating system images, there is more than one method for restoring system images. But restoring the system image will restore the entire backup—again, you cannot choose what is restored (it's either restoring everything or it's restoring nothing at all). Before you begin the restore process, ensure that the drive you are restoring the backup to is at least the same size as the drive where you created the system image backup. The drive can be larger; it doesn't have to be the exact size.

There are three methods for restoring a system image:

- Restoring a system image using the Recovery applet in Control Panel
- Restoring a system image using preinstalled recovery options
- Restoring a system image using a Windows installation or system repair disc

If the computer is not experiencing any problems but you need to get a new image on an existing machine, you can use the Recovery applet in Control Panel.

 RESTORE A SYSTEM IMAGE

GET READY. To restore a system image, perform the following steps:

1. Open Recovery by clicking **Start** and in the **Search programs and files** search box, typing **recovery** and then selecting **Recovery** from the resulting list.
2. On the Restore this computer to an earlier point in time page, click the **Advanced recovery methods** link.
3. Click **Use a system image you created earlier to recover your computer**.
4. You have the option to create a new backup at this point. Click either the **Back up Now** button or the **Skip** button. (For our purposes, we will click **Skip**.)
5. The computer restarts and boots into a Windows Pre Installation Environment. In the System Recovery Options dialog box (see Figure 8-17), click the drop-down arrow to choose a keyboard layout.

Figure 8-17

Choosing a keyboard layout

System Recovery Options	☒

Select a language:

English (United States) ▼

Select a keyboard input method:

US ▼

Next>   Cancel

6. The Re-image Your Computer Wizard launches (see Figure 8-18). Leave the default selection of **Use the latest available system image (recommended)**. Choose the **Location**, the **Date and time** of when it was created, and the name of the **Computer** that created it. If this is not the system image you want to restore, you can choose **Select a system image** and then browse to the one you would like to use. After you've chosen your system image to restore from, click **Next**.

Figure 8-18

Choosing which system image to restore from

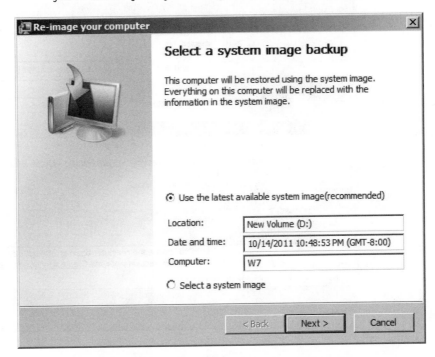

7. Additional restore options are displayed in Figure 8-19. From this page you can format and repartition disks. If the option is grayed out, you might need to install drivers by clicking the **Install drivers** button and then browsing to your mass storage drivers. If you click the **Advanced** button, you can deselect **Automatically restart this computer after the restart is complete** and **Automatically check and update disk error information**. By default, both are selected. Click **Next**.

Figure 8-19

Additional restore options

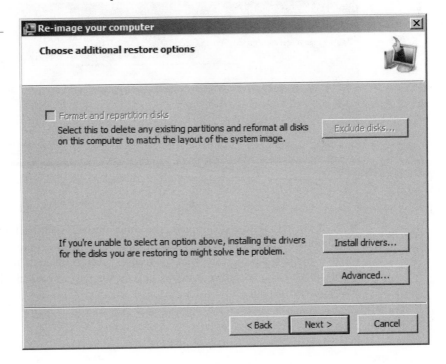

8. Click **Finish** on the last page to begin the system restore. A warning message displays (see Figure 8-20), prompting you to confirm that you want to replace all data on the drives to be restored. Click **Yes**.

Figure 8-20

A warning message

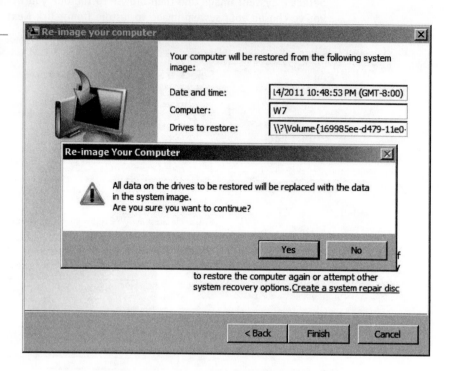

9. You can monitor the process of the restore via the progress bar that is displayed (see Figure 8-21). If you need to stop the restore, you can click the **Stop restore** button.

Figure 8-21

Monitoring the system image restore progress

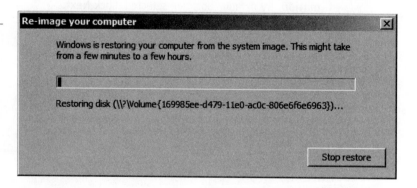

When the system restore is complete, the computer will boot back into Windows 7 and you'll be prompted to press Ctrl+Alt+Delete to log on. Once you're logged on, a Recovery dialog box (see Figure 8-22) indicates that the recovery has completed. You are provided with the opportunity to also restore your files. Click *Restore my files* or click Cancel, depending on what you want to do.

Figure 8-22

The system image restore completes

If you cannot access the Control Panel, you can restore your computer using a Windows installation disc or a system repair disc (if you have created one), as explained in the following section.

 RESTORE USING A WINDOWS INSTALLATION DISC OR A SYSTEM REPAIR DISC

GET READY. To restore your computer using a Windows installation disc or a system repair disc, perform the following steps:

1. With the computer shut down, insert the system repair disc and turn the computer on.
2. If needed, press any key to boot from the system repair disc.
3. Choose your keyboard layout (as previously detailed) and then click **Next**.
4. From the list of Recovery Tools shown in Figure 8-23, click **System Image Recovery**.

Figure 8-23

The System Recovery tools

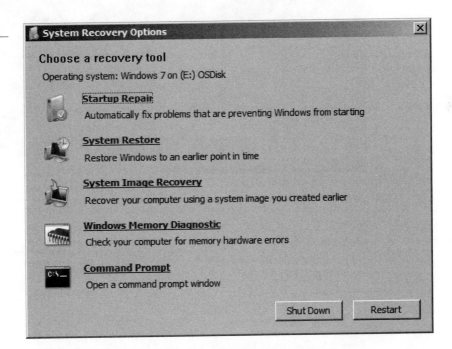

5. Continue following the wizard prompts as you did earlier in this section.

If you do not have access to the Control Panel and do not have a Windows installation or system repair disc, the next section explains how to restore from the preinstalled recovery options.

 RESTORE FROM THE PREINSTALLED RECOVERY OPTIONS

GET READY. To restore from the preinstalled recovery options, perform the following steps:

1. Shut down the machine (if it's not already shut down) and restart by pressing the power button. During the boot process, and before the Windows logo displays on-screen, press the **F8** key.

2. On the Advanced Boot Options menu screen shown in Figure 8-24, highlight **Repair Your Computer** (using the arrow keys if needed) and then press **Enter**.

Figure 8-24

The Advanced Boot Options page

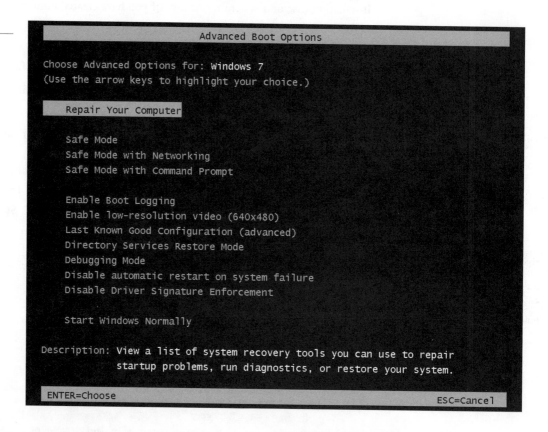

```
                          Advanced Boot Options

Choose Advanced Options for: Windows 7
(Use the arrow keys to highlight your choice.)

   Repair Your Computer

   Safe Mode
   Safe Mode with Networking
   Safe Mode with Command Prompt

   Enable Boot Logging
   Enable low-resolution video (640x480)
   Last Known Good Configuration (advanced)
   Directory Services Restore Mode
   Debugging Mode
   Disable automatic restart on system failure
   Disable Driver Signature Enforcement

   Start Windows Normally

Description: View a list of system recovery tools you can use to repair
            startup problems, run diagnostics, or restore your system.


ENTER=Choose                                          ESC=Cancel
```

TAKE NOTE*

You'll learn more about the Advanced Boot Options later in this lesson.

3. Choose your keyboard layout and then click **Next**.
4. Select a **User name**, type a **Password**, and then click **OK**.
5. On the System Recovery Options menu, click **System Image Recovery** and follow the same steps as you did beginning with Step 6 following Figure 8-18.

TAKE NOTE*

After a system image restore, it is normal for the computer to run slowly for a few hours while Windows checks for and applies updates to things like drivers and antivirus signatures. Opening Microsoft Outlook can also cause a major slowdown because the entire offline cache has to be rebuilt.

Using System Restore

THE BOTTOM LINE

If your PC begins experiencing unusual problems that don't clear up after a few reboots or some simple troubleshooting, you can use System Restore to roll back your system files and applications to a time when the PC was working properly.

System Restore uses the System Protection feature to create restore points. *Restore points* can be used to roll back your system to an earlier point in time; they are created automatically on a weekly basis and any time you make a change to your computer (such as installing a new application or device driver). System image backups stored on hard drives can also be used for system restores. Although a system image backup includes data files within the image, when you use the system image backup as a restore point, your data is ignored. To restore your data, you must use the restore feature from the Backup and Restore tool discussed previously in this lesson.

Anytime you are not sure about the potential impact of a change you are making to a computer, you should create a system restore. It is better to have a system restore and not need it than to need one and not have it.

 CREATE A SYSTEM RESTORE MANUALLY

GET READY. To create a system restore point manually, perform the following steps:

1. Ensure all open files and applications are saved and closed.
2. Click **Start**, right-click **Computer**, and then click **Properties**. The System page displays (see Figure 8-25).

Figure 8-25

The System page

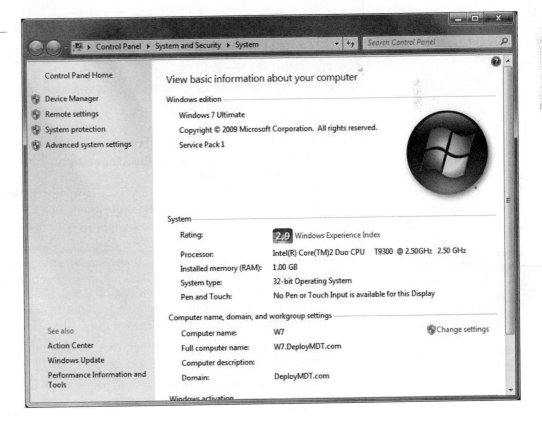

3. In the left pane, click **System protection**. If prompted by UAC, type your administrative credentials or click **Continue**.

4. The Protection Settings section displays drives on the computer and whether protection is on or off. Protection settings are enabled only on the operating system disk by default. To turn on protection for another drive, highlight the drive and click the **Configure** button (see Figure 8-26).

Figure 8-26

The System Protection tab

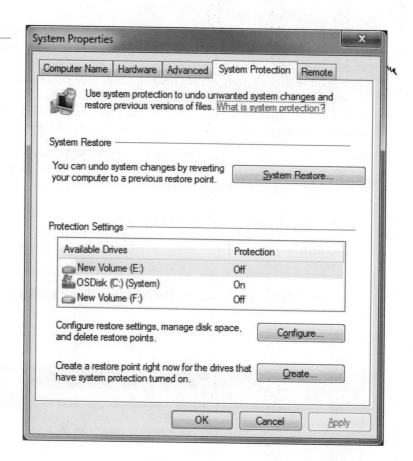

5. Figure 8-27 shows the Restore Settings for volume E. The default option is selected, which turns off system protection for that drive. You can choose to restore system settings and previous versions of files or you can choose to restore only previous versions of files. You can also adjust the maximum amount of disk space that can be used for system protections. Don't be overly concerned if you begin to run out of space; older system restores are deleted to make room for newer ones.

The **Delete** button at the bottom of the Restore Settings page deletes all restore points for that disk. Clicking this button displays a warning alert indicating that you can't undo unwanted system changes or restore previous versions of files on this drive. You are prompted to confirm that you want to continue. Clicking **Continue** deletes them all; clicking **Cancel** cancels the deletion process.

6. After configuring your restore settings, click **OK** to return to the System Protection tab.

7. Click the **Create** button to create restore points for all drives that have system protection turned on.

TAKE NOTE*

Turning off system protection deletes all restore points for that disk.

Figure 8-27

The Restore Settings for volume E

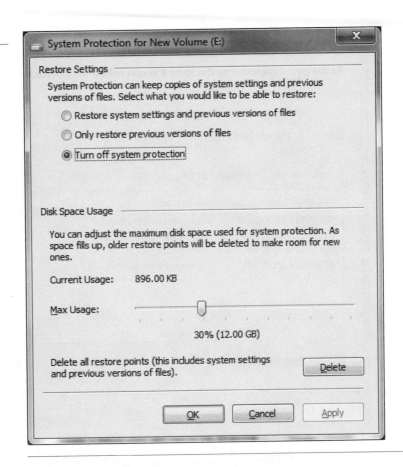

You now have new restore points for each drive.

Restoring Your System Using System Restores

When you need to utilize a system restore, there are a couple of ways to access them. In the previous section, you skipped the System Restore button on the System Protection tab; by doing so, you can now launch the Restore System wizard.

 LAUNCH THE RESTORE SYSTEM WIZARD

GET READY. To launch the Restore System Wizard, perform the following steps:

1. Click **Start** and in the **Search programs and files** search box, type **system restore** and then select **System Restore** from the resulting list. The System Restore Wizard starts.

2. On the Restore system files and settings page, click **Next**.

3. System restore automatically recommends the newest restore point to roll back to, but you can select a different restore point by checking the **Show more restore points** option. The descriptions of the restore points that were created automatically are based on the name of the event that triggered the creation of the restore point (see Figure 8-28).

4. Choose the restore point you want to roll back to. If no restore points are displayed, ensure that System Protection is turned on for at least the operating system disk and that there is enough hard drive space. On drives that are 500 MB or larger, you need 300 MB of available disk space; drives smaller than 300 MB need at least 50 MB of free space. You can check to see exactly what would be changed by highlighting the system restore you want to roll back to and clicking the **Scan for affected programs** button. The resulting page displays a list of programs and drivers that will be deleted and the programs and drivers that might be restored if you continue with this system restore.

Figure 8-28

Choosing a restore point

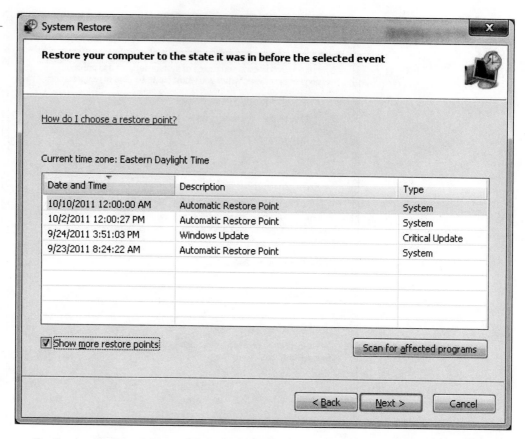

5. On the Confirm disks to restore page (see Figure 8-29), select the disks you would like to restore and then click **Next**. The warning message on this page alerts you to the fact that you must always restore the drive that contains Windows. Restoring others drives are optional.

Figure 8-29

Confirming disks to restore

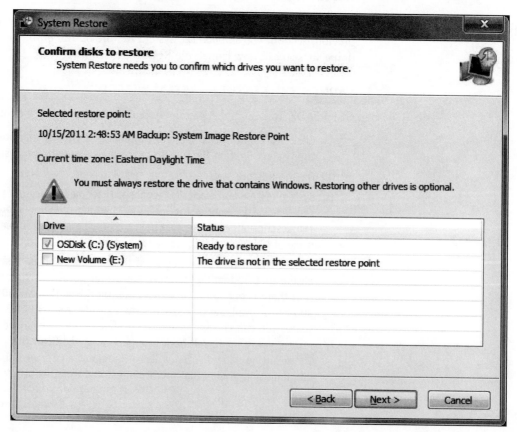

6. Ensure all files and applications are saved and closed. On the Confirm your restore point page, click **Finish**. Figure 8-30 shows System Restore initializing.

Figure 8-30

System Restore initialization

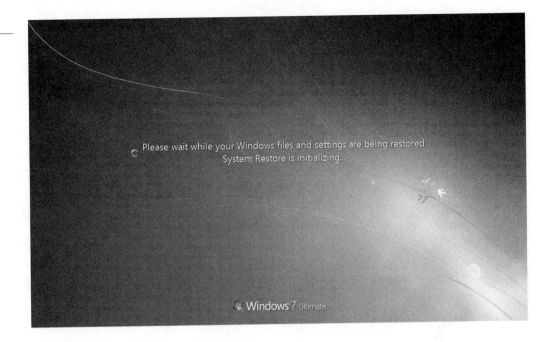

During this process, you will see the registry restored, temporary files deleted, and then Windows restarts. When the system restore is completed, an informational message displays, stating the system restore completed successfully. The system has been restored to the restore point you chose, and your documents have not been affected.

7. Click **Close** to end the system restore.

What happens if the system restore not only doesn't fix your issue, it makes it worse? If you can still boot the computer, you can go through the same process again and choose an earlier restore point to roll back to (if you have one). Or if you prefer, you can open System Restore, choose Undo System Restore, and then click Next. Review your choices and then click Finish.

If you would rather wipe your computer clean of all data and applications—which really should be only a last-ditch effort when every other solution fails—perform an advanced recovery.

 PERFORM AN ADVANCED RECOVERY

GET READY. To perform an advanced recovery, perform the following steps:

1. Click **Start**, type **recovery** in the **Search programs and files** search box, and then select **Recovery** from the resulting list.

2. On the Restore this computer to an earlier point in time page, click the **Advanced recovery methods** link.

3. The Choose an advanced recovery method page (see Figure 8-31) displays two options:

   • **Use a system image you created earlier to recover your computer.** Choose this option if you have a system image; this option re-installs your applications and system settings. If you do not have a system image backup, choose the Reinstall Windows option.

- **Reinstall Windows (requires Windows installation disc).** This option sets the machine back to ground zero (before you installed any applications or created any folders/files). If you have a backup, you can reinstall Windows and then restore your files from a backup.

Figure 8-31

Choosing the advanced recovery method

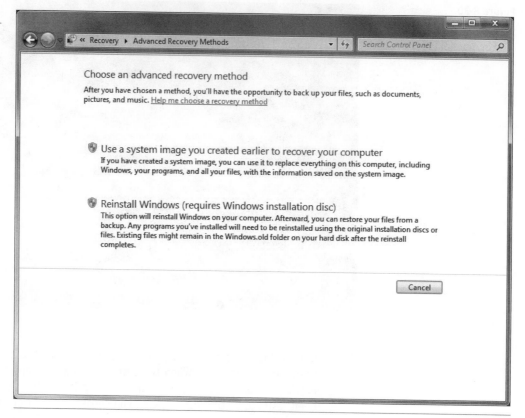

MORE INFORMATION

To learn more about System Restore, visit http://windows.microsoft.com/en-US/windows7/products/features/system-restore

■ Understanding Recovery Boot Options

↓
THE BOTTOM LINE

You might think if your computer doesn't boot, a restore or reinstallation must be done. But that is not always the case. There are some built-in recovery boot options you can try if your computer no longer boots.

CERTIFICATION READY
How are recovery boot options used to repair a Windows 7 installation?
6.1

Recovery boot options, also referred to as advanced startup options, provide you with tools to help you repair a broken Windows 7 installation. The options are found on the Advanced Boot Options page, which you access when the computer first begins to boot by pressing the F8 key. (You must press the F8 key before Windows begins to load.)

The following list explains each tool:

- **Repair Your Computer:** This tool is helpful when your computer will not boot due to corrupt or missing system files. In the event of missing or corrupt system files, this tool should begin working automatically. If you still suspect system files causing the problem, run this tool manually from the Advanced Boot Options menu. This option is not designed to repair hard drives or memory issues and it doesn't provide backups. Files used to repair your system files are stored on a Windows 7 Recovery partition. This partition is created by default and is a hidden partition, so you won't see it in Windows Explorer. However, if you open the disk management snap-in, you will see a partition with the label System Reserved and it will be 100 MB.

- **Safe Mode:** This tool starts Windows 7 in a limited state that loads only basic files and drivers. If you have recently installed an application and now your computer will not boot, you can start the machine in Safe Mode and then run the new application. If the application runs in Safe Mode, then it's likely that a .dll file or driver was installed by the application and it might be conflicting with OS drivers or .dll files. Tools that help you diagnose or resolve issues when in Safe Mode include System Recovery (to use a restore point), Control Panel, Device Manager, Event Viewer, System Information, and Registry Editor (to edit the registry).

- **Safe Mode with Networking:** This tool provides you with access to the standard Safe Mode options but also loads networking drivers so you can access resources on the network or the Internet. Avoid using this option if you are trying to repair the damage done by a virus because, in some cases, the infection can spread to network resources.

- **Safe Mode with Command Prompt:** Starts Windows Safe Mode, giving you everything from Safe Mode except the graphical interface so the only interface you will have is a command prompt. This is an advanced recovery mode, but it is useful for repairing systems on which the graphical user interface has corrupted.

- **Enable Boot Logging:** This tool boots Windows into a normal mode and creates a text file that lists all drivers loaded (or not loaded) during startup. The file will be named ntbtlog.txt and stored in the C:\Windows folder (or whichever drive you installed Windows on). The contents will look similar to Figure 8-32.

Figure 8-32

Drivers loaded during the boot process

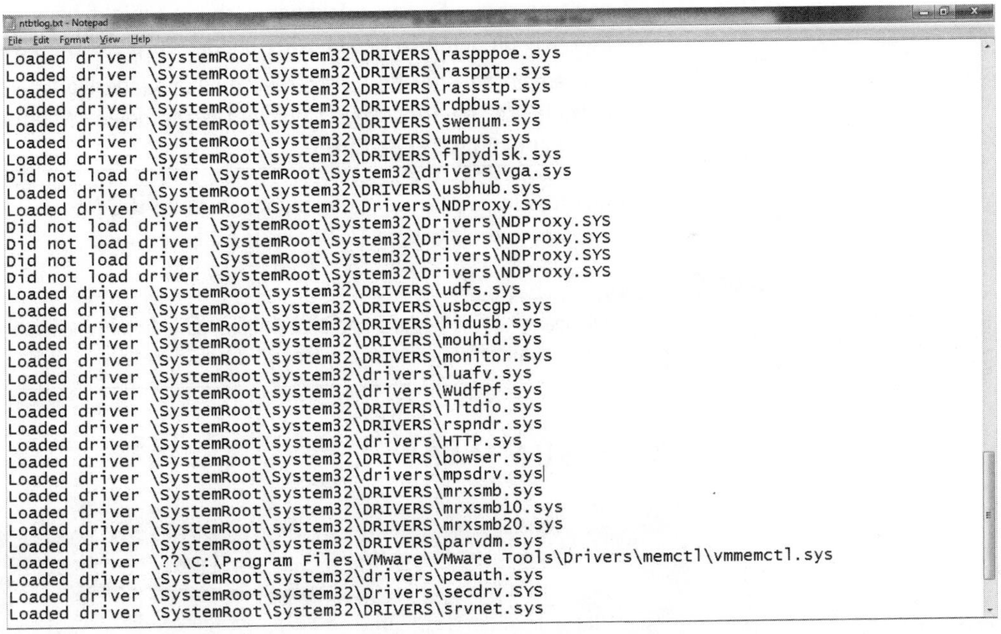

- **Enable Low-resolution Video (640x480):** This tool boots Windows normally but changes the resolution to 640x480 and lowers the refresh rate. If you suspect your video driver is misbehaving, choose this option to help lower the resolution and refresh rate to one that almost every driver out there can display properly. The drivers are tied to the actual monitor, so only install drivers for your specific type of video adapter.

- **Last Known Good Configuration (Advanced):** This tool boots from the last configuration that was known to work. When Windows shuts down successfully, system settings are saved in the registry. If you cannot restart your computer, you can choose to load the last known good configuration, which will load the system settings from the registry for the last time the machine booted properly. If you added new drivers or made changes to the registry and the computer no longer boots, those changes won't be included when you use the Last Known Good Configuration (Advanced) option.

- **Directory Services Restore Mode:** This tool is used only on domain controllers (DC), allowing administrators to repair Active Directory settings on a DC that is having issues.
- **Debugging Mode:** This tool starts Windows in an advanced debugging mode.
- **Disable Automatic Restart on System Failure:** If Windows encounters an error during the boot process, the automatic restart on system failure feature tells Windows to restart again. If your computer attempts to restart but cannot, and then it begins to restart again and again, this tool stops the loop behavior.
- **Disable Driver Signature Enforcement:** This tool allows you to install drivers that are not signed properly.
- **Start Windows Normally:** This tool simply starts Windows normally. Use this option if you have used a tool that returns you to the main Advanced Options Menu and you're ready to start Windows normally.

 ACCESS THE RECOVERY BOOT OPTIONS

GET READY. To access the recovery boot options, perform the following steps:

1. With your computer powered down, restart by pressing the power button. (If, however, your screen is displaying blue, power off the computer, wait a minute, and then power it back on.) As soon as you see anything display on your screen during the boot process, press and hold the **F8** key or press the **F8** key repeatedly. If you don't press the **F8** key quickly enough, you might have to shut the machine down and power it on again to get another chance to press the **F8** key.

2. The Advanced Boot Options screen displays (see Figure 8-24, previously). To select an option, use the arrow keys to move up and down. When you have highlighted the tool you want to use, press **Enter**.

If for some reason you cannot boot the machine to the Advanced Boot Options menu, you can also get these tools from a Windows installation disc.

 **MORE INFORMATION**

For more information about the Advanced Boot Options, go to http://windows.microsoft.com/en-US/windows7/Advanced-startup-options-including-safe-mode

SKILL SUMMARY

IN THIS LESSON YOU LEARNED:

- A backup is a properly secured copy of files and folders—and sometimes settings—usually saved in a compressed format. A backup is created so you can restore the files and settings in the event of data loss from a hard disk failure, accidental erasure or disk formatting, or natural events.

- Windows Backup uses the built-in Backup and Restore utility to enable you to back up and recover files.

- A system image is an image of an entire hard drive that includes all files needed to restore your operating system. By default, a system image includes the Windows folder, all system settings, programs, and files.

- If the drive your operating system resides on fails or the computer fails for any reason, you can use a system image on the same machine (replacing the hardware that caused the failure) or another machine to get the computer back up and running as quickly as possible.

- The Windows installation disc is provided by Microsoft or the computer manufacturer. You can create your own Windows installation disc if your organization purchases volume licenses of Windows 7 rather than individual retail copies.

- A system repair disc is a bootable disc you create in Windows 7 that contains Windows system recovery tools. You can use the repair disc to attempt to start a failed computer, or to restore a computer from a system image.

- Restoring a system image is usually necessary because of a computer catastrophe or a new computer. If a computer has crashed and you have a spare computer or a replacement hard disk, you can simply restore the system image. You can also restore an image to a new computer as a quick way to install the system.

- If your PC begins experiencing unusual problems that don't clear up after a few reboots or some simple troubleshooting, you can use System Restore to roll back your system files and applications to a time when the PC was working properly.

- System Restore uses the System Protection feature to create restore points. Restore points can be used to roll back your system to an earlier point in time; they are created automatically on a weekly basis and any time you make a change to your computer (such as installing a new application or device driver).

- Recovery boot options, also referred to as advanced startup options, provide you with tools to help you repair a broken Windows 7 installation. The options are found on the Advanced Boot Options menu, which you access when the computer first begins to boot by pressing the F8 key.

■ Knowledge Assessment

Fill in the Blank

Complete the following sentences by writing the correct word or words in the blanks provided.

1. Windows backups are _____ by default.

2. To store a backup on a network location you need to provide a _____ or _____.

3. Windows backups can back up data from drives formatted as _____.

4. You must be logged on as a(n) _____ to back up a computer or data.

5. You can restore an earlier version of a file using _____.

6. Repair discs are used to repair missing or corrupt _____ files.

7. A new device driver has been added and the system is not responding. You boot to the Advanced Boot Options menu and choose either _____ or _____.

8. You have enabled boot logging and now need to find the text file that contains your driver information. You should look in the _____ folder for a file named ntbtlog.txt.

9. The _____ service allows you to create restore points and backups of your system.

10. You can use a _____ to roll back your system to an earlier point in time.

Multiple Choice

Circle the letter or letters that corresponds to the best answer.

1. Backups of your data can be stored on which of the following? (Choose all that apply.)
   a. CD/DVD
   b. The same drive you are storing the backup on
   c. USB
   d. Hard drives
   e. Network
   f. Tape drives

2. When restoring a file using the Previous Versions feature, the permissions are set to which of the following?
   a. Permissions of the person restoring the file
   b. Full control to the person who is restoring the file
   c. Original permissions
   d. Whatever you set them to be

3. Which of the following can be included in a system image backup? (Choose all that apply.)
   a. User data
   b. The operating system
   c. All drives
   d. Data stored on a network server

4. What happens if you run out of disk space while creating a system image backup?
   a. The process fails
   b. You are prompted to delete files
   c. Temporary files and folders are deleted to make room for the new system image
   d. Older system images are deleted to make room for the new system images

5. Which of the following can be used to perform a system restore? (Choose all that apply.)
   a. Command prompt
   b. Recovery Control Panel
   c. Preinstalled recovery options
   d. System repair disc

6. You have performed a system restore from a restore point but your issue was not resolved. In fact, your computer is in even worse shape. Now the computer doesn't boot. Which of the following options are likely to restore the system? (Choose all that apply.)
   a. Roll back to another restore point
   b. Manually delete all files that changed
   c. Undo the System Restore
   d. Restart the machine

7. Which of the following methods can be used to access the recovery boot options? (Choose all that apply.)
   a. Using Administrative Tools
   b. Pressing F8 during the boot process
   c. Using the Backup and Restore tool
   d. Booting from a Windows Installation disc

8. Which of the following recovery boot options runs only on a domain controller and does nothing for Windows 7?
   a. Safe Mode
   b. Disable Driver Signature enforcement
   c. Directory Services Restore Mode
   d. Enable Low-resolution Video

9. When scheduling automatic backups in Windows Backup, which of the following can you customize? (Choose all that apply.)
   a. Whether daily, weekly, or monthly
   b. The day of the week
   c. The time of the backup
   d. Specific files to back up

10. Which recovery boot option should you avoid using if the computer you are attempting to boot has been infected by a virus?
    a. Safe Mode
    b. Safe Mode with Networking
    c. Repair Your Computer
    d. Safe Mode with Command Prompt

True / False

Circle T if the statement is true or F if the statement is false.

T F 1. You can choose exactly what you want to back up to a folder.

T F 2. Windows Backup backs up the Recycle Bin just in case you want to restore previously deleted files.

T F 3. You can control how much hard drive space backups can use.

T F 4. You must be an administrator to restore your own data files.

T F 5. You can restore individual data files from a system image backup.

Competency Assessment

Scenario 8-1: Scheduling File Backups

You provide technical support for PBJ&S, a small environmental consulting firm. Dina, the graphic artist, creates a lot of maps for client reports. Her Windows 7 Professional computer automatically backs up files every Sunday starting at 7:00 p.m. Dina reported recently that her computer was still backing up files when she arrived for work the last two Monday mornings. What can you do to help ensure that Dina's files are backed up by Monday morning?

Scenario 8-2: Installing from an Image

The owner of PBJ&S approved funds to purchase a new computer for Dina because an upgrade to her main mapping software requires more memory than her current computer's motherboard can handle. The new computer will be the same make and model but will have more memory and will have a much bigger hard disk. You also ordered a 1 terabyte external USB drive for backups. When the new computer arrives, how can you quickly get it up and running for Dina?

■ Proficiency Assessment

Scenario 8-3: Creating a System Repair Disc

Stanley works for your organization from his home office on a company-owned computer. He called your cell phone while you were at a restaurant having lunch. He said his computer has been having all kinds of problems lately and that it takes a long time for Windows to start. You suspect his Windows system files have become corrupt. Because you're away from the office, you can't set up a Remote Assistance session to troubleshoot Stanley's computer remotely. What do you advise Stanley to do?

Scenario 8-4: Resolving a Driver Problem Using Recovery Boot Options

You recently installed a new video adapter in Jeffrey's desktop computer using the driver supplied on the CD in the adapter packaging. When Windows starts, the words on the screen are unreadable. What is a possible solution for resolving the problem?

Windows Operating System Fundamentals: Exam 98-349

Objective Domain	Skill Number	Lesson Number
Understanding Operating System Configurations		
Configure Control Panel Options	1.1	2
Configure Desktop Settings	1.2	2
Understand Native Applications and Tools	1.3	3, 4
Understand Mobility	1.4	3
Understand Remote Management and Assistance	1.5	3
Installing and Upgrading Client Systems		
Identify Windows Operating System Editions	2.1	1
Identify Upgrade Paths	2.2	1
Understand Installation Types	2.3	1
Understand Virtualized Clients	2.4	2, 3
Managing Applications		
Understand Application Installations	3.1	4
Understand User Account Control (UAC)	3.2	2
Remove Malicious Software	3.3	7
Understand Services	3.4	4
Understand Application Virtualization	3.5	2
Managing Files and Folders		
Understand File Systems	4.1	4
Understand File and Print Sharing	4.2	6
Understand Encryption	4.3	4
Understand Libraries	4.4	4
Managing Devices		
Connect Devices	5.1	5
Understand Storage	5.2	4, 5
Understand Printing Devices	5.3	5
Understand System Devices	5.4	5
Understanding Operating System Maintenance		
Understand Backup and Recovery Methods	6.1	8
Understand Maintenance Tools	6.2	7
Understand Updates	6.3	7

Credits

The following photos were provided by third parties. All other images were provided by the authors and are copyright John Wiley & Sons, Inc.:

Figure 3-6 © Danita Delimont/Gallo Images/Getty Images

Figure 5-11 © Vicente Barcelo Varona/iStockphoto

Figure 5-12 © Lev Mel/iStockphoto

Figure 5-13 © Hans-Walter Untch/iStockphoto

Index